W9-ADY-125

Internet Commerce Metrics and Models in the New Era of Accountability

Sridhar Jagannathan

Jay Srinivasan

Jerry L. Kalman

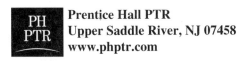

Prentice Hall PTR
Upper Saddle River, NJ 07458
www.phptr.com

ISBN 0-13-028186-7

Library of Congress Cataloging-in-Publication Data

Jagannathan, Sridhar.
 Internet Commerce Metrics and Models in the New Era of Accountability /
  Sridhar Jagannathan, Jay Srinivasan, Jerry L. Kalman.
  p. cm.
 Includes bibliographical references and index.
 ISBN 0-13-028186-7
  1. Electronic commerce. I. Title: Ecommerce. II. Srinivasan, Jay. III. Kalman, Jerry L.
 IV. Title.

HF5548.32 .J33 2001
658.8′4--dc21

                                                                    2001021440

Editorial/Production Supervision: *Jan H. Schwartz*
Acquisitions Editor: *Mary Franz*
Editorial Assistant: *Noreen Regina*
Development Editor: *Jim Markham*
Marketing Manager: *Dan DePasquale*
Manufacturing Manager: *Alexis R. Heydt*
Buyer: *Maura Zaldivar*
Cover Design Director: *Jerry Votta*
Cover Design: *Talar Agasyan*
Art Director: *Gail Cocker-Bogusz*
Series Interior Design: *Meg VanArsdale*

©2002 Prentice Hall PTR
Prentice-Hall, Inc.
Upper Saddle River, New Jersey 07458

Prentice Hall books are widely used by corporations and government agencies for training, marketing, and resale.
The publisher offers discounts on this book when ordered in bulk quantities.
For more information, contact:
Corporate Sales Department
Prentice Hall PTR
One Lake Street
Upper Saddle River, NJ 07548
Phone: 800-382-3419; Fax: 201-236-7141; Email: corpsales@prenhall.com

Printed in the United States of America
10 9 8 7 6 5 4 3 2 1

ISBN 0-13-028186-7   **3 2280 00759 8923**

Pearson Education LTD.
Pearson Education Australia PTY, Limited
Pearson Educatin Singapore, Pte. Ltd.
Pearson Education North Asia Ltd.
Pearson Education Canada, Ltd.
Pearson Educación de Mexico, S.A. de C.V.
Pearson Education—Japan
Pearson Education Malaysia, Pte. Ltd.
Pearson Education, Upper Saddle River, New Jersey

Dedications

For all their encouragement and support, I dedicate this book to my wife, Viji, my daughters, Sunita and Sushmita, my parents, the rest of my family, and all my friends.

Sridhar Jagannathan

To my parents

Jay Srinivasan

This is dedicated to my wife and fellow author, Deborah Bayles Kalman, who has opened more than doors for me.

Jerry L. Kalman

Contents

Acknowledgments

A book is not produced by authors alone. We would like to acknowledge the vision, commitment, and dedication of Mary Franz at Prentice Hall who saw the need for a book like this and made it happen. We also owe our gratitude to Jim Markham, our development editor, who cheerfully provided guidance, counsel, and oversight to convert raw electronic content into a navigable and useful book. As co-participants in this endeavor, our families have tolerated the endless hours that go into producing a book with patience and humor. Finally, it has been a pleasure to work with our co-authors who have participated with an abundance of talent and spirit.

—*Sri Jagannathan*

Introduction

"It was the best of times, it was the worst of times." Charles Dickens, A Tale of Two Cities

Imagine it is the summer of 1849. The setting is a saloon in a little California railroad town. As the business of a regular evening continues, a stranger with a wild-eyed gleam bursts through the doors and shouts: "There's gold in them thar' hills." In that electric moment, the realm of possibilities for everyone changed.

Fast-forward a century and a half. Substitute today and the new digital economy for the gold country in California. Just as the landscape for business changed at that instant in the 19th Century, here in the 21st Century we are seeing similar possibilities and challenges. Our wild-eyed stranger could be any of hundreds of entrepreneurs enamored with possibilities to strike it rich in the online world of e-commerce.

Ironically, in 1849 very few made their fortunes finding and extracting gold from the Sierra. In the Gold Rush, immigrants selling clothes, transportation, and banking services created businesses and most of the wealth, carrying such brand names as Levi's, Wells Fargo, and Bank of America.

Some 150 years later, the digital equivalent of those who sold picks and shovels, blue jeans, and other items to the miners are the ones who are reaping profits from the online Gold Rush of the last few years. We all know about the financial services side funding and supporting seedlings. Who are the modern-day equivalents of those who created the supporting infrastructure for gold mines throughout the West?

To take maximum advantage of the widening range of possibilities facing us despite bubbles bursting and shakeouts in the financial markets, we must understand that there are still numerous and potentially lucrative options available for conducting business on or through the Internet. Some are as visible as a mother lode vein of ore. Others are buried deep within the gold field and need hard work, diligence, intelligence, and a little luck in finding the right combination of resources to tap into the vast storehouse of riches available in the online world.

E-commerce, however, is not an automatic moneymaking machine. It is an environment that requires a strong sense of customer service. It also requires hard work and application of sound business disciplines, such as measuring important processes and outcomes—what we call metrics. To understand how to take these important steps toward building online success, we need to change our view of e-commerce and put it in some old, and some new, contexts.

From its early days, Internet-enabled commerce was a random collection of business thoughts and ideas, technologies, decisions, and partnerships. To be successful today, these random collections must morph from a series of loosely connected "atomized" units of business functionality into a more robust and seamless whole. These units must combine and operate cohesively to fulfill an entrepreneurial or corporate objective. In this introductory chapter, we trace a few of the more pertinent evolutionary traits of the Internet, and lay groundwork for the construction and analysis of e-commerce business models.

Evolving E-Commerce

For the Internet and electronic commerce, 2000 marked a watershed year. Activity online in page views was soaring. Victoria's Secret scored more than two million unique visits for its Web-cast fashion show live from Cannes, France. After a predictably slow start, *NBCOlympics.com* reached a high-water mark of almost 11 million visits on the day when Laura Wilkinson won the gold medal for platform diving, forcing a favorite from China to settle for silver.

Needless to say, the American presidential elections pushed site traffic to some of the highest levels for CNN, the television networks, and other general news sites, often eclipsing offline media statistics.

With the proliferation of sites, service businesses, and venture capital, online statistics were hitting us from all directions. "Numbers to Know" were part of the regular fare from the media that report on electronic commerce, coming from such diverse sources as market research firms, online tracking services, investment bankers, and even government agencies. With a little shareware on a server, even you can log trends at your site . . . and then use the statistics to justify someone placing a banner ad on your home page.

It was, indeed, the best of times. Page views for many merchants were increasing, purchases of all goods and services were strong, and new software and hardware arrived on the market at a rate that often outstripped an ability to install it.

There were also storm warnings, indicating that the worst of times were just around the corner. The stock market in March and April 2000 woke us up to an incipient meltdown that would strip billions of dollars in valuations from online companies.

Toward the end of 2000 and into 2001, the bloom was definitely off the Internet rose.

Venture capital funding of e-commerce companies rocketed from $7 billion in 1998 and $32 billion in 1999, to $15 billion in the first quarter of 2000, but soon plummeted. NASDAQ values for IPOs of online companies turned sour, dragging down funding prospects for those in the queue. With the IPO market following NASDAQ, it wasn't long after when valuations of companies for mergers and acquisitions followed suit and dropped like a stone.

When IPOs dropped from an average of 30 deals in March 2000 to about 13 in May 2000, it was clear to all that the easy times for funding were gone. Even for the companies that did make it out, no longer was the explosive first day in the IPO a guaranteed success. This IPO shutout led many underwriters to postpone or withdraw registrations with the SEC.

By the start of 2001 major players were e-liquidators—vultures who swooped down on dead and dying dot coms, snatched up a morsel or two of intellectual property and customer lists, and brokered them off to survivors. More than 40 such firms operated at year-end, focusing on online ventures.

A respected trade magazine, *The Industry Standard,* was tracking online ventures going out of business! In early 2001, the publication's Web site listed more than 80 companies, many with high-profile names that ceased operations in 12 months.

With declining cash assets, a grouchy capital market, and regular headlines heralding an online apocalypse, Internet executives at last started to face reality. Companies scrambled to cut down bloated marketing programs. Customer acquisition costs, which ranged from $70–$80 per customer in the U.S., were pared down, and the focus shifted in part to customer retention.

Changing Business Models

To demonstrate their nimbleness, companies started to modify their businesses. Venture capitalists with mounting losses in their portfolios among both pre-IPO and public companies started encouraging mergers. Wal-Mart.com, backed by Accel Partners, purchased the assets of HomeWarehouse.com. Similarly, Idealab company Paymybills.com bought out another Idealab-backed company, Payme.com.

Consolidation through mergers and acquisitions became the norm, replacing IPOs and heavily funded start-ups as the operative mode for the corporate finance world. By the end of 2000 and into 2001, many highflying Internet companies were down in the penny-stock trading range, and some faced delisting from NASDAQ. Huge drops happened across the board, but the heaviest came in consumer-to-consumer (C2C), business-to-consumer (B2C), and eventually business-to-business (B2B) market plays.

All ships were being lowered by the tide. Those that were "relatively" healthy appeared to be infrastructure suppliers in enterprise architectures, network hardware, and data center management. But they, too, would begin to see softening in market valuations.

The landscape was becoming flooded with layoffs and bankruptcies. By early 2001, the bloodbath was painful, especially in Silicon Valley, where newly-minted millionaires started papering the job market with their resumes.

Carpenters have a saying: "Measure twice, cut once." These craftsmen know that accuracy reduces waste and saves time. Most consider their tape measures, levels, and squares to be power tools, even though these devices are largely mechanical or without moving parts. Moving up the skills ladder, architects use blueprints and renderings to guide construction of a building.

In electronic commerce, we also have tools—powerful tools. Some tools and crafts measure site performance, as noted above. Some measure corporate performance. Some measure markets. And we also have templates and business forms, called business models, which provide us with architecture to guide us in constructing a business . . . often in market areas where none existed before.

This is part and parcel of what makes online commerce new, fascinating, and exciting.

Most of these numbers can be quite useful. Victoria's Secret attracted almost two million site visits to the fashion show in Cannes in 2000 without much of a hiccup. The first time around in 1999, however, higher than anticipated traffic brought the site to its knees.

And in all that traffic, as with those who went to *NBCOlympics.com* site, there were visitors who were meaningful and within the target zone for the merchant. But there were many more who were not. In anticipation of heavy traffic, Victoria's Secret correctly forecast a need for a robust infrastructure of servers, software, and communications services that would be scalable. This is not a trivial expense.

Does it make sense, however, to have the needle pegged at high site-visits with only a small number being target customers? Does a million-plus page views a day justify the investments to support traffic consisting of an audience where more than half, conservatively, will never influence a purchase decision, let alone make a purchase?

Investments to build the Victoria's Secret, IBM, and NBC brands are huge in time and dollars. To gain customer trust, confidence, and exposure to generate awareness to get customers to these sites are also considerable feats. These investments in site design, navigation, infrastructure, branding, and awareness can often push one important metric—customer acquisition costs—through the roof!

When those making decisions about whether or not to invest in these companies see little or no return, they pull back on their investments. When management sees internal rates of return for invested capital dropping or turn negative and stay there consistently, they withdraw support for projects. When suppliers and service providers see customer volumes drying up, they begin to look for new strategic partners.

And when the business model du jour loses favor and becomes stale to users, they look for the next category for online news, information, education, and entertainment. Fickle as they rightly are, investors vote with their feet.

Shakeouts are inevitable. They are even healthy, though painful, for those caught in the up and down drafts. Those that survive do so for several reasons: first, management knows how to manage in tough times; second, the business is founded on a reliable architecture and solid business principles; third, there are often voices in the wilderness within the company who just might be in touch with the realities of the day and hold a vision of what the future "really" holds; and fourth, they are nimble enough to recognize when a business model needs modification.

In the latter instance, management uses internal and external metrics to give them early warning clues about everything from sea-state changes to impending economic tsunamis. Their peers often consider the few who are tuned in to their businesses and the markets as idiot savants.

A guide on how to envision, set up, and manage a business for the bottom line is what this book is about. It is about finding the right business model, or architecture; determining the operational aspects that provide the most useful benchmarks for success and then measuring them. It is about metrics, models, and the experience to use them.

In the rest of this chapter, however, we look at broader Internet trends with a new view to the future.

Connectivity

Sadly enough, one half of the world's population has never made a phone call. New communications technologies can change all of that, and none too soon. Participating in the explosion of global communications can only help those disadvantaged cultures with little opportunity to participate in economic expansion. Consequently, connectivity continues to grow globally on an impressive scale.

Major carriers such as Global Crossing and Teleglobe are developing transoceanic and transcontinental networks. Substantial investments in Internet infrastructures are also being made in China and India.

Connectivity is soaring in every major economy around the world, and this is adding large numbers of new users to the online space. As more and more low-cost PCs and Web-enabled cellular phones reach consumers through retailers, discounters, kiosks, and cyber-cafes, usage of Internet and e-commerce technologies is expected to explode in their wake.

Ironically, connectivity in many advanced countries is constrained by too little "hard-wiring" of businesses and homes from what we in the U.S. refer to as COs (central offices) maintained by the local telephone company. These businesses and residences are turning to wireless technologies in many regions to take up any slack in the last mile to the intended point of access.

This explosion in online connectivity is fueled in part by innovations like DoCoMo from NTT in Japan, which is setting up strategic alliances around the world to handle anticipated market expansion. DoCoMo, a leader in the Japanese market, offers Web-enabled cellular-style phones, devices that are catching on rapidly there.

Meanwhile, as customer demands for access are occurring, so are their requests for higher and higher speed connectivity. Fueling this boom are bandwidth-hungry applications such as video streaming, downloading of pictures and music, interactive conferencing, and gaming.

Overall, long distance Internet capacity is slated to be well in excess of anticipated peak demand in both the U.S. and Europe. In fact, some analysts predict that through 2004, two-thirds of European and one-third of U.S. bandwidth in the long haul market will go unutilized. These two authors, however, predict that there will still be bottlenecks and shortages in the "last mile" at access points closest to the customer. Those shortages are expected to continue for at least three or four more years until broadband is more widespread.

Hard drive and DRAM producers are counting on demand for their technologies to keep them in the memory business. However, as advances in memory technology keep giving PC manufacturers more and more to work with, software companies, in turn, use up as much of this resource as possible with ever-larger products. Unfortunately, bandwidth appears to be headed down a similar path: the more bandwidth given to end users, the quicker those distributing content and services online deplete it.

Dial-up for consumers will still be much more than 50 percent of all Internet access methods over the next three years. While Digital Subscriber Line (DSL) technology continues to lag behind cable modem installations as of Q3 2000, DSL installation growth rates are climbing rapidly. Yankee Group expects there will be five million DSL users and 7.6 million cable modem users in the U.S. by 2003, still a small fraction of those using dial-up and other access methods.

Business to Consumer (B2C) Commerce

B2C commerce involves transactions initiated by a consumer and conducted with an online retail establishment. Merchants can include a software company, a book or music store, a travel agency, or a bank. B2C commerce commanded tremendous media space in the last couple of years because of its high visibility and the threat that it seemingly posed to traditional brick-and-mortar businesses. It was thought that the digital nature of the products sold and the pervasive nature of the sites enabled new players to change prevailing business models. They set about deconstructing, or taking apart, the value chain that made up the traditional retail model, and then sought to rebuild it around their perceived competitive advantages.

Pure B2C is no longer a threat to offline establishments. Statistics released in late 2000 and early 2001 show online customers are making choices between merchants and not an either/or between online and offline. In fact, during the 2000 holiday season, many click-and-mortar, or hybrid stores, did better as a teamed online/offline business speaking with one voice to the customer!

B2C commerce is differentiated from offline commerce in many different ways, and the deconstructed value chain is one predominant underlying theme. The other is convenience.

By the way, the term "retail vs. e-tail," as with most things concerning the Internet, is a reflection of a compact lexicon. E-tail is the virtual online retail world, one composed of mouse clicks. It is the challenger to the brick-and-mortar retail establishment. We will use e-tail to indicate pure-play online merchants. The other classification is click-and-mortar, which refers to hybrid operations consisting of both an online and offline store.

Amidst the clutter of pure-play Web sites some retailers stand out: Amazon.com, eBay, Charles Schwab, and Edmunds, to name a few. The keys to their success in generating both "mind space" as well as loyal clientele are many and varied.

These sites offer the products and services wanted by customers, amplified by the provision of all the things made possible by the Web. These inherently positive traits for e-tailers include: 1) convenience, 2) selection, 3) quality, 4) content, and 5) service. These attributes are neither unique nor peculiar to online B2C businesses, but are seemingly defendable against brick-and-mortar competitors.

Let's look briefly at these five traits in a little closer detail.

- *Convenience:* A good online store is ubiquitous and available 24x7x365. Once the novelty value of online shopping wears off, it is convenience that drives customers to the Web. Supporting features reflect the principles of good Web site design—user friendliness, availability of information, and good search capability. The quality of user experience foretells repeat visits to the site, ending possibly in a transaction and a suggested visit by a friend.
- *Selection:* A good, if not exhaustive, selection is mandatory. Unlike stores in the physical world, though, selection is virtual because of the relative ease of storing information about products versus the products themselves. Intuitive navigation and a good search tool makes location of product by attribute easier, and

this hastens conversion of browsers into buyers. Breadth of product is especially important for drop-ship stores.

- *Quality:* On the Internet the reputation of a retailer is considerably enhanced if sites are constructed upon foundations of quality. At eBay, for instance, the auction site has a robust system of user ratings on both buyers and sellers: one point for positive comments, zero for neutral responses, and minus one for negative feedback. Anyone racking up a score of minus four forfeits the right to use the service.

  Thus, quality refers to the quality of the product or service sold and its delivery, as well as in generating customer feedback. The integrity of this gesture is measured by how well the merchant acts upon them. It has implications for the quality of relationships all along the value chain—from suppliers to end customers.

- *Content:* Information content in an online market can be measured along several dimensions: information about the customers and their needs, information about the products or services, and information that users have and share.

  The Web presents many opportunities to gather and disseminate information from a variety of sources. Information about customers and their buying patterns can be monitored continuously to customize offerings that reflect understanding gained from that knowledge. Information about products being sold is dependent on availability of exhaustive catalog information and responsiveness to customer inquiries. Breadth and depth of content (catalogs of products being measured this way) are also important in rating content quality, and are intimately linked to selection.

  In fact, if it is not obvious by now, we must state here that all of these traits, qualities, and factors are interrelated. They are very difficult to remove, isolate, and examine out of their original context. This is one of the unique qualities associated with the online world: its interlocking relationships.

  The last content dimension, the willingness of users to share their knowledge, is especially pertinent to a Web presence owing to its singular ability to link a product's quality or specification to comments of other users. As noted above, quality is dependent upon customer feedback. With Amazon and eBay, integration of content and quality takes the form of reviews and feedback by customers on products they may have purchased or sold and then self-rated.

Because content is so important, we devote an entire chapter to it, Chapter 4, "The Content Stack."

- *Service:* Service, specifically customer service, is an important but largely missing ingredient on the Internet. While automation produces efficiency, it can also make the experience impersonal. In turn, this results in low customer retention.

On the Web, good customer service can be addressed with feedback, prompt handling of questions and complaints, and in how well the merchant provides a smooth, trouble-free method to handle returns and refunds. When handled well, this often turns a negative experience into a positive one. It is ironic that on the Web the term personalization can mean customized automation within the online glossary.

Business to Business (B2B) Commerce

As is obvious, B2C is highly visible, but it was not the first area of online commerce, nor is it the biggest. Forrester Research estimates the B2B market will cross $1 trillion by 2003, suggesting boundless opportunity for this segment over the next decade. As organizations in every industry see more and more end users picking up offerings through online commerce, it is only natural that they look for opportunities in their day-to-day operations to challenge conventional ways of doing business. If they don't, a competitor tuned into the same market dynamics will. Because of these insights and observations, B2B is being transformed. Such a transformation in B2B is rippling through the value chain and affecting every player at every point back through the continuum—from retail and its relationship with end-customers back into the supply chain. This view in Figure 1.1, a demand-based environment, is a continuous loop, facilitated by the Internet.

Interestingly, the same dynamics driving B2C noted above (convenience, selection, quality, content, and service) are powerful drivers in B2B as well. These dynamics happen on a broader scale, and the numbers can be much greater (in terms of transaction size, etc.).

In a supply-based view, the value chain consists of the complete spectrum of producers and their support communities from raw material origins to final consumption. It is a model that describes a series of value-adding activities encompassing the supply side (raw materials, logistics, production) through the demand side (outbound logistics, marketing, sales).

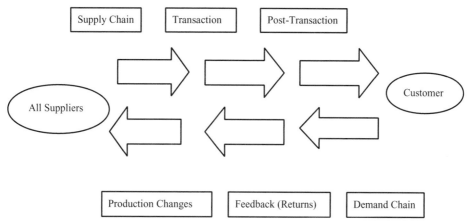

Figure 1.1 The Value Chain, Simplified

The B2B value chain is much more complex, but because of this complexity it lets us understand existing organizational structures and future possibilities for their transformation to eliminate costs and gain value. Typically, this involves identification and decisions about non-value-adding activities or highlighting gaps that exist between one group of activities and another.

Gaps occur when handoffs take place. These gaps are most often information-based. They occur where problems or inefficiencies arise and things simply "fall through the cracks;" as for example, when a customer query about a product return and credit results in an indifferent response or lack of accountability. Many people in the service sector are building complete businesses around the handoff of information between one player and another.

The Internet provides enormous opportunities for integration of functions and responsibilities all along the value chain, and this is referred to as *disintermediation*. Disintermediation occurs when entities in the supply chain that add little or no value are taken out. In the offline world, such intermediaries exist because they make possible relationships with suppliers or customers that an organization cannot reach by itself. With online connectivity, one-to-one relationships are more easily managed. The information flow is shortened to encompass only those with a need-to-know and a need-to-use!

It is natural for management to want to consolidate value chains and remove cost. Flattening steps through the value chain to foster faster and more accurate exchange of information, collaboration, and tighter integration are becoming a reality. "Partner integration" introduces the latest innovation in business strategy, breaching external boundaries.

When Dell accepts an order for a computer, it notifies its supplier for disk drives that a new unit has been ordered. This removes several handoff points in Dell's supply chain.

The Intersection of Content and Community

When shifting our view from the broad categories of B2C and B2B, we see that there are common factors that continue to be drivers in each. As Chapters 4 and 5, "The Community Stack" illustrate, content and community are two of these important drivers leading to a condition where e-commerce can occur.

Offline we select our communities of common interest for many reasons, and those reasons are replicated online in virtual environments. The Internet, in its relatively short popular history, is revealing an intriguing concept: The most popular sites are those that permit some kind of interaction, whether communication (e.g., chat rooms) or transaction (e.g., auctions). Those that contain static information have considerably less appeal than those that are dynamic and even interactive. In these chat rooms, auctions, and other environments, there is a high degree of interaction (content generation) and this builds a sense of community among the participants. This reiterates a point that the Internet establishes and reinforces connections between people; their sense of community grows out of connecting through shared content.

Users in communities intensify the value of their participation as potential buyers of products and services. To a customer, commerce sites that aggregate content from a variety of sources establish context, integrate content and communication, and enhance community value when they are asked to participate in some way. *Edmunds.com* is an example of a B2C Web site that articulates the basic elements of content, context, communication, and commerce.

To vendors, an online community provides like benefits: reduced search costs, higher customer propensity to buy, efficient targeting of potential customers, and a better basis to tailor and add value to existing products and services (Hagel and Armstrong). Reduced acquisition cost is another benefit enjoyed by the merchant and those in the supply chain.

When we isolate content and community to analyze them separately, the importance of metrics for each becomes more understandable. From this understanding of the dynamic interaction between the two comes the ability to leverage them.

The Emergence of Marketplaces

Online marketplaces are virtual forums that enable buyers and suppliers to meet, exchange information, and perhaps even contract to purchase a product or service. If this sounds like an example of the convergence of content and community for commerce, it is!

Network economics and the opportunity to reduce the costs of acquiring and utilizing information are advantages of marketplaces. They come in different shapes, sizes, and market focuses and reflect sourcing characteristics, constituent bias, product or service orientation, and industry or market view. They also differentiate around value proposition, transactional model, domain expertise of the host, degree of market neutrality, value-added services, technological infrastructure, and so on.

Business-to-business marketplaces have superficial similarities to business-to-consumer marketplaces. There are suppliers and there are buyers. There are catalogs, search mechanisms, ordering, payment, order tracking, and delivery. These similarities, valid at the highest aggregate level, hide important differences and processes below the surface; the differences are explored in Chapter 6, "The Commerce Stack."

In its simplest sense, intermediaries facilitate interactions between buyer and seller organizations while enlarging the overall market and its attractiveness to both. Efficient marketplaces faciliate transactions and promote liquidity. Liquidity, in this context, reflects the "attractability" of the marketplace for both buyers and sellers.

So what are the attractions?

Several, ranging from price competitiveness to product variety, information content, ability to engage in supplier contracts, simplifying the purchasing process, etc. In trying to accommodate suppliers and buyers and position themselves as marketplaces of choice, intermediaries often serve as catalog aggregators (some call this a portal), digital exchanges, and the now-popular auction sites, online business forms that are discussed at various points throughout the book. Intermediaries are equally effective in B2B as well as B2C.

In addition to facilitating transactions, intermediary-driven marketplaces also offer a range of value-added services such as a technological infrastructure, directory services, content management, advisory services, and trust relationship and transactional services that include pre-qualification, credit verification, payment mechanism, escrow, insurance, fulfillment, and settlement.

Intermediaries coalesce around one of these biases: seller-centric and buyer-centric.

A "seller-centric" marketplace, or seller hub, often has a dominant supplier or distributor on one side and a large number of buyers on the other. Seller-centric markets support purchases of maintenance, repair, and operations (MRO) products and services; however, there are many others that deal with primary goods needed by Original Equipment Manufacturers (OEMs). OEMs like Intel, Cisco Systems, and Dell all host their own private marketplaces, which feature content aggregation, set up purchasing rules and order requisition standards for their customers, manage workflow, and provide some backend integration into financial systems, payment, and fulfillment.

Organizations have long-term relationships with their suppliers that they would like to preserve. "Buyer-centric" marketplace solutions, or buyers' hubs, are the initiatives of large buyers and generally enforce participation on suppliers who risk losing vendor status if they don't participate. General Motors, Ford, and Daimler Chrysler formed Covisint, shown in Figure 1.2, to create a front-end to a marketplace where their collective purchasing requirements can be placed in front of a number of qualified suppliers. Such a marketplace could jeopardize many long-term relationships between members of the automotive supply chain, but if the automakers can make good on their claims of taking as much as $4,000 in costs out of each car, the customer wins and the system becomes more efficient.

Obviously, businesses are complex operations and purchasing tends to be equally complex. Purchase value, both at an item level and at a consolidated level, tends to be high. It therefore requires spend limits by function or position, approvals, information about pricing, contracts, suppliers, payment, and fulfillment. There is also the audit trail, requiring documentation, verification, and analysis.

In a perfect world, all these different elements are seamlessly tied together, providing senior management with important metrics about *who* spends *how much on what, when, where,* and *why.*

Price and Pricing Mechanisms

Whether B2B or B2C, marketplace or single buyer-seller transactions, how we pay and with what are important finalizing elements in online commerce.

Electronic commerce technologies and business practices enable online stores and marketplaces to provide major innovations in pricing. Many are variations on pricing

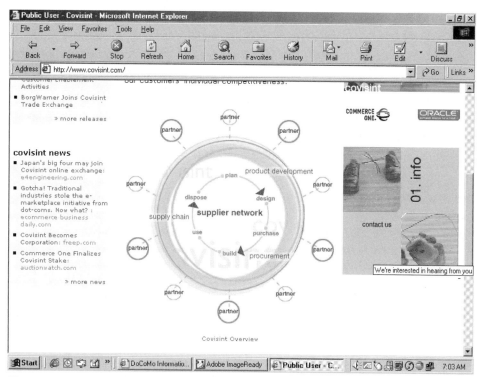

Figure 1.2 Covisint, an Online Exchange for the Auto Industry

schemes that existed down through the history of commerce: barter, negotiated purchasing, bid-ask mechanisms, etc. Appearing on the Web, they are often portrayed as magically new and different. Not so.

Among the popular pricing mechanisms are fixed price, "name your price," and a variety of auction formats. Fixed price, sometimes based on terms and conditions, is standard in B2B, but has many variations and combinations in B2C.

Auctions are very old market-making mechanisms that are now being used in both B2C and B2B markets. Typically, auctions work by spatial matching, that is, either the buyer or seller bids against availability while conforming to a floor or ceiling price. Depending on the type of auction, prices can rise or fall from a designated point. Auctions enable efficient management of inventory and a means to secure revenue for unwanted or excess stock that cannot be easily sold through a fixed price mechanism. In a few commodity-like situations, dynamic pricing is beginning to play a role, adjudicating between demand and supply.

The ability to change prices and bring in different pricing mechanisms to support them is a significant innovation brought about by these new technologies. If there was ever any credence in using the term "new economy," it is in this area.

Flexibility to adjust demand and supply to keep both in equilibrium are long sought after by economists. Flattening the value chain to allow vendors at the top-most end of the value chain to be closer to sources of demand hopefully adds enough visibility for each producer along the way to maintain inventories and adjust supplies as required by those downstream.

Emergence of Services: Outsourcing as a Way of Life

One of the most interesting aspects of the Internet evolution is the proliferation of new and different services, so much so that the "service provider" label is now a standard part of the Internet vernacular. Starting with Internet Service Provider (ISP), we have seen the emergence of the Application Service Provider (ASP for networked applications), Content Service Provider (distribute centralized content), Customer Service Provider (CSP), and so on.

Fundamentally, the Internet allows merchants to expand value in modular and spatially distributed ways. Each module of service, as we will see, gives rise to a set of vendors specializing around that service. Thus, it is no longer necessary or even prudent to consolidate one's physical and human resources in company-owned and operated locations.

Growth of data centers mean that corporate servers can be located outside a company's IT center, gaining several strategic advantages for both host and hosted. ERP (enterprise resource planning) software vendors foresaw the Web-enabling wider use of their applications, expanding their markets. Similar services are now available for desktop office applications, further reducing the burden on in-house IT staff.

In addition, a variety of third-party marketing services are available, such as DoubleClick and AdForce, for launching online advertisements and Responsys.com for email marketing. Other examples of services are BizRate for customer satisfaction monitoring, SalesForce.com for sales contact management, BeFree.com for affiliate recruitment, and Employease.com for human resource management.

Services are so important to articulation of business models, evolution of community, and handling transactions and payments that they are a common thread that runs through this book. Services touch on every aspect of electronic commerce, perhaps like in no other form of commerce. In many sectors of electronic commerce, the service providers are those who are selling picks and shovels to the miners, a reference that harkens back to the Gold Rush days and mentioned previously. In the 1850s, megafortunes were made by a jeans manufacturer, a stage coach line, and a bank formed by an immigrant from Italy (Levi Strauss, Wells Fargo, and Bank of America) while many of the gold miners ended up penniless and with no legacy at all.

Customer Acquisition

As with offline merchants, the holy grail of online commerce is to secure and retain customers. Any inability of online businesses to acquire paying customers successfully, and retain them, is at the root of instability and shakeout in the Internet space.

In B2C, the problem is simple: too many merchants for too few customers. Very few are good at brand differentiation. There are too many competitors in a small niche and this exacerbates low customer propensity to purchase, aggressive price reductions, and lack of organized shopping environments, all of which contribute to small revenue streams and low customer retention. Most of the time company revenues (not earnings!) barely equal their customer acquisition costs, guaranteeing that increasing volume would not solve this problem.

Many B2B environments are linked to B2C, and they fare worse. In a sense, the B2B customer acquisition problem is inverse to that of B2C. Whereas in B2C a lack of stickiness is an issue, for B2B, established relationships often make customers *too* sticky. This leads to corporate reluctance to try newer offerings, even if such offerings have higher value ("Nobody ever got fired for buying IBM," goes the old saying).

It takes much more effort to change established and time-proven corporate practices. Moreover, in many cases the touted advantages of intermediaries and marketplaces failed to impress, let alone secure financial advantages for B2B and other exchange participants.

How to improve customer acquisition with each tactic and strategy are subjects for different books. In this chapter, we look at the overall dynamic of customer acquisition and show the interrelationship between tactics to help you develop a mechanism on which any method can be analyzed.

Goals and Objectives of This Book

There are several ways to measure success of an electronic commerce site, ranging from hard traffic numbers (which can be difficult to validate) and intangibles associated with positioning and branding, to fixed numbers associated with a Return on Investment (ROI) and increases in revenue, market share, and overall profitability.

The objective for any electronic commerce site is to get qualified customers to the right place and then make their shopping experience as efficient and easy as possible. It is also important to make the site as intuitive as possible to direct the customer through a minimal number of navigational steps, yet enable that person to make a decision in a timely manner. For an e-tail consumer, too many page views, clicks, and scrollings can get in the way of commerce taking place, and too few can leave the customer with an "incomplete" feeling. Striking a balance between getting the cash register to ring immediately and encouraging a leisure stroll down virtual aisles is important.

For a corporate customer, the emphasis needs to be on providing the content, relationships, and processes in the right context. A corporate purchasing decision may be based on a procurement specification, requiring data from multiple supplier catalogs. A decision to procure may be contingent on vendor references, pricing discounts, service agreements, and purchasing automation.

Just as there are two types of qualified visitors—those who have visited the site before and newcomers—there are also many ways to measure who they are and their interests. Similarly, there are also many ways to measure and evaluate their importance to a venture. Because many browsers are still new to the online world and perhaps even intimidated by online shopping, any objectives for the first six months of a venture should be modest.

Perhaps more so than offline merchants, e-tailers and those in B2B have many opportunities to measure the effectiveness of their work. This capability provides a wide gulf between the online and offline world, giving a strategic advantage to the merchant that chooses to use it. Ironically, the tools that we use to measure success vary widely from online to offline, and even in the online world, between B2C and B2B. This book is dedicated to those participants in electronic commerce who want to understand, analyze, and innovate their way to success.

Power Tools for the Online Business

Just as the carpenter measures twice and cuts once, we are advocating a similar attention to the accuracy of your efforts. That same carpenter also has available a wide set of power tools to make sure that the measurements are accurately used. In the pages that follow, we are also suggesting that the entrepreneur and innovator in electronic commerce set about using quality measurement and the appropriate tools of electronic business and, perhaps more significantly, business in general.

With new online power tools, B2B and B2C merchants alike can adjust supply to meet demand, shift promotional emphasis from one product or offering to another, change vendors, and help customers track orders and shipments. Very little, if any of this, was available to the offline merchant before the advent of the Internet and the Web.

Here are some expectation-setting thoughts to guide exploration into whether or not to use an aggressive set of metrics to judge success levels.

1. Build site traffic and page views to engender confidence on the part of those who are early adopters (relative to the target population) and thereby stimulate word-of-mouth referrals.

2. If you are a B2B site, continue to build existing relationships while fostering new ones with a friendly style of allowing purchases to happen. The same applies to B2C after a customer becomes involved, and is expanded upon by encouraging use of a credit card or personal account to make the process as simple as possible. B2B customers, of course, have purchase orders as their primary medium of transactions.

3. Ease regular customers into the online experience with your firm.

4. Encourage requests for further information and building of a dialog between the customer and the firm.

5. To facilitate the site being customer-friendly in the same manner as an offline presence, put real people trained in sales and technical support, if need be, online.

6. Add names gathered at trade shows and other places where customers appear to the database for special promotions, catalog sales, and future email of offers. In addition, the database provides the parent firm with an opportunity to customize offerings around personal tastes and preferences of each customer.

E-Commerce Power Tools

- Metrics: If it moves, measure it!
- Purchasing simplicity
- Interaction
- Customer database
- Personalize
- Raise switching costs
- Raise barriers to entry with all of the above
- Do what the competition does, but better

7. With intelligent information in the database, personalization programs, such as birthday and special event calendars, can be leveraged. Even in business-to-business marketing, this kind of personalization works wonders.

8. Raise barriers to exit for customers and barriers to entry against competitors. These are primary defensive weapons any merchant can use; by "locking in" a customer, it makes it harder for competitors to dislodge that customer.

There are several metrics and power tools that are borrowed from established business practices. ROI is a metric requested by the investment community, financial services organizations, and others and it could be measured in several ways. While seemingly simple, after a period of inflated expectations and dashed hopes from poor performance on the part of some failed dot coms, this metric should be an important part of any business plan.

Lest you think that these are metrics that apply mainly to B2C, think again. Good merchants, worldwide and across many categories, in one way or another, must be database-intensive to select one tool from the above. Raising switching costs is extremely important to assist customer loyalty in technology products. Slightly changing the pin-count on an electronic device can be the difference between locking in repeat business and losing it to competitors who "knock off" a semiconductor design.

Reduced cost of doing business is a frequently cited benefit of doing business online. Savings are anticipated from a variety of business process improvements, ranging from:

- lower overhead costs
- lower Selling, General and Administration Expenses

- reduced processing time for orders
- elimination of paper catalogs and brochures
- reduced support personnel
- lower marketing expenses

Significant transaction costs are often achieved in banking, travel, and online brokerage firms. Electronic commerce enables a reduction in the cost of a banking transaction from more than a dollar to approximately one cent, offline versus online. A business travel reservation offline costs $10, while an online transaction was 20 percent of that. Online brokerage transactions were $10 versus $50 from a full-service broker.

Increased revenue is another reason for investing in electronic commerce. Sources of new revenue come from:

- new customers/accounts/buyers
- new products and services to existing customers
- opening up global markets
- individualized marketing directed at existing customers

Raising levels of customer satisfaction is also important through:

- timely and up-to-date information to customers
- more detailed product information than through a catalog
- 24 x 7 availability of the firm for customer information
- online tracking of orders and shipping
- reduced order entry errors

Other reasons include faster time to market (combining the benefits from having an Extranet with the Web site) and increased information flow through the company (the Intranet). All of these vectors are important to consider for any electronic commerce venture.

As is obvious, each way of looking at a business activity varies because of the different combinations of business models, operating styles, and market conditions. This means the metrics used can be highly variable, both in terms of the math used to quantify results as well as the analysis needed before using the math! These variations are reflected in the diverse ways metric analyses are presented.

Organization of the Book

Overall, this book is designed to provide a framework for how to understand and cope with the many issues that arise in building and sustaining an electronic commerce business by examining prevalent business models on the Internet. More specifically, the intent is to provide details about ways to build business models that can then be pieced together in a building-block fashion to construct, understand, and analyze complex business relationships in the new world of electronic commerce.

In the early chapters we set up a framework that establishes benchmarks you might use as the starting point for evaluations. The middle chapters focus on key concepts of electronic commerce such as customer acquisition and product pricing. Finally, there is a trial analysis of a sample company we call Ebiztro.com to show how all can be brought together.

Assembling these units into a cohesive view of an enterprise is achieved by defining the online business model in terms of four horizontal stacks and one vertical stack. The four horizontal stacks are platform, content, community, and commerce, as described in Chapter 2, "The Five Stack E-Commerce Model," and illustrated in Figure 1.3. The vertical stack is services, which provides value for each of the horizontal stacks. Metrics and examples to illustrate what we refer to as atomic business models are provided wherever possible.

Services are vertical because they can be introduced into every horizontal stack, usually when a make versus buy decision point is at hand. Services are pervasive throughout the new economy, and they potentially touch every enterprise that uses online

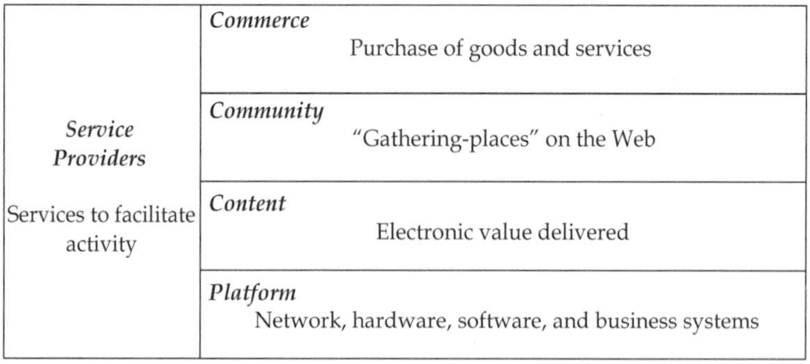

	Commerce Purchase of goods and services
Service Providers	*Community* "Gathering-places" on the Web
Services to facilitate activity	*Content* Electronic value delivered
	Platform Network, hardware, software, and business systems

Figure 1.3   The E-Commerce Stack

processes and technologies. Integrating services and service providers shortens time to market and often reduces capital costs.

There are other benefits as well as trade-offs for implementing outside resources. We touch on them in the remaining eight chapters as appropriate.

Chapter 2, "The Five Stack E-Commerce Model," looks closer at the model and identifies value in each part of the stack and the role that it plays in the big picture. In this chapter, we present a complete profile of the online company and the supporting elements it does and can use.

Chapter 3, "The Internet Platform," takes a comprehensive look at the Internet Platform in greater detail, listing and integrating the many hardware, network, and software components associated with an e-commerce enterprise. The Internet Platform consists of many technologies and technologically-based service providers, each of which also has a different business model. Make versus buy decisions exist at every node in this platform.

Chapter 4, "The Content Stack," looks at the nature of content—its source, aggregation, categorization, and distribution to users. In a very fundamental sense, the Internet is a vehicle for the intelligent movement of content. There are three types of content, each with a different reason and role in the online community. Content can be static, dynamic, or interactive, and some merchants integrate all three at one time or another into their sites.

Chapter 5, "The Community Stack," provides perspectives on community evolution and structure for B2C and B2B environments. Online sites bring people together into virtual communities. These virtual communities have tremendous economic potential for merchants, but coalescing users into a community requires perhaps more patience than working with other stack elements.

Chapter 6, "The Commerce Stack," focuses on e-commerce and lays out the business models under the categorization of stores, marketplaces, and ecosystems. This classification encompasses both B2C and B2B environments. Also provided is a discussion of the hybrid store of the future.

Chapter 7, "Pricing Models on the Web," complements Chapter 6 with a detailed look at pricing models that are made possible on the Internet and their applicability to different e-commerce contexts. With new pricing models there are also many new transaction mechanisms that allow merchants to shape an accurate pricing strategy. Metrics in this area can be very precise.

Chapter 8, "Customer Acquisition Models for E-Commerce," analyzes customer acquisition models and provides a graphic example of the pitfalls of e-commerce marketing. Permission marketing and banner ads are two marketing techniques unique to the online world, and an extensive analysis is included that uses several metric tools. Often overlooked is the power of the brand and correctly assembling resources to begin the branding process.

Chapter 9, "Application of Business Models," assembles the components of the puzzle and establishes the methodology for constructing more complex business models. A complete e-commerce store, Ebiztro.com, is modeled using the techniques of the book and illustrates the learning that comes from usage of business models, metrics, assumptions, and analysis.

The Five Stack E-Commerce Model

There are many ways to describe a business venture, ranging from the way it serves customers to the way it sets up its operations. In this chapter, we look at the many different forms of classifying online and offline activities. These classifications are often used to help the uninitiated understand some of the new dynamics associated with conducting business online—or where there are crossovers with their offline counterparts.

Some elements described here, for example, the five stacks, are greatly expanded upon in succeeding chapters. This discussion of the Five-Stack Model is designed to provide a high-level view of an e-commerce ecosystem. As you read through the remaining seven chapters, salient points will be expanded upon and integrated with others. In the argot of online, view this chapter as your home page.

Internet-enabled commerce consists of business kits that create and exchange value. These business kits contain "atomic" units of business functionality that are joined together, much like pieces of a building, to fulfill a corporate objective. A business model is much like a building in that both have foundations and floors. Floors have support pillars running through them bearing the weight. Each floor has walls, flooring, and artificial ceilings housing an infrastructure consisting of electric cables, plumbing, ventilation ducts, etc., that make the building whole and livable.

To continue the analogy and clarify some popular terms, e-commerce is what the business does and how it is accomplished. The business model is the overall architecture of the structure: how it is built, the design, and its face to the customer. E-business comprises all the infrastructure elements that electronically make up the support system for the venture.

E-commerce represents five elements consisting of four horizontal and one vertical stack. Starting from the bottom up, the four horizontal stacks are: **Platform, Content, Community** and **Commerce,** as shown in Figure 2.1. The vertical stack is **Services,** which supports and augments the functionality of the horizontal stacks. Each stack, horizontal and vertical, also represents several crossovers: from tangible (e.g., hardware) to intangible (software), from publishing and broadcasting (content) to interactivity and communication (email, chat, conferencing, e-commerce).

Not every Internet business model requires all the stacks; however, it is generally true that higher-order business models require lower-order stacks, such as platform and content. As one example, content in the form of catalogs is often needed to facilitate e-commerce. Platform, or infrastructure, must be in place and deployed effectively to support all the other stacks.

The **Platform** stack is critical because it encompasses both technology and the basic business elements. It is host to the hardware and software as well as the functions and processes required to successfully run a business. More globally, hardware also includes the information technology systems consisting of desktop computers, servers, modems, routers, hubs, switches, storage devices, monitors, cables, etc., that together form the Network portion of the platform. Software includes operating systems, application software, integration software, etc. A large organization integrates all of these even if it were to outsource many IT functions, and more so if it chooses to run all the activities in-house. In the disembodied

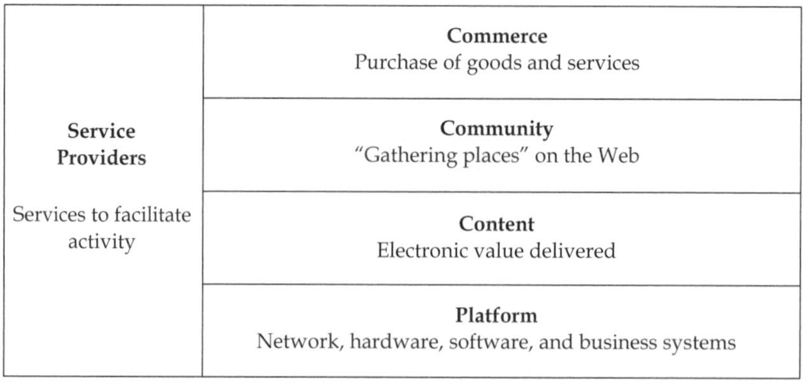

Service Providers Services to facilitate activity	**Commerce** Purchase of goods and services
	Community "Gathering places" on the Web
	Content Electronic value delivered
	Platform Network, hardware, software, and business systems

Figure 2.1 The Five-Stack E-Commerce Model

world of the Internet, the platform floor of a small entity specializing in one facet of its engagement online may actually be spread across several other third-party entities that perform specialized tasks and have the infrastructure (platform) to support them.

The next stack above is **Content,** and this is where one begins to see value added and delivered. The Internet is not some pie-in-the-sky technology that has no relevance to mainstream business. Content turns the Internet into a delivery mechanism, a medium, and a channel that can continue and expand business. At the most basic level, content is everything that an enterprise chooses to "publish" about itself: its mission, management, lines of business, products, financials, etc. Extending that further, it is meaningless and insufficient to be just a publisher—unless that *is* the organization's main business—without exploiting the Internet to further its goals, such as sell more by attracting a larger audience and enabling their purchase and delivery of products and services of their choice.

Content is also the database of products, the employee files on an Intranet, the history of customer accounts in a marketplace, all of which coexist in the public and private parts of the enterprise. The platform stack links them.

Above content sits **Community,** which expands the company's reach while narrowly focusing the interests of its constituency, or membership. A networked community has geographic scope that brings diversity of views not possible in a small physical community, asynchronous contact, timelessness of reference material (from archiving of content), and flexibility. Communities on the Internet actually predate the Web and the commercial era of the 'Net. The Well in the San Francisco Bay Area is one example of an online community that linked diverse interests together. Communities increasingly perform complementary roles in commerce environments. There are, of course, communities that do not have a commercial orientation and these are generally dynamic content repositories on specific topics or issues. Cluetrain is one that comes to mind that is non-commercial but trying to shape the commercial.

The topmost is the **Commerce** stack, which represents the purchase of goods and services on the Internet. Imagine what it takes to complete the purchase of your groceries when paid for with a credit card. First, there is selection of items from the various aisles and putting them in your shopping cart. At checkout there is scanning of each item by a clerk to log prices and keep a running total to tally amount due. Eventually, you manually swipe a debit or credit card with appropriate authentication (followed by your signature); the approval process and printing of the receipt follows. You then "take" possession of the groceries just paid for. Internet commerce occurs when you strip out all the complexity that lies hidden behind each transaction, an almost exact duplication of the whole process used to purchase your groceries. Only all of it happens online and immediately, and your tangible purchases are scheduled for delivery in due course by any of several logistics services that include UPS, FedEx, or even the USPS, though each of them are highly unlikely to handle groceries.

The **Services** stack represents value-added activities for each of the other stacks, providing for enhancement or outsourcing of the value. These facilities can be viewed in one way as what adds additional strategic advantage or distinctive competence to the venture. Thus, for example, one may think of a community operator or manager—such as on AOL's various forums—as performing a service to facilitate community interaction. Another example would be the provision of third-party authentication, commerce enabling, and escrow services to facilitate electronic commerce in the financial services arena.

Together, these five stacks of Platform, Content, Community, Commerce, and Services form fundamental building blocks underlying the "dot com" companies.

Additional building blocks that serve as other infrastructure elements include:

- network management tools
- security infrastructure for authentication and verification
- back-office systems for database management and enterprise integration
- commerce-enabling systems for hosting, transaction facilitation, and order processing
- intra- and intercompany integration
- applications that make possible a particular business model such as a marketplace, a storefront, or an auction center

This constant evolution and morphing of businesses and the resultant blurring of boundaries calls for a simple means to understand and appreciate the underpinnings of a business to be modeled. The five-stack paradigm serves this purpose well.

The Role of Context

The stacks shown in Figure 2.1 do not imply a hierarchical relationship. An electronic commerce transaction may require both content and community. A service offering quite often requires a community.

There are two important considerations. First, the Web enables and, in many cases, compels the consideration of multiple choices. Second, these choices are exercised in the "context" of the opportunities.

Let's visualize, for example, an online investment site. This hypothetical site could have *content* in the form of information about investment matters, corporate news, financial analysis, stock performance analysis, quotes, and the like. A *community* is then built around discussion forums that focus on specific sectors or industries—semiconductor, automobiles, telecom, etc., or investment vehicles like tax sheltered mutual funds, hedge funds, etc. There might even be a *commerce* angle built into this site, either in the purchase of relevant books or in links to online brokers to facilitate placement of a buy or sell order. Naturally, there is an underlying *platform* that provides the transaction and database engines. And our hypothetical site could offer additional *services*, such as tax planning, portfolio management, etc.

Each facility represents a specific and conscious feature-set offered by those managing the investment site to support the community of customers, build upon its focus, leverage its membership, and provide additional value to users with enhanced services. Context builds on the synthesis of the community's overall identity, bolstered in part by interactivity that arises from each user's desire to seek and share information collectively about investment matters. Site operators as well as the community of investors leverage the group's collective expertise for individual gain.

It is precisely the sum of these stacks that gives us Context, and that phenomenon allows us to identify business and e-commerce opportunities by defining and forming relationships between the different "floors" where none might have existed before (Figure 2.2).

Thus, a model that focuses only on content and commerce elements may exclude the context and, therefore, the benefits that accrue by integrating community and services. Where is one likely to see such a narrow model? A simple catalog business, for instance, would be one. Think for a moment of the L. L. Bean catalog in the offline world. You get a seasonal catalog in the mail that features several products categorized in different ways to support merchandising strategies. L. L. Bean includes several pictures and items within the same product category having characteristics (size, color, shape, etc). There is also an inserted form that lets the customer place an order, figure the cost, and authorize payment with a credit card. To complete the transaction, you send the form in the mail (or call an 800 number) and, sometime later, take delivery of the items ordered.

Now imagine the whole process replicated on the 'Net: there is the online catalog, some kind of selection mechanism, and payment for items in a "shopping cart." Because

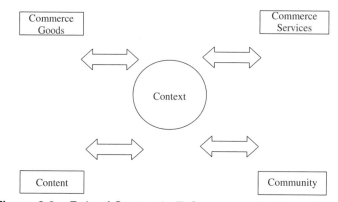

Figure 2.2 Role of Context in E-Commerce Business Models

this is a simple catalog model, other value-adding features that occur when community and services are integrated are not quite necessary.

Land's End, a strong offline competitor to L. L. Bean, has an online site that does successfully blend content, commerce, and services by letting the shopper configure a virtual model for trying on clothes and getting dressing advice/hints, etc. That service, enabled by a robust platform, enhances content in the catalog by making it a personal experience for a community of one, a specific shopper!

The Internet Platform Stack

At the beginning of this chapter we noted that a company's Internet "infrastructure" consisted of integrated hardware and software as part of the Internet Platform. Pause and think about this for a moment. If we are actually discussing a business run on the Internet (and, certainly, that is the focus of this book), IT hardware and software do not, in and of themselves, make a business. There is more to business than simply the geeky aspect of an Internet operation.

A business has physical facilities and communication facilities. A business also has a mission, strategies to achieve its mission, processes to enable the strategies, and several layers of support structures to ensure that processes are well defined and operate smoothly. Technology acts as one possible enabler of business, but it does not exist in a vacuum. Numerous dot.com failures attest to an inadequate recognition by entrepreneurs

Figure 2.3 Elements of the Internet Platform

of the need to enable the proper **business infrastructure** to support the role of technology in their businesses.

- The Internet Platform results from the integration of two elements: the Information Technology and Business platforms, as shown in Figure 2.3.

In the context of a unique business premise built on a genuine market need, which is then supported and bolstered by information technology within and without an enterprise, we have a genuine Internet Platform. The online platform, or foundational building block, grows by adding the appropriate technology to the strategic direction of the venture to create the reason for using the Internet.

IT Platform

The IT foundation of the company enables internal functions to take place, customers to interact, vendors to communicate, etc. With the Internet, the lifeblood of a company shifts from paper-based communication to the workings of its IT infrastructure, much like electricity enabled companies to take advantage of the industrial revolution. Broadly, the IT Platform may be divided into two parts: the Network Platform and Software Platform. Both of these platforms are purely digital and are not meant to exclude the physical hardware such as modems, routers, servers, etc.

Network Platform

The Network Platform is the communications infrastructure that is integrated into the IT Platform for an Internet-based operation. Just as highways, utilities, and river dams are the infrastructure of a nation, so too are networks for Internet businesses. The Network Platform supports on and off ramps to the Internet for consumers and businesses, encompassing global and local access. Table 2.1 shows the network infrastructure in terms of each different type of medium, its value, use, and future. Selection of each or any drives a series of other decisions about supporting hardware systems and services designed to support each. The network infrastructure, along with a more complete discussion of important hardware and software, is expanded upon in Chapter 3, "The Internet Platform."

Thus, while speed of access and download are always desirable, there are always trade-offs. Not all customers might have broadband access available, for example. An online consumer catalog that depends on extreme uses of bandwidth might build its infrastructure around high-speed interconnects, but may be at the mercy of slower speed distribution by copper-based dial-up connections by ISPs. A B2B catalog operation that entrusts end-point access to businesses with T1s will not face such a problem.

As with all other decisions on implementing an e-commerce business model, context becomes important!

Software Platform

On a PC, software is essentially of two types—operating system software (Unix, Windows, AppleOS, etc.) and application software (word processing, spreadsheet, presentation, etc). A third, utility software, is often overlooked or confused with application software. In a networked environment (and the Internet is one form of this), the types of software increase to include desktop OS, network OS, enterprise applications, etc. Further along the chain, an Internet-based operation additionally has e-commerce packages. Table 2.2 describes these.

Software systems vary in use from the "client" on up through various network nodes to ISPs and others in the e-commerce food chain. The more removed the enterprise is from B2C transactions, the more likely software increases in functionality, and with it complexity and cost.

Business Platform

The business platform consists of elements that comprise what it takes to set up a business around its processes and support structures to implement the specific offerings of the com-

Table 2.1 Technology Options for Connectivity to the Network

Medium	Value	Used By	Prognosis
Fiber	Very high data transfer rates in regular fiber.	Major backbone carriers to carry voice and data traffic.	Excellent growth likely with adoption of Wave Division Multiplexing technology (WDM).
Copper	Very high local coverage in the U.S. Enables low to moderate bandwidth connections.	Individuals, businesses.	Poor to moderate. Analog modems are giving way to Digital Subscriber Line (DSL) and cable. An interim technology, ISDN seems relegated to history.
Cellular	Low to moderate with more dense coverage in metropolitan areas. This is increasing in importance as new wireless technologies are deployed.	Mostly for voice traffic, but some new capabilities are on the horizon.	Good potential for lightweight mobile Web-enabled devices.
Satellite	Moderate to high with potential for sweeping universal coverage.	Not generally useful or available today for Internet traffic, despite inroads made by some ISPs.	With increasing numbers of Low Earth Satellites, there is a good case for and likelihood of a satellite based IP network.

pany. The business platform encompasses the needs of any company (Internet or otherwise), as well as its sustainable strategic advantage to carry out its business intent. The business platform consists of its physical support structures, including space, office furnishings, and internal communications along with outside services such as credit card facilities, banks, accountants, and lawyers, etc. Just as with our brick-and-mortar cousins, certain capabilities are required to meet the bare minimums for safely, securely, and efficiently conducting business with customers. Most of these issues cannot be covered in depth in this book, except to point out areas where outsourced facilities may exist to substitute for those usually found with the in-house business infrastructure.

Table 2.2   Types of Software

Software Type	Application	Prognosis
Operating System	Core foundation layer to install and/or build other software on.	Will stabilize to one or two basic types with UNIX dominating heavy duty back-end servers and NT and Linux serving intermediate layers.
Enterprise Applications	Front-office, back-office and "Web-office" applications; warehousing, logistics, manufacturing and distribution systems.	Disintermediation of these monolithic applications will occur; integrated suites will need to become flexible to match dynamic reconfiguration and adaptation. Application Service Providers (ASPs) will provide a "buffet" of offerings.
E-Commerce Software	Store builder tools, Web site management, content presentation, personalization, and customization.	Huge proliferation of applications for variety of purposes; will be available in hosted versions or ASP-based "pay-per-use" models.
Presentation Software	Browser "platform" to accept content on the screen. Capable of multimedia and serving as a launching pad for other functionality.	Rapid evolution anticipated particularly in mobile versions. Applicability to hand-held Web devices. SGML standards based content management and display.

The Content Stack

Content is an important element leading to e-commerce—it adds value to interactions and provides a reason for transactions of goods and services. Just a few years back, large libraries, such as those at universities, were considered the primary repositories of content. Clearly, the Internet and its two billion pages have turned into the world's largest repository of content. The Internet provides access to content of both a historical nature, which is being rapidly converted into digital formats, as well as newly minted content, which starts out digital.

Content may be categorized in a variety of ways, but mainly online content is of three types: static content, dynamic content, and interactive content (see Figure 2.4). Static content is created and, apart from periodic updates where necessary, simply exists as a

Example: Non-Profit Agency Channel Marketing

One does not normally associate a non-profit agency with leveraging content. We include this reference to show that not all e-commerce is applicable for commercial ventures. Non-profits are simply presumed to exist on the sidelines of everyday commerce, focusing on some niche aspect of society, evangelizing an issue, and prodding social conscience. But, as with any business, the circumstances of its operations are not all that different or unique. Consider, for instance, one of its operational attributes—channel marketing. This may be encapsulated within a set of "functional requirements" that articulate what channel marketing is expected to undertake.

Overall functional requirements: Provide information, create media "buzz," attract new and existing support online, and track usage and contributions. Attributes:

1. Content management
2. Content updates and special donor drives
3. Focus content on core and special initiatives
4. Provide mediated community space for active donor involvement and new users
5. Provide context and content for media usage
6. Alliance program management with corporate and foundation entities
7. Corporate tie-ins for payroll deduction and matching programs
8. Integration and cross-linking to corporate Web sites
9. Affiliate programs with corporate sponsors and e-tailers
10. "Pass through" shopping with integrated contributions
11. Manage traffic, track usage, and contributions
12. Extend "brand" to other non-profit causes through active partnerships

A non-profit agency focusing on whole foods, for example, has its marketing drives clearly defined. Online a lot of its charter revolves around content specific to organic foods, health updates, scientific research news, community space for people to ventilate their views, alliance/affiliate and co-branding with manufacturers and sellers of organic foods, online shopping catalog, etc. Thus, this enterprise relies heavily on electronic content to be credible on the Web, and engage in a dialog between various constituencies!

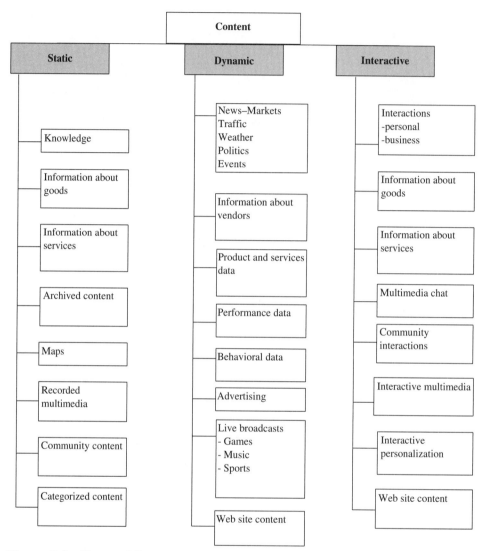

Figure 2.4 Types of Content

repository. Examples are maps, recorded multimedia, categorized content, and most "brochureware" sites. Dynamic content takes the concept one step further: it is constantly changing. We may think of news of any type, weather forecasts, advertising, live broadcasts, etc., as being dynamic. Lastly, interactive content actively solicits and is enriched by user interaction. The Internet, in sharp contrast to radio and TV broadcasts, is especially suited to content interactivity. Multimedia chat, community interactions, online shopping and online brokerages typify uniquely interactive content.

While not comprehensive, Figure 2.4 makes it clear that online content generation and management is a very large industry supported by a variety of ancillary technologies, providers, and services that cater to the aggregation and dissemination of content.

Static Content

All over the world efforts are underway to convert historical data (on paper or other media) to electronic form. Libraries and research institutions are posting their archived content to searchable environments. Human knowledge of all forms—arts, sciences, history—is being rapidly made available on the Internet. Manufacturers of goods and providers of services are converting offerings of informational or transactional nature to the Web. Current and ancient maps of the world depicting oceans, continents, and cities are available on demand. Old recordings of music and events are being systematically digitized for replay. All this is leading to huge requirements for systematic cataloging of information, that is, providing the ontology, which is often the most efficient search basis for retrieval of data.

Dynamic Content

The Internet excels in the provisioning of dynamic content. With increasing transactions on the Web, there is a strong need to have dynamic content about products and services. In this new economy, manufacturers must provide all the content that helps consumers make a buying decision. Such requisite content could include online product descriptions, photos, pre- and post-sales information, customer testimonials, comparisons, reviews, and recommendations.

The dynamic nature of the Web also demands good "end user" experiences. Colocation and cohosting facilities improve content delivery by situating themeselves on the major Internet arteries. Even more creative are efforts provided by content generating firms like Akamai and Inktomi. Bandwidth heavy content such as images and multimedia are streamed from their content servers situated on the "edges" of the network to minimize latency effects.

News

Those who are the primary sources of "fresh" news must update their sites on a regular basis to demonstrate the dynamic nature of their content. News reporting illustrates the degree of change that the Web brings to making dynamic content available to users, showing that news gathering and distribution organizations are now vulnerable. "News" is freely syndicated from news collection agencies, such as Reuters, directly to portal environments or to the user's Web browser. The residual value of "expertise" and "opinion" in offline forums is thus less valued as the content is directly assimilated. The sports industry is moving to providing real-time content and, with adequate bandwidth, we are likely to see the rapid escalation of the computer as an environment to view sporting events that use streaming audio and video on full screens.

News content is made for the Internet. As an intangible commodity that can easily exist as digital bits, its delivery via the 'Net is highly efficient and, most importantly, timely because news by definition has an extremely short life expectancy—its value is inversely proportional to the time of delivery. That means instantaneous delivery has greater value.

Consumers could pay for news content delivered via the Internet at a higher rate than other media. This aspect of value is, of course, closely associated with perhaps a lower cost of distribution, which contributes to profitability.

Value also increases from features unique to this form of delivery—the ability to customize and personalize, and the ability to alert and notify consumers of and when content is available for them.

News content is mostly originated by media organizations such as AP, UPI, Reuters, CNN, The New York Times, Time, Newsweek, ABC, CBS, NBC, and so on. Not surprisingly, these media giants are parlaying their news gathering prowess and financial muscle to the Internet. Many of them provide the bulk of the content to portals such as Yahoo!

Interactive Content

By far, the greatest promise of the Internet lies in the potential of broad-scaled interactivity that fuels a wide sphere of human interactions equal to or exceeding those in the offline world. Content-based interaction is still limited to text exchanges and asynchronous queries. Face-to-face communications with voice and video, voice over Internet, chat environments, instant linguistic transalations, voice-based email, and browsing services are already revolutionizing online experiences. The Web is beginning to acquire a "human face on demand," which can go a long way toward facilitating e-commerce transactions. In the non-profit world, community town halls and group meetings on the Web can be expected to be much more fruitful, efficient, and pleasant.

With interactive multimedia may also come interactive personalization, where the end user specifies the vehicles and constructs in which content is to be delivered interactively, such as multichannel streaming, live multiway broadcasts, and interactive gaming.

The Community Stack

If content is the "oxygen" of the Internet, community is surely the "adhesive." It binds people to issues. It forms the basis of our response to fashion, sports, entertainment, and just about every aspect of our involvement with other people. On the Internet, communities take the form of "virtual" relationships centered around interests that bring each of us into the relationship in the first place.

Community Elements

A community, whether in the world of the consumer or B2B, has a basis in the four important elements, as shown in Figure 2.5.

- *Common Interests:* This is the primary basis for forming a community. Members share a particular, narrow interest: family, lifestyle, hobby, programming, corporate purchasing, efficient manufacturing, etc. Communities can be narrowly or broadly focused, depending on origins, needs, and constraints. For instance, a community focused on new moms may not have the same focus as toddler parenting, although there could be a partnership that "graduates" members to a related community. Inevitably, communities need motivated founders and team leaders who ensure success of the community. This is similar to a neighborhood that needs a gregarious family to arrange various civic activities. Communities that fail often do not have leaders who provide the glue to maintain the spark of common interests among community members.

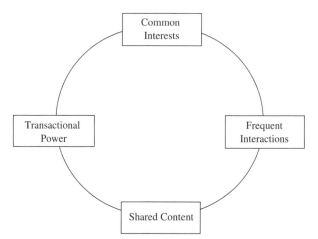

Figure 2.5   Community Elements

- *Frequent Interactions:* A community starts building when shared interests are combined with frequent interactions. In the early days of online, communities were electronic bulletin boards, which by today's standards were primitive and limited to text-based threaded discussions. Several of those early electronic communities were extremely successful in meeting the needs of the community. They still bear testimony to the potential in the new Web environment with its pervasive ability to connect to the community members over a lengthy period of time.

- *Shared Content:* As a community grows with increased members and frequent interactions, its shared content grows into a dynamic, and often valuable, database. For example, if there is a community of 1,000 members, out of which say 100 members interact everyday, then the content of the community grows at a rate of 3,000 messages a month. In addition, the Web-based community excels in organizing its needs around its own form of pertinent utility: specific information, resources, searchable indexes, cataloged content, and threaded communication trails. By common consent, all these are now the shared content of the community, available to all 1,000 members. Thus, a new community member is rewarded with a personal library in the area of interest and is granted access to specialized resources (i.e., the other community members) for guidance on more detailed issues. In a community, the compensation for active and knowledgeable members is "respect" and "recognition."

- *Transactional Power:* As a community grows and its purchasing potential increases, it becomes attractive as a venue for vendors willing to supply goods and services. These vendors fall into two categories:

    1) Member-Benefit Model: These vendors sell at "community-negotiated" prices for product categories that do not necessarily relate to the community's specific focus. For example, a community on *DadsOverForty.com* could have travel packages, financial investment offerings, cars, etc. Here, the community exploits its buying power to obtain preferred terms for its members.

    2) Community-Focus Model: In this case, the vendors cater to the specific and often narrow interests of the community. For example, a community of overworked Silicon Valley employees, BurntOut.com, may have segments in its community categorized as: Depressed, Family Stressed, Office Politics, Options Worthless, etc., and there may be vendors with offerings in each specific area. Furthermore, they can be tied into the threaded discussions of the community through keyword indexing of content and commerce, always in appropriate contexts. Team leaders play a critical role in enabling such transactional features because they recognize and extract suitable benefits from vendors on behalf of the community.

Both of these models leverage any spending propensity of its members. This interaction by the community on behalf of its members gives it a community buying power, which has the potential to lower the price of goods and services.

Consider, for example, that Macy's has a President's Day Sale for Wonder Washing Machines at a price of $299. Just as the doors are about to open, a community "activist" identifies that there are 200 potential buyers for the Wonder Washing Machine because it is more environmentally friendly than competing brands. On behalf of these potential buyers, he is then "authorized" to speak to Macy's management to seek a preferred price, which is lower than the listed price. At that instant, this "community" has gained buying power and, with judicious exercise of power, market advantages.

In the physical world, creating such a buying community is difficult to do. This allows merchants to set the much-accepted fixed price notion for transactions. Online, such aggregations are easily viable in both structured and instant formats, forcing online vendors to be much more responsive to these attractive offers.

Types of Communities

Authors Hagel and Armstrong ("Net Gain") brought to the fore the need, potential, and power of communities on the Web. While we devote Chapter 5, "The Community Stack," to a more complete discussion of communities, it is important to show their relationship here to other stacks.

Broadly speaking, there are two natural types of communities:

- Business communities
- Consumer communities

The Business Community

Business communities are divided into three categories: vertical, horizontal, and topical, as shown in Figure 2.6. Historically, businesses structured themselves vertically (e.g., vertically integrated corporations as in the automobile or chemical industries) or horizontally (conglomerates such as GE that have a presence in many industries). In the physical world, the rise of lobbying groups to represent, say, the pharmaceutical industry or the movie industry (vertical) and trade, tax, etc. (horizontal) are evidence of the particular merit in each of these two forms of communities.

Topical communities, more recent in their appearance, owe their existence, at least partly, to increasing complexity in our professional and personal lives. Even here, topical communities such as IEEE, the American Management Association, and the American Medical Association existed prior to the emergence of the online world.

Vertical Business Communities

These communities are narrowly focused on a single segment or subsegment of an industry. Early origins of such groupings came up in the research, education, and software development sectors. With online interaction becoming ubiquitous, such vertical communities are being formed in every aspect of business. These communities share knowledge across companies and increase the aggregate efficiency of the industry segment. Best practices are more easily adopted, and expert groups develop to resolve common industry issues. These vertical industries also become proficient at lobbying for their interests in the appropriate corridors of power.

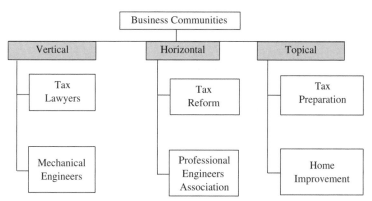

Figure 2.6 Business Communities are Divided into Three Main Categories and Subcategories

Horizontal Business Communities

These communities are influential across many vertical industries. They are particularly noteworthy in their role in shaping tax laws, environmental regulations, export procedures, trade practices, and real estate procedures. Here, expertise in these areas is valuable across a broad swathe of industries. Such horizontal communities may serve a very valuable role, particularly in content aggregation and creating a need for enhanced search algorithms. A resulting body of content may become valuable in and of itself. To demonstrate its power, it can stand alone for leverage outside the community, by itself.

Consider for example a community on Marine Pollution Law. A body of content (law, regulations, case law, applicability, current pending cases, risk mitigation scenarios) coupled with community members who have expertise in this area may serve a valuable role to oil companies, government, the press, and the public at large. In the event of a marine accident, such a body could quickly assemble online and weigh in on the issues. By weight of its expertise, it could also provide clarity to the issues.

Topical Business Communities

Here, the focus is on specialization needed for executing within a particular business context. Without a doubt, there could be viable and powerfully active communities for Project Managers, Java Programmers, Linux Users Groups, etc. This enables community members to learn rapidly from each other, particularly in areas such as these marked by rapid change. Cohesion because of a shared interest in a topic also provides community contact among peers, which is useful in recruiting and for expanding employment opportunities. Peering relationships, contribution to discussions, resolving problems, and earning recognition are hallmarks of a good topical community.

Consumer Community

Consumer communities are also online associations of individuals who interact for personal and collective benefit. Such emergence of communities mirrors origins of social institutions, which created villages, towns, countries, associations, lobbying groups, and political movements. With free flow of information and easy access to the Internet, individual thoughts become the underpinnings of online communities, drawing strength almost magically for pervasive interaction. A consumer community evolves much like a multihued quilt—from isolated strands of fiber to a strong fabric with strength and character.

Consumer communities can be broadly divided into three subcategories as follows (see Figure 2.7):

Geographic: Such communities focus on specific geographic areas associated with one's residency, such as the San Francisco Bay Area, Palo Alto, etc. The geographic boundaries cannot be so broad as to dilute the sense of belonging to that physical space. The content associated with geographic communities deals with lifestyle issues such as traffic and schools, local events, politics, and initiatives. Community members help each other in settling down, adjusting, relocating, and helping as needed.

Demographic: These communities deal largely with "stage-of-life" issues driven by age, lifestyle, ethnicity, and parenthood status. The links are often shared or similar life experiences, and their camaraderie engenders an attitude of "we are in this together." In such communities the emphasis is less on content and more on the scope of interaction. Community members may provide counseling, job postings, training, and mentoring.

Topical: In topical communities, the focus is on efficient execution of one's chosen activity or hobby. These include communities focused on activities like model plane flying, origami, nature hikes, religious practice, trading, music, etc. This narrower focus allows and demands far greater specialization, giving rise to community "gurus" who mentor and enable cohesion and attraction. In the absence of such leaders, topical communities are vulnerable and may often wither.

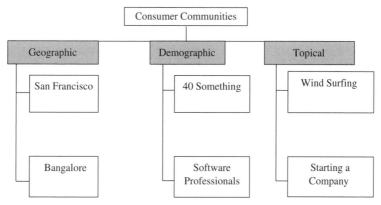

Figure 2.7 Consumer Communities

The Commerce Stack

Internet commerce spans a very large set of transaction possibilities crossing numerous constituencies. In one sense, we can create commerce opportunities around four broad sets of constituencies:

- Big Businesses
- Small/Medium Enterprises
- Community
- Individuals

Big Businesses

Large companies have substantial resources to execute against corporate objectives. Their management interacts with the external world to acquire basic materials needed to develop and market their offerings and then sell the finished goods or services. Large corporations have five primary stakeholders: employees, shareholders, community, partners, and suppliers. Of these, the last two, partners and suppliers, form a visible part of their business interactions. Partners and suppliers make up what is termed the value chain, and it can be other big corporations like themselves as well as smaller businesses. In addition, business engages both with a community at large (local, national, and global) and with individuals as customers.

The very size of big business poses enormous complexities in every aspect of the organization—in the number of departmental interfaces, levels of hierarchy, management control and reporting, and responsiveness to external stimuli. The links to the external world are likewise complex.

Small/Medium Enterprises (SMEs)

Smaller businesses are much more limited in resources and strategic reach. However, on the Internet model, SMEs can acquire larger reach and scope.

Reach is defined as the number of people, or customers, that a SME can realistically have a relationship with. In some ways, this reflects a concept called network economics—the greater the connectivity, the greater the value in becoming connected. In the pre-Internet days, reach was for the most part limited by geography. Smaller businesses do not have the wherewithal that larger companies have in spending heavily on brand promotion. Today, a company on the Web can have the world at large as its market. It has many channels open to it to enlarge its customer base, often putting it on equal footing with its larger competitors.

Scope is the ability to extract greater value from the business of selling a good or service. As simple as it sounds, scope is often limited in the brick-and-mortar world, particularly for a small business seeking many different paths to extract value. On the 'Net, however, a business is defined not so much by what it produces or services, but by the way it serves customers and the value of its informational content. As we saw above, information content can be customized and personalized, made interactive, and combined with other services and additional information to enhance value.

Community

In the previous section we saw that there are many different kinds of communities that gather around and within the Web. There are communities within the B2B world. Recently, digital marketplaces formed to buy and sell commoditized products among themselves. In those exchanges, the aggregations of individual business members produce, add value, and consume each other's products and services. Similarly, consumer communities are aggregations of individual customers, often found in buying pools or on popular auction sites, who themselves produce content, add value, or deliver goods and services to other consumers. Communities, obviously, are both sources of e-commerce offerings as well as consumers of them. As the online world goes through a series of rolling shakeouts in a form of digital Darwinism, the fittest representatives in an e-commerce community have the best chance of surviving. Those who do survive most likely will be those with a keen appreciation for and understanding of the important role metrics play, a topic that we discuss later on.

Communities are very important in the new, emerging world of e-commerce. The days of large and undifferentiated sites that appeal to a low common denominator are rapidly fading. The more successful businesses, large and SME, are recognizing the value of identifying with communities of interest to leverage customer acquisition cost and reduce operating expenses formerly thrown at marketing projects.

Individuals

Individuals achieve enormous new leverage with the proliferation of Web sites. Individuals are no longer seen as mere producers in the workspace and consumers in the off-work environment. The individual can become a "producer" by utilizing his or her knowledge, skills, expertise, and talent to offer new goods and services to the market. Consider, for example, an export/import manager at a large corporation. Such an individual can offer expertise on the Web through sites such as *www.guru.com* or *www.expertcity.com* to other businesses. Or a business development manager can provide guidance to an entrepreneur for writing a business plan. Or a handyman could reach out to construct a community playground in his off-hours.

Individual productivity, which was held captive inside a structured business environment, can also expand reach and scope, leading to new channels of revenue for an *individual acting as a business unit.* Such new reach for individual "productivity" can enormously alter the dynamics and economics of everyday commerce, especially for SMEs.

Figure 2.8 illustrates the "solution space" for e-commerce among these four broad constituencies of Big Business, SMEs, Communities, and Individuals.

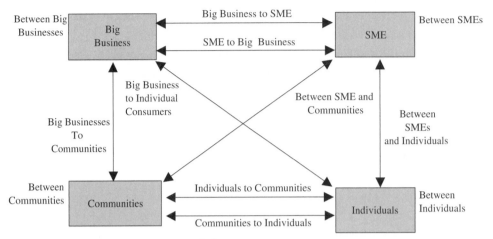

Figure 2.8 Solution Space for E-Commerce

The more traditional description of this solution space is in terms of the following:

1. Business-to-Business (B2B)
2. Business-to-Consumer (B2C)
3. Consumer-to-Consumer (C2C)

Business-to-Business

B2B is commerce between business entities, small and large. It also includes business transactions between business and the government, sometimes referred to as B2G. The list of transactions included in this category spans everything from sourcing everyday items like printer toner and paper to machinery parts, raw materials, capital equipment, finished goods, and services. The B2B world is said by many market research firms to be as much as ten times greater than B2C; however, most studies that put a number on it are equally wide ranging.

B2B commerce can take place directly between business entities or indirectly by means of a marketplace. Online, direct trade between business partners is an extension of Electronic Data Interchange (EDI), which arose in the late 1970s and early 1980s and is based on private networks. Where EDI-based commerce already exists, it is expected to move gradually over to the Internet to take advantage of the open environment and avail lower cost connectivity.

Marketplaces go by different names—exchanges, vertical markets, auctions, hubs, depending on several nuances including functionality. Basically, exchanges provide an open trading community and they seek to match buyers and sellers. Vertical markets are exchanges focused on a single industry or segment; and hubs are collections of contextual exchanges across several vertical market segments as well as horizontally across functional or process dimensions. Auctions are both transaction methods and forums to dispose of used equipment, excess inventory, or clearance items. Marketplaces also provide services, such as contextual search, vendor-managed catalogs, transaction processing, hosted procurement, managed bids and quotes, buy-side integration into enterprise systems, and so on.

Business-to-Consumer

The B2C space captivated the attention of consumers and alerted merchants to the possibilities of the Internet as a new and dynamic channel to sell goods and services directly to consumers without a physical store presence. In this business model, the online merchant typically provides a catalog of goods with adequate representations of features, functionality, and options. The consumer purchases the goods in a self-service model, often without any direct interaction with the merchant. Decreased customer service costs associated with self-service are certainly compelling in contrast to the often untrained or overworked customer service representatives in retail stores and mail-order business houses. However, the explosive proliferation of online stores created a huge problem associated with customer acquisition. Online stores, thinking the path to their virtual doors was paved with riches, advertised heavily in offline and online media to gain visibility. As further inducements, borne partly out of naiveté, they rushed to provide free shipping and substantive discounts to acquire a customer. This led to customer acquisition costs of over $75, on average, in the U.S. In a subsequent chapter, we will model the various methods of customer acquisition, mapping the corresponding costs and consequences to the enterprise.

Consumer-to-Consumer

In the offline world, this is the world of the classifieds and the garage sales. This marketplace for used goods and personal services is relatively local or highly focused in trade media, but the connectivity and interactivity enabled by the Internet has caused this segment to explode online. This is well illustrated by the explosive growth of activity at *eBay.com* and *QXL.com,* as well as numerous others in this general category.

C2C businesses have unleashed previously captive "inventory" of goods and services into the marketplace, leading somewhat to cannibalization of commerce from the B2C segment, a process called disintermediation. For example, a consumer looking to purchase a dining room set can shop as easily at an online mall as bid for similarly used merchandise at the eBay site. Potential buyers of a dining room set can read a sufficiently elaborate description, see a picture, and obtain reviews about the seller to gain trust in the potential transaction. In the offline world, there are constraints to such substitution due to the reduced information available about a used product, or the absence of a picture or the validation of a seller. In many states, laws prohibit some merchandise from being sold directly to end users by manufacturers—automobiles in Texas, for example.

Furthermore, the current model of C2C could easily evolve into a barter system. In a barter environment, goods and services can be directly exchanged on a product-product, product-service or service-service basis; or a sale can be denominated in an artificial currency like Flooz and Beanz. Thus, a seller would be credited in an ersatz currency that could be used to acquire other products and services within the barter economy.

Methods of Commerce

Another important distinction in e-commerce business models can be made between the different methods of commerce:

- Direct Commerce
- Intermediated Commerce
- Affiliated Commerce

Direct Commerce

In direct commerce a merchant sells goods without any intermediaries, or distributors and retailers, to a business or a consumer. In this model, the merchant has ownership of the goods and may have manufactured the goods or had it manufactured and branded. Direct commerce, such as between WalMart and its retail customers or between Office Depot and its business customers, incorporates many elements of their supply chains that lead up to the sale. With these highly integrated environments, there are broad effects on corporate planning, specifications, logistics, inventory control, merchandising, account management, and sales management. When Nike subcontracts with an Indonesian enterprise to assemble shoes to Nike's specifications, it is engaging in direct commerce. At large sourcing operations, such as at General Motors, Ford Motor, Boeing, and GE, there are direct transactions with thousands of producers, suppliers, partners, and government agencies.

In the past, these myriad interactions were managed semimanually. Some rudimentary automation took over repetitive tasks while whole processes continued to be handled manually. With the advent of EDI, the elements of procurement and manufacturing transactions involved in large, direct commerce began to be automated. Both parties to a transaction had to invest in EDI (software, hardware, data formats, etc). The Internet now provides an open alternative that is low cost, has lower overhead, is flexible, and scalable. Moreover, a business is not tied to one other partner like Siamese twins but free to explore opportunities at large.

Interaction of a business with its suppliers and partners constitutes the half of the value chain termed the supply chain. The supply chain involves sourcing raw materials and semiproduced goods, logistics, and inventory management.

At the other end of the value chain are customers with whom the business has interactions. Electronic commerce does not do away with the traditional aspects of engaging the customer—from identifying who the customer is to ensuring there is repeat business following their satisfaction with the product or service sold to them.

The front end of the supply chain often consists of traditional sales and marketing. Market research sought to identify and categorize the buying public; then marketing initiated programs to position the product or service, and sales did the job of actually selling them. While these roles have not disappeared with the advent of the Internet, it is possible to engage the consumer in a manner never before achieved. The 'Net makes possible customization and one-to-one marketing on a much larger scale, again opening scope and reach to the merchant. As we've seen, informational content can be packaged to add value to a product or service.

Direct commerce has three interlocking elements: front-end operations, site operations, and back-end operations. This outward-facing information structure enables connectivity within and outside the enterprise, and throughout the entire value chain. It is referred to as the "extended enterprise" (Cherry Tree & Co. Research, *Spotlight Report on*

Extended Enterprise Applications, January 2000). The front-end includes Customer Relationship Management (CRM) applications. Site operations include enterprise applications (such as ERP, and MRP). Back-end includes Supply Chain Management (SCM) applications, all of which are shown in Figure 2.9.

Front-End Operations

Every business has a so-called "front end" responsible for acquiring, engaging, and ensuring that customers are satisfied with the product or service. To companies such as Intel, Cisco, and Dell Computer, which have large—and rapidly growing—Internet-based businesses, the front end is crucial and complex. The complexity arises from the number of products, features, and possible configurations that would normally be the territory of a traditional sales force charged with selling to a particular type of client. The Web makes it possible now to offload a good chunk of this responsibility to the customers themselves. For companies producing a complex array of products that have several possible combinations, self-configuration is a valuable service to customers. Customer service in the form of customization and one-to-one relationship management is another area of immense importance in B2B commerce. This is the area of CRM that proactively manages new and existing customers face-to-face, via the Internet, or through more traditional direct mail or telemarketing.

Site Operations

Intraenterprise operations in an online, B2B commerce environment take three forms: Core Backbone, Core Business, and Business Value Add. The core backbone of an

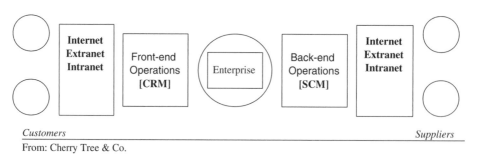

From: Cherry Tree & Co.

Figure 2.9   Direct Commerce

enterprise information infrastructure handles security, network and server availability, performance management, and transaction management. Each of these directly affects the quality and throughput of commercial transactions.

Core business is the distinctive competence of an enterprise, what it sells or services, and the reason for commerce. It consists of goods, services, and content directly and indirectly related to its products and services. It also includes the supply chain that supports the enterprise.

Business Value Add encompasses an umbrella of services such as loyalty programs, gift certificates, value and personalization that provide incentives and other inducements for customers to prefer the merchant. Many times, the value added by the online environment is a compelling reason for customers to buy from an e-commerce vendor. Convenience and lower cost are two benefits that accrue from business value-add programs.

Back-End Operations

Back-end operations are largely invisible but crucial for commercial enterprises, especially those that are large and complex. It includes enterprise systems integration, supply chain management, planning and execution, administration, and forward and reverse logistics. The success of the enterprise rests to a great extent on its ability to handle, or achieve, integration with external entities. These include suppliers and partners, transportation systems, warehouses, vendors, and retailers.

Intermediated Commerce

An intermediary can play a matchmaker role between the buyer and seller. Given the prolific nature of the Web and the abundance of sellers, the power of an intermediary is in the ability to provide a multiplicity of solutions to a potential buyer. Thus, the buyer, instead of navigating to one seller's Web site and then to a competitor's Web site, is instead motivated to go to an intermediary who consolidates the offerings of many sellers. The intermediated sector of online B2B commerce is in a state of rapid evolution, but three kinds of "intermediated marketplaces" operate today:

- affiliates
- hubs
- exchanges

Affiliates

Affiliate marketing, or affiliated commerce, is much like the model that Amway and Tupperware use to bring in the customer for the sale. Online, this is used by Amazon to secure a selling outpost of several hundred thousand affiliates who merchandise and drive the sale to Amazon. Such models are spreading rapidly through the B2C and B2B marketplaces. Affiliate marketing firms such as BeFree and Commission Junction create environments whereby merchants and Web site partners can get affiliated.

Hubs

Hubs are essentially aggregators of either information alone (denoted as infomediary hubs) or for transaction (denoted as transmediary hubs). They may be vertical in scope, consisting of catalogs that pertain to suppliers from one industry. Trading hubs are marketplaces that may include vertical or horizontal markets, and also focus on some dimension of business such as process or function. SciQuest.com (*www.sciquest.com*) is a marketplace for scientific products, aggregating products from several hundred suppliers. Such markets pull together suppliers and their product lists, specifications, prices, delivery, ordering mechanism, and financial settlement. Hubs could be horizontal in scope, providing a wide selection of suppliers for a vast marketplace. FedCenter.com (*www.fedcenter.com*) aggregates a large number of suppliers for departments of the U.S. government to provide a supplier base for an expansive set of categories.

Exchanges

Exchanges, as we saw above, operate similarly to primitive stock exchanges and seek to match buyers and sellers, sometimes using a bid/ask mechanism. Esteel.com (*www.esteel.com*) brings together buyers and sellers of steel to form a dynamic market, where the price is set by demand and supply imbalances within the marketplace.

All indirect commerce marketplaces, particularly hubs, draw sustenance from fragmented markets (of buyers and suppliers). To provide a business value add, they bring domain expertise in specific industry segments to ameliorate inefficient procurement practices, while offering a greater choice of products and variations in pricing. They promise cost savings from streamlined processes that include sophisticated search tools, extensive vendor-maintained catalogs conforming to specific standards, requisitions, business rules, workflow management for approval routing, invoice matching, ship status and delivery details, payment, and integration to back-end enterprise financial systems.

The Service Providers

One of the most fascinating aspects of value creation on the Internet is the broad spectrum of Service Providers, many of whom owe their existence to perceived online merchant needs. Service providers create a wide range of outsource capabilities that allow an online player to substitute owned assets or internally performed units of work with those that are externally contracted or carried out. These outsourced services in every aspect of business provide individuals, entrepreneurs, small businesses, and large businesses with new options on the way an *atomic business functionality* is achieved.

All of which boils down to a simple consideration: *Is there an external alternative in every specific, narrow aspect of business?*

The remarkable answer is an impressive **YES!** As shown in Figure 2.10, service provider functionality spans across all other layers of our e-commerce stack, stretching over Platform, Content, Community, and Commerce. As a consequence, the Internet now allows the creation of completely "virtual" businesses that can own almost no infrastructure, no physical assets, no unique content, and no employees other than the owner, and yet are able to earn real revenues.

Is this possible?

Absolutely.

It is now possible for an entrepreneur residing in a seaside condo in Tahiti to run an online business with zero owned hard assets and be on par with a traditional company, competing equally on the Web. What does it take? Money, of course. A brand. And an ability to make smart choices about the service providers that can provide the outsourced functionality to create the "virtual" business.

Can such an enterprise be profitable? That's a harder question to answer and we will get into these issues in further detail in subsequent chapters.

It is important to understand that profitability has more to do with successful execution of the business model and less to do with physical assets—the trappings of traditional enterprise. It is possible and sometimes likely that physical assets—buildings,

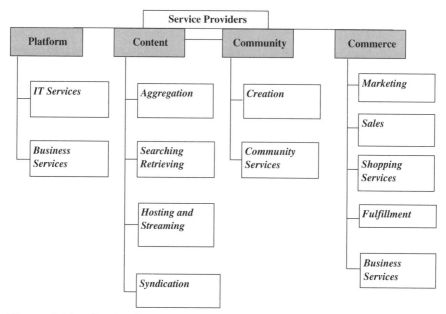

Figure 2.10   Service Providers Support and Supplement the Other Four Stacks

warehouses, plants, even employees—may detract from theoretical efficiencies that may be possible through outsourced functionality.

Does it make sense to go completely virtual? In most cases never, although "virtual" businesses may make sense for "remote entrepreneurs."

Consider the former hotbed of entrepreneurs, Hong Kong. A well-heeled businessman in Hong Kong could set up a dynamic online retail store, selling predominantly to the U.S. market with completely outsourced infrastructure, products, and services. For most businesses, this theoretical business limit of zero hard assets except for cash is not the relevant case in point. More relevant are the choices available to outsource for assets or functionality that are either not available internally or exist inefficiently.

In the first case, assets or functionality that need to be created cost time, and your time to build versus buy may yield significant competitive advantage to an adversary (the late mover disadvantage). In the second instance, inefficient in-house execution wastes money, which could be put to better use elsewhere in the business process. Do such substitution options exist in the offline world? Indeed they do, but not as obviously, efficiently, or as prolifically.

Platform Service Providers

Platform service providers provide functionality that enables the Internet platform for companies' Web strategies. The key elements are *IT services* consisting of Internet service providers, application service providers, e-commerce solution providers, consultants, and *business services.*

IT Services

Independent Service Providers (ISP)   There are thousands of companies around the world that provide access to the Internet. Access methods range from relatively slow dial-up phone lines and wireless to high-speed frame relay, cable, and other broadband services. Typical issues that govern end-user choices are: bandwidth available, network performance, quality of service, and security. Depending on which are most important and those relatively of lesser importance, just about any grade of service is available depending on the communications budget.

Application Service Providers (ASP)   The second group of providers in this stack provides access to selected software applications over an Internet connection. ASPs provide many business applications over the Internet or through a secure network to companies. This model enables the business customer of the ASP to concentrate on its core competencies. The ASP takes care of all aspects of software, hardware, and infrastructure that are required for these business applications, charging a monthly fee for their use. ASPs provide access to software like PeopleSoft's human resources applications, SAP's manufacturing software and Siebel's Customer Resource Management solutions, and office applications software similar to Microsoft Word, Excel, and the like. In addition to providing access to these packages, the ASP also automatically updates and supports the application to assure customers that they are receiving the latest, upgraded systems available.

Two types of ASP models exist:

- Traditional applications with consulting—This is the model followed by Corio for ERP and CRM applications; and Interliant for groupware, office suite, and e-commerce applications. These ASPs minimize implementation time of proven mainstream applications for their customers by giving a hosted package.

- Web-based applications—With these companies, ASPs create and roll out business applications written for the Web. Typically, these are lower-end office suites and some e-commerce applications such as transaction processing, shopping cart management, intellectual property, etc.

E-Commerce Solution Providers (ESP) Providers in this category go a step further. The ISPs provide the basic access; ASPs provide software on top of the access; and ESPs provide almost complete online business solutions. ESPs build and maintain the online store, provide customer service to the customers of their customers, and provide additional services like order management, logistics, fulfillment, etc. Customers of ESPs concentrate on just one thing—customer acquisition—in addition to developing and producing their product.

With ASPs, the customers maintain their individuality and brand. But merchants using an ESP have several options. They could become part of a suite of merchants hosted by the ESP. In this case, they can choose to retain their brand and individuality with linkages to multiple merchants, or they can become part of a cluster of similar merchants and use an integrated shopping cart. On the other hand, a business entity may choose to retain, maintain, and enhance its brand while using all the solutions supplied by the ESP.

Consulting Services E-commerce consulting services are booming businesses. The few knowledgeable and experienced consultants and consulting firms are in high demand, able to command salaries beyond the dreams of avarice. This segment is not limited to just IT professionals, but to the various business constituencies that a merchant needs to draw on to figure out how to use the Web to a speedy advantage.

Several types of consulting services may be distinguished:

- Strategy Consulting—Typically these are firms like McKinsey or Bain, which have targeted the "big picture" and now increasingly focus on identifying complete Internet components essential for a company's business.
- Implementation Consulting—Like the Big 5 Accounting Firms, these companies focus on implementation services, typically after a strategic assessment. Their focus is on ERP, business realignments, and process re-engineering.
- IT Consulting—Traditional firms such as IBM have large armies of consultants who focus on IT systems in general. These are being refocused to Web-based initiatives.

- E-commerce Consultants—A new breed of consulting firms, strongly wedded to the Web, are now proving themselves, such as Applied Theory, Scient, Razorfish, and Agency.com
- Programming Services—Consulting companies focused on providing manpower or carrying out small software projects are now moving to Web technologies and integration with new software applications that require integration with business practices.
- Maintenance Services—Given the 24×7 nature of the Web, the need for uptime and maintenance is very high. A rash of companies promise maintenance of machines, backups, recovery, and continuous monitoring.

Business Services

Business services for enabling the platform stack are typically targeted at small entrepreneurial startups and focus on providing communication tools, online calendar systems, contact book, file systems, and a simple Web site. On top of these are suites of business productivity software such as Web-based office products for word processing, spreadsheets, etc. Layered above these are financial and human resource applications and e-commerce enabling.

Other niche categories consist of advertising (through an ad server or a network); affiliate marketing (with affiliated merchants and Web sites); online design bureaus for advertising; printing services for business cards and T-shirts; and mass email and snail mail services for direct marketing, payment systems for employees and vendors, etc.

Email is the most popular use of the Internet. Many business users outsource their email hosting and management. Apart from routine email, messaging has expanded to include the concept of "integrated communication centers" that encompass internal and external email, fax, and voicemail. Again, these copied the business model of email providers. Real-time chat, address book, calendar, and a to-do list now come integrated with most of them.

New to the scene are group messaging, collaboration tools, and conferencing functionality that often include Internet telephony. While the entities are new, the concepts take simple email models one step further and include most services that came before it. Thus, group-messaging services incorporate all of the prior services such as email, address book, calendar, and chat.

Example: Corporate Web Site Management

Functional Requirements: Maintain and manage corporate Internet Web site to enhance image, provide information about company products and services, engage stakeholders, and enable commerce.

- Web site design and development
- Database and middleware
- Enterprise integration
- Web site hosting
- Web site testing
- Content generation and management
- Content delivery
- Commerce application
- Customer relationship management
- Supply chain management

Content Service Providers

Aggregation

Aggregation as a service model deals with collecting content on behalf of an online business. Such content may be offline such as phone books, catalogs, dental records, etc. Or it may be online tracking content consisting of browsing behavior, shopping patterns, etc. Thus, any content that could potentially be used on the Web could be contracted from a suitable aggregation service.

Directory Services

As with most everything pertaining to services on the Net, variations of directory services may be considered software as well. Search tools include everyday search engines and directories such as Yahoo!, Alta Vista, and Excite, metasearch engines such as HotBot, Dogpile, and WebCrawler, and parametric search engines offered on business marketplace portals to perform complex searches on product catalogs. Increasingly, search as a stand-alone service offering has largely disappeared, and most sites now offer it as part of a bigger service. However, a quality search tool remains an important part of a site and is also a reason for site traffic.

In the consumer category, Yahoo! is perhaps the best known directory owing to the success of its portal, which rose out of an initial, basic search tool. Ultimately, the company/site expanded to free email, chat, categorized information, weather, news, and so on.

Search engines continue to evolve as they come to grips with exploding information on the Internet, and this makes cataloging both an art and a science. A familiar problem with any generic search tool is their proclivity to serve up anything vaguely resembling what is being searched for. Apart from sheer volume that this engenders, the accuracy of the find is often mediocre at best and is likely buried within.

Newer search tools use a combination of technologies—"spiders" that seek out new sites and/or human analysis and cataloging to make a qualitatively better "hit rate." In the spider category, search results are based on rankings of the number of links to an item(s) at other sites, relevancy, and prior retrievals. Human intervention search sites such as About.com and even Yahoo! provide context in categorizing links.

Search services have inherent attributes that argue for their incorporation within a larger service. Users do not expect to pay for such a service. Existing technologies are easily replicable, and newer ones continue to unfold making recent entrants a potential risk for existing players that are not aligned or partnered with other enterprises. From the perspective of the service provider and given the abundance of information on the Internet, their marginal value is low; thus, they run the risk of becoming irrelevant. All this points to an unavoidable conclusion: Channel presence is critical and must be secured through partnerships, alliances, or other means.

Directories seek to mimic the ease of use and access to information that print substitute cousins provide in the offline white and yellow pages directories. Some, such as anywho.com, in fact, get their results from both sources in the non-virtual dead tree world. Web directory sites such as infospace.com, superpages.com, and worldpages.com contract with Acxiom Corp. (*www.acxiom.com*), a clearinghouse, to supply information scanned from phone pages. For this reason, directory enquiries on the 'Net are often as incorrect as the information culled from outdated sources. Email directory sites, on the other hand, use site users and partnerships to compile directories. They suffer from a lack of exhaustiveness.

Delivery Services

These electronic equivalents of "store and forward" entities are dispersed throughout the world. They are repositories, placing content reasonably close to the end-user so that the content can be quickly streamed. Examples are Akamai Technologies (*www.akamai.com*) and Digital Island (*www.digitalisland.com*), which provide value (see Figure 2.11) in the following manner:

- Content is distributed throughout the Web and concentrated in areas where there is a high density of users.
- User's proximity to content provides a better end-user experience, thereby facilitating downloads of rich content such as video and audio.
- The total demand for delivery of content is not throttled through a single server or network pipe at the business location, but rather is distributed, thereby securing greater reliability and efficiency.

  The responsibility for enabling and operations of servers and networks for content delivery rests with the delivery service. Scaling to other countries or regions becomes simpler.

Syndication

In this service model, a syndication company acquires as much content as possible in several categories. It then resells the content (whether static or dynamic) to a variety of Web sites, which then subscribe for a range of services from a menu of choices. For example, a syndication service may offer a variety of games, quizzes, jokes, etc., for syndication (see Figure 2.12). A Web site focused on B2B may syndicate office humor and use a few jokes a day to provide variety on the site.

Community Service Provider

These services are oriented towards creating and maintaining communities on the Web. Portals such as Yahoo! provide Yahoo!Clubs (*www.clubs.yahoo.com*), which let a group of people create a public or private environment. Business-centric community service providers such as Egroups (*www.egroups.com*) provide services facilitating working communities focused on shared content and interactions.

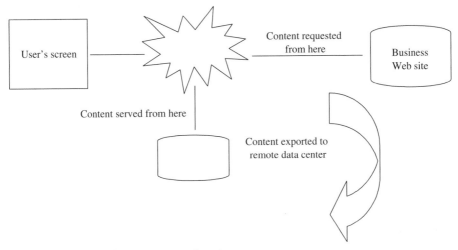

Figure 2.11   Content Delivery Service

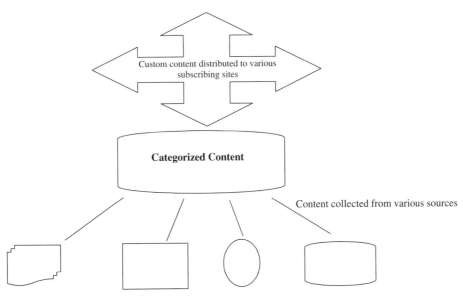

Figure 2.12   Content Syndication

Commerce Service Providers

Commerce service providers provide an outsourced ability to conduct e-commerce. Such services are available in every aspect of e-commerce, ranging from enabling suppliers to satisfying and ennobling customers. For simplicity, these are categorized under the categories of marketing, sales, logistics, and business services.

Marketing

Marketing services position a product or service in front of a potential customer for consideration. Online advertising services such as DoubleClick (*www.doubleclick.com*) and Adforce (*www.adforce.com*) provide online advertising in a variety of environments (banner advertisements, slotting in portals, contextual links, etc.), and some even manage an advertising campaign on behalf of a business. Other marketing services, such as online market research, are easily available as outsourced services. Direct marketing companies like Responsys.com (*www.responsys.com*) and yesmail.com (*www.yesmail.com*) provide Web-based software to target customers by email, based on opt-in or permission marketing against a mail-list where the users have agreed to receive mail for merchandising purposes.

Sales

Many aspects of the sales process can be outsourced. One of the most dynamic and powerful is the affiliate selling model discussed earlier. Stores "syndicate" their content to other Web sites, which serve to lead in a customer or make the sale directly on their site. The complete sales process can be outsourced, as at Amazon's Z Stores (*www.amazon.com*) or at Yahoo!Stores (*www.stores.yahoo.com*). These environments have all services required to create and maintain a store, including catalog maintenance, shopping cart, electronic wallets, credit card approval, and order status maintenance. In addition, there are also outsource services that provide live customer service functionality from customer contact centers.

Logistics

Third-Party Logistics services are coming into vogue to provide many aspects of logistics that encompass all functions following a click on the buy button: fulfillment, warehousing and inventory management, such as SameDay (*www.sameday.com*); delivery services such as local delivery by Kozmo (*www.kozmo.com*); and returns management, such as with iReturns.com (*www.ireturns.com*). Fourth-Party Logistics services expand this model with additional Web-based services for order tracking and management of inbound orders as well.

Business Services

This broad, all-encompassing category covers a wide swath of just about every aspect of a business' service requirements that could be outsourced. Many consider any implementation of professional services on the Internet as reintermediation to include parts of the value chain that do not comprise a company's core competence. This is the opposite of disintermediation, which occurs when parts of a conventional value chain get removed altogether such as, for example, an online bookstore that carries no inventory and sources from wholesalers who drop-ship directly to customers.

Many ancillary business services needed at every level of an organization, from janitorial services to strategic management consulting, are available on the Internet through e-commerce. The most visible ones include advertising and marketing, business and IT consulting, Web design and development, education and training, and various other hosted services. Advertising services, for example, enable Web sites to be advertised dynamically through online networks and affinity channels while marketing seeks to leverage knowledge gained from customer profiles, tracking data, and purchase patterns to tailor product/service to market needs. In the realm of IT, most companies now routinely outsource

Example: Corporate Services Reintermediation

Functional Requirements: Manage outsourced services for self-service employee benefits

- Provide contracted content for full range of employee benefits
- Enable employee options and integrate with corporate HR and payroll systems
- Customize for HR management of updates to benefits
- Manage interface with third-party entities for one-stop experience to customers
- Provide detailed default and customizable reports for benefits administrators and controllers
- Provide notification and feedback options
- Provide online, persistent access for employees' to their personal data

management of networks, applications development, and Web design and site development. The Internet makes remote site monitoring and project management possible. Professional services in this category have mushroomed to take advantage of the trend. This model, likewise, can serve corporate training.

Summary

This chapter takes a top-level view of the often dynamic nature of an e-commerce environment, showing how the various elements work with each other. To isolate and overemphasize one to the exclusion of others in the real world is how service organizations are built. Our intent is to show that atomic building blocks create e-commerce, identifying them as five distinct stacks associated with the platform, content, community, commerce, and services. It is critical for every e-commerce player to understand the possibilities and important relationship each stack has to the others and know what is essential to handle with internal resources and what is desirable to outsource.

Business functionality is becoming ever more atomic, with modular functionality available for purchase or hire. A successful e-commerce business constantly needs to examine the atomic business elements that pertain to its particular way of operations and look for ways to reduce cost, enhance functionality, and achieve greater efficiencies of scale and scope.

CHAPTER 3

The Internet Platform

An e-commerce business needs a solid foundation on which value may be created. This is the Internet platform. The Internet platform consists of the physical infrastructure, network infrastructure, computer hardware, software, and integration elements required to manage an Internet-based business model successfully. In this chapter we take a look at the underpinnings of the platform infrastructure and provide details on how to construct or otherwise obtain such a capability to execute the company's business objectives and strategy. Sample cost estimates and the beginning of a series of metric analyses are offered as a starting point for determining the best business path for the start-up.

The physical infrastructure is everything "physical" an enterprise needs to run its business and is needed to a greater or lesser extent by virtual companies just as much as brick-and-mortar companies. The physical infrastructure includes office space, furnishings, communications facilities, etc. The network section primarily addresses connectivity to the Internet as well as connectivity inside the enterprise. The hardware section focuses on servers required for accepting customer requests for Web pages, processing user information, and manipulating data and images. The software section is subdivided into office, enterprise, and e-commerce software. Integration elements address interaction issues between a company and its partners, such as content providers, suppliers and fulfillment partners, and those upstream of the company we consider members of the supply chain.

Physical Infrastructure

There is nothing esoteric about the physical infrastructure. Every business requires office space, office furnishings, security, communications equipment, and so on. At the start-up stage, particularly, this may entail a capital expenditure or a recurring cost such as a lease expense. For the sake of financial completeness, a very brief section is devoted here to the physical infrastructure in running a business. This section is relevant for business planning purposes to project cash outlays needed or applicable to early start-up situations where economies of scale have yet to take place. Although these are not high-tech issues, these costs are both insidious and significant over a period of time. Damaging effects of such costs accrue typically without significant management scrutiny, and can drain the company's cash reserves if not planned for and managed properly.

The following represent some key elements of the physical infrastructure:

- Facilities (physical space for offices)
- Furnishings
- Communications

Facilities

Let us consider the physical space requirements for a small start-up company that is in a growth mode. How much rental space should the company contract for? Too little may result in lack of available new contiguous space as new employees are hired. Forced growth in a non-contiguous space (such as in a different floor of a building or in a different building) can result in operational problems—unanticipated glitches in office wiring, networking, phone communications, break-up of departmental groups, etc. On the other hand, acquiring excessive space could result in additional negative cash flow in the form of increased monthly rental costs.

Ideally, a company should plan for about a six-month growth within an existing space and negotiate with the landlord for rights to expansion. For planning purposes, and assuming either open floor offices or cubicles for most of the staff, an allocation of 100 to 150 square feet per person should normally be sufficient. This allocation also includes common areas such as corridors, kitchen, and meeting spaces.

Office space assumes critical importance, especially when a tight real estate market, as in Silicon Valley or Boston, hinders a start-up's ability to focus on its core business.

Shortage of available space may require firms to locate farther and farther away from strategic partners and nearby human and technology resources. Location, lease structure, sublease options, and time to find and secure space are all distractions that have to be resolved before a start-up can begin to make meaningful progress.

Furnishings

Furnishings are normally capital costs that are associated with new hires. This includes space utilization elements like cubicles and desks, chairs, phones, etc. What is acquired and installed depends largely on the level of funding, company operating style, and what is "allowable" by investors.

Communications

In the world of the connected employee, communications become significant. Redundant though it might appear, it is essential to note that most employees need to be "connected." Employee connectivity provides significant corporate efficiencies. Every time that an employee cannot be contacted to retrieve a piece of data, to provide support, to lend advice, or to make a decision, workflow associated with a specific business activity comes to a halt. For example, if the manager cannot approve a sales proposal to a client, the client commitment cannot be sealed and may result in the failure of a sale. Similarly, connecting most employees to the Internet and providing email access ensures that they have the information they need, understand their internal and external customers, and carry out their responsibilities more effectively.

Beyond Internet connectivity, issuing pagers and cell phones to employees ensures that they are "online" and available on demand. Of course, too much of a good thing can lead to adverse consequences such as employee burnout due to company demands during off-hours, or excessive cell phone usage without an increase in productivity. Depending on the business need and the appropriate local prices, an average communications cost per employee can be determined.

Infrastructure Example

Table 3.1 provides an example of a computation for eBiztro.com's planned company size of 80 employees. The rental cost is assumed at $1 per sq. ft per month, $1,000 for

Table 3.1   Infrastructure Costs Example

Physical Infrastructure Costs for eBiztro.com	
Number of Employees	= 80 (over a 6- month period)
Area required per person	= 100 sq. ft
Total rental space needed	= 8000 sq. ft
Rental cost per month	= $1 per sq ft
Total rental cost	= $8000 per month
Furnishings per employee	= Phone, cube, chair
Furnishing cost	= $1000 per employee
Total furnishing cost	= $80K
External phone line ratio	= 1:4
Total external lines needed	= 80/4 = 20
Cost per line per month	= $20
Phone line cost	= $400 per month
Network bandwidth	= T1 line; 1.5 Mbps
Cost of bandwidth	= $400 per month
Capital costs:	
Network hardware	= $80K
Computers and servers	= $200K
Physical infrastructure	= $80K
Total capital costs	= $360K
Monthly Costs:	
Rent	= $8000 per month
Phone	= $400 per month
Internet connection	= $400 per month
Total monthly costs	= $8.8K per month
Average monthly cost	= $110 per employee

furnishings per employee, and a monthly phone line charge of $20, after installation charges are absorbed. Elements vary by geographic market, and are used here for illustrative purposes only.

The Network Infrastructure

As we all know, the Internet is a system of several million computers on global information highways connecting to local highways, which in turn connect to major arteries, sub-arteries, streets, lanes and, finally, businesses in those lanes. In a sense, most businesses exist on the fringe of the super highway. Placing a business in proximity to the major arteries maintained by ISPs or interconnect nodes called Network Access Points (NAPs) improves network performance.

One computer knows the "address" of another computer by a globally unique system of IP addresses (Internet Protocol), giving every computer on the network a unique address. However, a system of numerical addresses is clearly difficult for human interaction. Thus, a system of domain names was created whereby a registry is maintained of an URL (Universal Resource Locator) consisting of an alphanumeric name (such as *www.mybiz123.com*) that is mapped uniquely to a specific IP address. This registry is then globally populated through Domain Name Servers (DNS) located throughout the world. When a user types in the URL, this is converted to an IP address, which is traced on the Internet, and the communication between the two computers then continues. This mapping is illustrated in Figure 3.1.

Most companies connect to the Internet through an ISP. Internet connectivity to an ISP is commonly through a phone line or a frame relay dedicated connection. Less common, but viable, are connections through a cable modem or wireless. However, it is becoming increasingly common to locate the Web site of a business at a co-location facility. Such a facility is typically connected to the main cross-country networks to provide

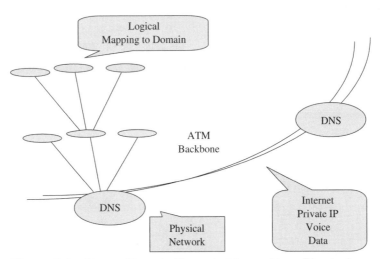

Figure 3.1 How a Domain Name is Mapped to a Physical Computer

high-quality connectivity to businesses that colocate their servers with them. Typically, such facilities charge both for the amount of rack space occupied by the servers and network bandwidth required to service the customer needs. Hosting services that are adjacent to or even support the network backbone are very expensive, but if system performance is an issue, it is well worth the added monthly fees.

Trade-offs between cost for proximate access and more remote access need to be assessed and factored into operating expenses. As noted in Chapter 2, "The Five Stack E-Commerce Model," it is possible to outsource many functions, including almost every aspect of the network infrastructure. Co-location fees are more expensive than self-hosting, but with self-hosting there are other costs, including addition of staff to develop and maintain the servers.

Network Layout

For discussion purposes, Figure 3.2 provides a simple network layout showing the hardware and network components associated with business connectivity to and from the Internet. The firewall is programmed to allow only certain types of traffic from and to the Internet. Typically, traffic is routed to the Web server, which then interfaces with other servers to provide content or enable transactions.

A special name, DMZ (Demilitarized Zone), is given to this part of the network to signify its separation from the rest of the company's network.

The internal Local Area Network (LAN) is extended through a series of routers and switches to provide high-speed connectivity to desktops, workgroup servers, file servers, transaction servers, high-speed disk arrays, back-up storage devices, etc.

Businesses normally have to deal with network issues like firewalls, routers, switches, and network connectivity, all of which are critical because they require a series of trade-offs between system security and costs. Generally, the greater the level of security, the greater the expense. Here are some of the elements that go into setting up a system to be secure, yet operationally efficient.

Firewall

A firewall is a sentry system, regulating the nature of traffic and restricting unauthorized traffic. It protects interconnected networks from unauthorized intrusion that could result,

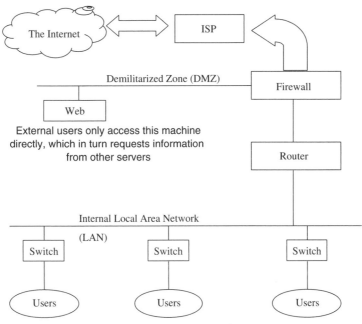

Figure 3.2 A Typical Network Layout for a Business

at the very least, in a "denial of service" attack or, at its worst, in highly compromised security and corruption of data. With an increasing prevalence of hacking on a global basis, the need for robust firewalls has increased dramatically. Software-based and hardware-based firewalls are currently popular.

Whatever the case, software- and hardware-based firewalls reside at the junction between the two networks, one of which is usually a public network such as the Internet and the other a private network called an Extranet, or internally as an Intranet. A software-based firewall may be more configurable, but potentially vulnerable to hacking through holes in network systems, the operating system, applications, or employee sloth. A hardware-based firewall is considered more hackerproof, but may allow less flexibility and upgradeability. A hardware-based firewall is a more preferable way to go, but this kind of firewall can cost as much as $10,000.

Firewalls serve as censors of traffic in both directions and, besides halting hostile traffic, serve other purposes as well. These include logging and triggering alarms to access restricted servers, file locations, or documents; filter packets based on IP addresses and port numbers, by attribute, and by protocol. Firewalls come in two flavors—network level firewalls and application level firewalls. The former are based on criteria about IP addresses of individual packets of information, both source and destination. The latter are generally hosts running proxy servers where data does not directly pass from one network to another.

Routers and Switches

A router is a traffic cop adjudicating and managing inbound and outbound traffic flow from and to the Internet. Each gateway to the Internet would need a router. Additional internal routers may be needed for larger organizations. Routers are sized and priced by speed, configurability, controllability, number of ports, and number of interfaces. A typical 16-port router sells for about $2,500.

A switch and its country cousin, the hub, are for internal networking needs. These are sized by the number of ports and support for regular Ethernet (low speed, 10 megabits per second), Fast Ethernet (high speed, 100 megabits per second), and Gigabit Ethernet (very high speed, 1 gigabit per second). A 16-port switch costs about $150.

Wiring offices and hooking to computers requires some skilled technical effort. Wiring an office includes pulling Ethernet cable or fiber lines through ceilings, hooking to the network, and optimizing performance. Then, after the wiring is in place, someone needs to get permits from city and/or county building and safety departments because of fire codes and regulations, which most people fail to consider!

Network Connectivity

Connection to the ISP is charged monthly, and is based on the bandwidth required. Globally, the cost of Internet access is falling steadily; in urban areas in developed countries it is approaching utility rates. The amount of bandwidth required depends on the type of business carried out by the company. Connection options include frame relay, a phone line with modem-based dial-up connection, an ISDN line, a cable modem, or a DSL phone line.

The analog modem approach is bandwidth-constrained and is limited typically to about 56 Kbps (a normal page of about 50 lines is about 25 K bits, and to download it in one second would require a bandwidth of 25 Kbps). The ISDN line allows a bandwidth capacity of about 128 Kbps; however, ISDN is rapidly falling off the radar screen as cable and DSL take its place. The more advanced DSL (Digital Subscriber Line) technology and associated variants collectively referred to as XDSL provide greater bandwidths, ranging from 1.5 Mbps to about 6 Mbps, than analog or ISDN. Frame relay is based on dedicated digital connections to the ISP, and can range from a T1 (about 1.5 Mbps) to a T3 (45 Mbps). These connections start at approximately $1500 a month, depending on bandwidth, and go up from there.

Two issues with bandwidth that are of particular concern to start-ups (who do not have a history to help them figure out how to plan for bandwidth) are peak and average usage. Consumer-oriented sites especially can have a difficult time dealing with this.

Again, for the start-up planning for possible crash-inducing spikes, it is useful to keep both peak and average usage in mind and negotiate with ISPs either by contracting for burstable bandwidth over and above the negotiated kilobit per second rate or going for a preset bulk data transfer to take care of peaks. The latter addresses the problem of bandwidth and the unpredictability of peak usage. As with everything concerning the new technologies, however, contracting for a monthly maximum for data transfer with the ISP also means a start-up must estimate peak usage and how many times it may occur during the month. A wrong prediction, as, perhaps, with a new marketing campaign, may mean the best plans go awry when several peak loads during the course of just a few days exceeds the monthly rate.

Table 3.2 contains sample costing for various networking expense items.

Table 3.2 Sample Costing Model for a Business Network (*eBiztro.com*)

Network Hardware Costs for eBiztro.com	
Number of employees	= 80
Wiring cost per desk	= 1 person-day
Total work effort	= 80 person-days
Cost per person-day	= $800 (network technician)
Total wiring cost	= $64K
Router cost (2)	= $5.0K
Firewall cost (2)	= $10K
Switches (8)	= $1.0K
Total cost	= $80K

Computer Hardware

Computer hardware consists in part of desktop computers, a variety of servers, storage devices, and Uninterruptible Power Supplies (UPS). Desktop systems have become increasingly standardized with immense power at one's disposal. Until very recently, desktops typically meant a stand-alone computer system, connected to a network to obtain data and external connectivity. In such a system, the desktop applications such as Microsoft Word, etc., were installed on the local computer. This view could become archaic in the next few years *if* a new breed of "network computers" comes into use.

With a network appliance, the intelligence for the application would be hosted on a server and distributed through the network. Thus, the word processing software would reside centrally on a server and provide the software on demand to the network computer. The function of the network computer is then to serve as a high-speed display and interaction device. Given the consistently low cost of regular desktop computers, the jury is still out on the effectiveness and cost-savings associated with network computers. Indirect savings associated with centralized management of office and enterprise software, however, may be appreciable.

Servers are essentially heavy-duty computers geared for continuous operations and optimized for performance. The industry trend is to distribute special functionality across several machines rather than consolidating them in a central, large machine. This provides discrete control and minimizes loss of functionality in case of failure. Servers in "rack-mountable" configurations enable such modularization.

The following is a list of the various server types:

- Web server—accepts and responds to Web page requests
- Application server—executes programming logic for interactions, transactions, etc.
- Database server—stores data in a relational table structure, such as customer data, orders, transaction history, vendor data, purchasing information, etc.
- Media server—stores and pushes out multimedia content
- File server—stores files
- Storage devices—are often configured in a Storage Area Network (SAN)
- Mail server—manages inbound and outbound email
- Remote access server—enables dial-in access
- Development server—maintains internal development environment

- Test server—facilitates testing before release
- Standby server—specific fail-over device
- Print server—manages and distributes data streams to various printers
- Load balancer—makes sure no one server in a server farm becomes overloaded and compromises network performance

Servers are often distinguished by the type of operating system they host. The prominent ones, particularly at the lower end of the scale, are Windows NT/2000, UNIX, and Linux. In general, NT systems drive Intel machines from Dell, Gateway, and the like. UNIX systems are sometimes associated with a particular hardware manufacturer, such as Sun and its Solaris operating system, IBM AIX, or from HP/UX. The Linux operating system is either free or nominal in cost, and is finding its niche in either embedded systems (such as in firewalls) or in corporate environments with large server farms.

Server costs are largely driven by CPU and memory considerations. A typical dual CPU, 1GB memory server with NT, Solaris, or Linux could cost from $2000 to $6000, depending on packaging, disk drives, and other components. Table 3.3 lists the estimated hardware costs for a small company.

Outsourcing Server Functionality

It is now quite common for a lot of server functionality to be outsourced (see Table 3.4). In particular, the business may have its store or Web site at an ISP. In that case, the servers

Table 3.3   Sample Computer Hardware Costs

Computer Hardware Costs for eBiztro.com	
Number of employees	= 80
Cost per desktop computer	= $1000
Total desktop costs	= $80K
Number of servers*	= 20
Cost per server (NT)	= $6K
Total server cost	= $120K
Total computer cost	= $200K

* The number of servers is highly variable and depends largely on the operating model for the company and degree of outsourcing, as we see in the following section.

Table 3.4   Sample Hardware Costs with Server Outsourcing

***Computer Hardware Costs for* eBiztro.com**

Number of employees	= 80
Cost per desktop computer	= $100
Total desktop costs	= $80K
Number of servers	= 20
Number of servers outsourced	= 16
Number of servers in-house	= 4
Cost per server (NT)	= $6K
Total server cost	= $24K
Total computer cost	= $104K
Total monthly server cost	= $8K
Total annual server cost	= $96K
Total cost after one year	= $200K

required at the company offices may be limited to those who manage the network, provide file services, enable email, and provide for office functionality. Web-centric servers, including database servers, application servers, and Web servers, would reside at the ISP location and would scale based on end-user traffic.

An approximate and conservative rule of thumb is that the monthly cost of a server at an ISP facility is about 1/12th the cost of the company-supported server. In other words, if a server of a given CPU, capacity, etc., costs $6000, then expect to pay about $500 per month for that server at an ISP facility. The capital cost of the hardware is expensed and stretched over a year, which may be useful from a cash management standpoint. The other indirect benefit comes from reduced staffing required for in-house IT systems, management and administration.

Software

Software is categorized as Office software and Enterprise software. The purpose of this simplistic definition is to flesh out some of the costing aspects for software acquisition. An e-commerce business has a considerable range of other software types that are needed, including that for managing networks, security, email, development, testing, transaction management, and so on.

Office Software

Office software refers to the standard "office suite" needed to support an employee (see Table 3.5). This includes personal productivity applications such as word processing, spreadsheet and presentation software, email for client communications, a Web browser for Internet applications, database tools such as Access, anti-virus software, handheld device applications, etc. Increasingly, these are being made available as browser-based environments, which makes it easier to have a "clean" desktop with all maintenance, licensing, and upgrades made on the server. Also, hosted models for office software are becoming available and may become more commonplace with increasing bandwidth and assured security.

Enterprise Software

Enterprise software (in its more complete versions often known as ERP—enterprise resource planning) typically integrates a suite of "industrial-strength" software applications designed for a wide-ranging set of operating interactions. These can be broadly categorized as customer-facing, back-office, and supply-chain applications.

Customer-Facing Applications (CFAs)

Customer-facing functions encompass marketing, sales, customer service, support, and customer relationship management. In the world of e-commerce, applications that support each other are being rapidly redefined to take into account the dynamic and interactive nature of sales and customer service processes. At the same time, linkages to other sales and marketing channels need to be integrated to present a "common voice" to the customer, irrespective of whether the customer is in a B2C or B2B environment.

As an example, consider an online customer who calls about a promotion seen in a newspaper advertisement. The call center handling the call may need to acknowledge the

Table 3.5 Software Costs for Desktop Applications

Office Software Costs for eBiztro.com	
Number of employees	= 80
Cost per office suite	= $250
Total office suite costs	= $20K

linkages between the newspaper campaign and the customer's immediate desire to complete the transaction. Customer Relationship Management (CRM) software, which often reconciles these issues, is evolving rapidly to stay in tune with concurrent demands to manage online and offline customer relationships.

Traditionally, CRM focused on marketing, sales, and call center automation. The focal point of these software components was on enabling customer service and sales staff employees. In contrast, the rapid evolution of Web technologies places emphasis on customer self-service. Thus, traditional CRM vendors are facing the challenge of Web-enabling their offerings. In the meantime, new challengers are providing highly focused Web-based offerings, which chisels away at the competencies of the mainstream vendors.

The main areas of CFAs are:

- Sales force automation and management
  - Self-service, configuration, requisition, purchasing
  - Sales force tools including mobile and stand-alone
- Marketing management
- Personalization and collaborative filtering
- Email campaigns
- Targeted advertising
- Customer service
  - Contact management
  - Live help (chat, voice over IP, video over IP, call-back)
  - Help desk
  - Field service dispatch (repair, warranty)
- Email management (automated responses, intelligent routing)
- Knowledge-base utilization
- Search technology for content and price information
- Software agents for immediate or delayed responses
- Relationship management (with partners, affiliates, vendors)

Implementation of CRM, as one component of CFAs, can vary widely in terms of vendor time, and cost.

Baseline Measurement for CFA

1. **Number of customers** that might use the system per day. This could be computed based on daily Web traffic and measurements of customer behavior.
2. **Volume** (calls per hour, chats per person, emails per day). It is important to identify the characteristics of demand in terms of time of day, day of week, and seasonal effects, such as at Christmas.
3. **Staffing requirement** for CRM applications. This depends on the traffic in each CRM inbound channel (voice, chat, email) and assessing the likely amount of time spent in interaction with the customer. For example, an email may take five minutes, a chat session 10 minutes, and a phone conversation 15 minutes, on average.
4. **Knowledge-base construction** (categorization, indexing, retrieval). Proper knowledge management and training leads to reduced time in responding to the needs of the customer, as many customer queries revolve around the same issues.
5. **License cost** per user (named or unnamed user), in a traditional ERP model.
6. **Hosted cost** per user in a leased model (in the ASP model discussed in Chapter 2).
7. **Interface requirements** with marketing partners.

Back-Office Applications

These are internal company functions such as manufacturing, production planning, order management, logistics, fulfillment, inventory, financials, human resources, etc. ERP vendors usually have stable offerings in serving several functions in this arena. These products are still not fully integrated and are often "asynchronous" to the online customer transaction, especially in high volume e-commerce environments. Such separation between the Web store and the back-office applications affects performance and availability. These applications also require more integration to set up and maintain as each interconnect between applications and with third parties raises additional security and privacy concerns.

Supply-Chain Applications

These focus on interactions with outside partners such as vendors. The emphasis here is on procurement, purchasing, vendor management, materials planning, scheduling, etc., all of which provides the basis for a robust exchange of information with external players. Frequently, this requires different modes of interaction. For instance, older and more established players may require EDI (Electronic Data Interchange), especially in high-volume environments. More recent merchants may prefer data interchange using XML (Extensible Markup Language). Smaller players may require faxes and "snail mail" documents.

Supply chain applications enable visibility into and throughout the supply chain allowing, for example, an automobile manufacturer to anticipate and manage changes in sales for particular models in specific areas. Tier 1 vendors of basic materials, for example, can see "through" the changes spilling backwards from the dealerships and take appropriate decisions that help to reduce overall industry carrying costs.

The major enterprise suites belong to SAP, Oracle, PeopleSoft, and J.D. Edwards. Traditionally, ERP applications were very pricey, very bulky, very complex, and very expensive to implement. With implementation cycles of several months to several years, the anticipated benefits of improved operational efficiency and enhanced user benefits were slow to manifest. Furthermore, implementation cycle time often approaches the major upgrade time of the applications, that is, the implemented functionality is often outdated when it goes live. This leads to the "implementation treadmill," where a new upgrade cycle follows on the heels of a prior implementation cycle. Moreover, adverse publicity from implementation complexities, overrun budgets, and a spate of lawsuits from aggrieved companies implementing ERP are breaking the cycle of infallible growth among the primary ERP vendors.

Application Service Provider

ASPs were discussed in the prior chapter in the broader context of the services they provide. Many of them are building their business models around resolving some of the problems associated with traditional ERP implementations. However, there are many more ASPs that function well beyond ERP implementation.

Enterprise applications are generally hosted in a central environment at the company level. In the ASP model, this same functionality of applications can be "rented" to subscribing businesses. In this "pay by the sip" approach, the commitment of the ASP is to provide business functionality "on tap" in a scalable, high-availability environment.

The key value propositions of an ASP providing ERP modules are:

- The ASP operator puts a bundled solution together. This consists of a selection of any or all hardware, software, network, security, technical services, and implementation services. Such a bundled solution may not necessarily be the one preferred by the customer (for example, a Unix lover may not be in favor of a NT-based ASP environment), but standardization and cost optimization from a capital cost and operations cost standpoint could clearly govern this choice for the ASP. The savings are passed on to the customer.
- The business applications available are provided as packaged offerings—ERP applications, e-commerce solution sets, office suites, third-party services, and integration.
- Standardized solutions are the norm. The intent is to make businesses adapt to standardized off-the-shelf processes rather than force the applications to adapt to "custom" business processes. This may be considered by businesses to be a disadvantage because it reduces their options to customize software applications and business processes unique to them. In the long run, taking as much as possible off the shelf is desirable. It allows the ASP vendor to maintain a standard set of applications with simple points of integration to the customer. This permits easy maintenance and upgrade of the ASP applications, which are useful across the board to all classes of customers.
- There is a single point of resolution for all customer problems, namely, the ASP operator. This may require the ASP operator to work with the ERP vendor and the e-commerce software vendor to resolve problems, but the customer does not have to peel the onion to identify the cause of a software glitch.
- "Pay by the sip" models reduce upfront costs, which may be particularly significant for start-up e-commerce companies looking to preserve cash.
- To be effective, both parties must make a commitment to a Service Level Agreement (SLA) that sets the acceptable levels of performance by the ASP that the customer is willing to pay for. The higher the up-time, the greater the cost.

Does it make sense to use an ASP? Under certain conditions, yes. In Figure 3.3, we consider ASP offerings in the context of products and services.

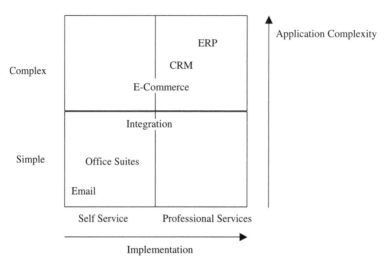

Figure 3.3   Categorization of Software Applications by Complexity

As application complexity increases, implementation complexity increases too. An enterprise application forces greater resources to be spent by the business in implementing it, which detracts from its core business objectives.

The ASP model (see Figure 3.4) may therefore be relevant under the following considerations:

- To obtain rapid implementation—decreased "time to functionality." For e-commerce companies trying to reach a commercial value quickly, time may be a critical resource. It may therefore be wiser to obtain strategic or supporting functionality through an ASP model rather than to devote a greater order of human resources for in-house implementation.
- To reduce implementation risk, which would come from dedicated resources of the ASP operator or from trusted partners.
- To move to "pay for use" scaled selection of resources rather than pay for often-unused licenses, which is not uncommon in the traditional ERP model.
- To reduce the disruptive impact of an ERP implementation within the company.

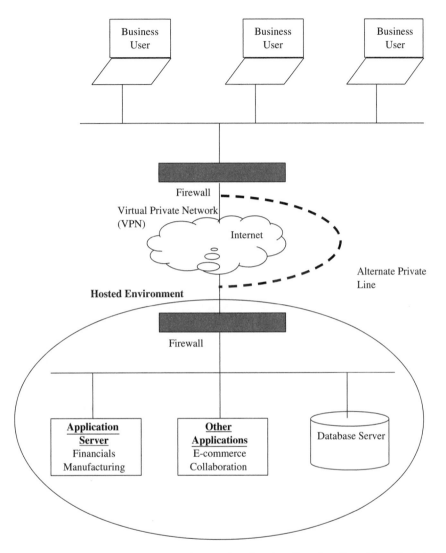

Figure 3.4 A Typical Layout for an Application Service Provider Model

In spite of these benefits, a decision to go ASP is not to be taken lightly. The following issues should be carefully considered:

- Facilities maintained by ASP should be evaluated. These include data centers, networks, and redundancy arrangements for failure of power, communications, and networks.
- SLAs for redundancy, availability, and performance should be scrutinized for implications to the business. Contingency arrangements for loss of service should be planned for.
- Guarantees of security for data transmissions, virus intrusion, and loss of privacy should be spelled out.
- A complete understanding of cost should be available including immediate implementation, and monthly operational and upgrade costs.
- Contract terms should be clearly spelled out and the consequences disseminated to key parties, such as executive management, operations staff, accounting, and IT staff.
- Given the upfront investment made by the ASP operator, it is not uncommon to find onerous "Exit Conditions" placed in the contract. The e-commerce company should reserve the right to terminate and understand the technical, operational, and financial consequences of termination. Such an understanding should include ownership of data, migration support to another environment, access to hardware, rights to software licenses, and customizations.
- Support of vendors to the ASP, their relationships, and mutual commitments should be understood. Clearly, any instability of the ASP transmits instability to businesses using the ASP.
- Future potential—ability to grow, support new requirements, global expansion.
- Ability to support your e-commerce business model and its evolution is important.
- References should be carefully evaluated; this is a very immature industry.
- Installation or set-up times.

Baseline Measurement for Evaluating ASPs

1. A **detailed list of applications** and functionality supported by the ASP. This should drill down to the granular detail. For instance, if an ASP is offering an EDI module, the detail might specify the types of EDI transactions supported,

the vendors supported, the method of interaction (such as Value Added Network or EDI on the Web), availability of redundancy, integration to core applications, and costs associated with any required interface construction, customization, and maintenance.

2. Number of **users to be supported** ("named" users or total number allowed), cost per user per month, cost of adding new users.

3. **Number of interfaces** that need to be built and the cost of interface construction, testing, and maintenance. In addition, the contract should specify the responsibilities for the interface when the vendor upgrades the application or the client requires changes to the interface.

4. Extent of **customization** required for each application (enhancement of basic functionality, integration requirements, support for preservation of customizations, custom queries, and reports).

5. **Implementation** detail—process, functionality, and data conversion need to be specified in complete detail, including responsibilities and manpower allocation for identified tasks. Implementation of an ASP model consumes time of the ASP vendor teams, the client, and any outside consultants brought in.

6. Detailed **testing plan** for connectivity, interfaces, customization, data integrity, and application functionality.

7. Meeting provisions of the **SLA.**

Illustrative Scenario for an ASP Implementation

The choices facing a company in trying to gain ERP functionality is to either implement in-house or to use an ASP to host the ERP applications (see Table 3.6). In this utilization scenario, we contrast implementation issues for a company deciding between an in-house ERP solution and an outsourced ASP solution. The metrics utilized are intended for illustrative purposes. What is more important is the methodology to be used in identifying the issues, allocating the costs, and understanding the consequences.

Here are some important conclusions:

1. In-house implementations are typically more exhaustive and expensive. ASPs focus on quick implementations, since there is greater leverage in charging for the hosted applications as soon as possible.

Table 3.6   Illustrative Comparison Between In-House and ASP for an ERP Application

Applications: ERP Financials and Basic Supply Chain
Nature of Implementation: Phase I of ERP and E-Commerce Integration
Number of Users: 50

	In-House Implementation	*ASP Solution*
Overall design	10 person-weeks	6 person-weeks
Base implementation	20 person-weeks	12 person-weeks
Integration to e-commerce application	16 person-weeks	10 person-weeks
Customization of ERP applications	16 person-weeks	4 person-weeks
Data transfer	2 person-weeks	2 person-weeks
Testing and training	6 person-weeks	6 person-weeks
Total elapsed time	6 months	4 months
Total IT labor time Cost per person-week (at the rate of $200 per hour)	70 person-weeks $8000	40 person-weeks $8000
Capital Costs: Total IT labor cost License cost (50 users) Hardware cost Total capital cost	$560K $500K $40K $1100K	$320K $320K
Monthly Costs: Technical support Salary to support ERP ASP hosted cost ASP lease line Total monthly cost	$6K (15% of license fee per annum) $24K (4 person-team) $30K	(bundled in price) $12K (2 persons) $50K ($1K per user) $1K $62K
Total cost over 1 year Total cost over 2 years Total cost over 3 years	$1.46M $1.82M $2.18M	$1.06M $1.81M $2.55M

2. Internal interfaces, such as to home-grown applications, are often more cumbersome due to lack of documentation and standardization. The ASP vendor, on the other hand, focuses on consistent methods of integration between hosted applications and in-house applications.

3. With in-house applications, there is often a strong tendency to modify base applications to accommodate internal business processes. The ASP provider often places stringent restrictions on customization to hosted applications because they are not easily supported during application upgrades. Thus, the "wish-list" for customization with hosted applications automatically shrinks, resulting in faster but less customized implementations.

4. In-house applications require license fees to be paid upfront. The normal ASP model is for the license cost to be built into the monthly hosting fee.

5. Total elapsed time for implementation may be about 50 percent greater for in-house implementation as compared to an ASP solution.

6. An in-house implementation requires continuing post-implementation support, such as an applications DBA (database administrator), an application technical engineer, and a functional lead. In contrast, with an ASP, a functional lead may suffice.

7. Overall capital costs for an in-house ERP implementation may be about 100 percent greater than the corresponding ASP implementation cost.

8. The monthly operational cost of an ASP solution may be 50 percent greater than the corresponding in-house cost.

9. There is greater tendency and potential for "endless implementation" (project creep) with an in-house solution. This also leads to greater maintainability problems.

10. Overall costs of an ASP solution are lower in earlier years and greater in later years. In a simplistic sense, and excluding considerations such as enhancements, new module implementations, technology changes, personnel turnover, ASP stability, etc., we estimate that the in-house solution is favorable after about three to four years in a cumulative cost analysis. However, cash flow analysis favors the ASP model, with known, systematic outlays of expense. This trade-off between capital costs and operating costs for the two models is shown in Figure 3.5.

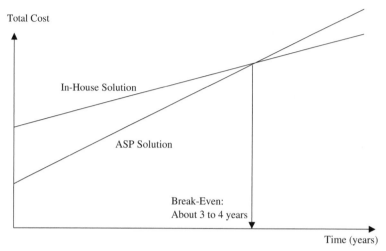

Figure 3.5 In-House Versus ASP

E-Commerce Platform

In an e-commerce environment, the three important dimensions of attraction, interaction, and transaction need to come together in the context of a prospective customer and an online merchant. The specific context may vary quite widely depending on the type of business. For example, the attraction context of an online store is a customer who is marketed to using advertising or direct marketing. In contrast, the attraction context for a business marketplace may involve membership in a community, partnerships, and positioning within a marketplace.

As is readily evident, it is difficult to isolate any one dimension without affecting other stacks. That is the beauty of online, because a complete e-commerce system is a closed ecosystem and when one element or dimension is affected, it has a multiplier effect on the others. In Figure 3.6, we map these three dimensions.

Attraction

This provides the primary basis for obtaining customers and getting them to an online site. Attraction may be provided by an online campaign with email, third-party site referrals, seeded positions within search environments, or banner advertisements. And/or it

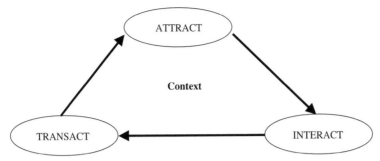

Figure 3.6 Elements of Attraction, Interaction and Transaction

can result from offline advertising in newspapers, magazines, billboards, radio, or TV. Don't overlook cross-references or cross-linking from other sites, promotions, coupons, etc.

Once attracted to try out the online site, there needs to be a sufficient online compulsion for the first time visitor to stay, which is often termed stickiness. In a B2B setting, the attraction to customer participation may revolve around such issues as strength of vendor participation, ability to continue contractual relationships with preferred vendors, back-end technological integration with order management and payment systems, workflow management, etc.

Interaction

The second dimension deals with working interactively with the online customer to create a context for engagement. This dimension may be accentuated through site navigation, graphics and other aesthetics, personalization, customization, merchandising, marketing, and entertainment.

Transaction

Most e-commerce environments want a transaction to occur that results in direct or indirect financial remuneration. For an online retailer, this may be an order; for a portal, it may be a referred transaction or a click on a banner advertisement; for a community, it may be an interaction with other members of the community.

For the three dimensions of attraction, interaction, and transaction, we identify the value provided in several categories such as providing content, navigation, etc. The shaded areas in Table 3.7 designate where such value is predominantly provided. For instance, content is the basis of attraction, which can be advertising or positioning to bring in a customer. Content does not play as much of a role in the transaction, though order tracking after the sale could be a form of content.

At this point, an e-commerce site should review the navigation needs of a customer. Simple, consistent, logical navigation is critical, as the confused user will just click away. A poor navigation on the front page is analogous to a retail store without its aisles properly numbered and identified. Haphazard advertising and irritating pop-ups often jar the casual visitor and discourage interactivity.

To a large extent, Amazon.com (*www.amazon.com*) and Yahoo! *(www.yahoo.com)* demonstrate the effectiveness of good navigational, or user interface design (UI) principles. Business and consumer portals can offer the options of customizing user navigation, often done through preferences in an e-commerce engine.

To engage the customer, the content has to be compelling. For example, an online retail store may discount a new product; an e-commerce marketplace may promote a new gadget with an advertisement; an exchange may provide a detailed perspective on a new supplier.

Table 3.7 Value Provided in Attraction, Interaction, and Transaction

	Attract	*Interact*	*Transact*
Content			
Merchandising			
Navigation			
Customization			
Personalization			
Configuration			
Payment Systems			
Customer Service			
Order Management			
Fulfillment			

These are examples of merchandising, and merchandising bridges the gap between attraction and interaction. The intent of most merchandising is to drive a user reaction in the form of a drill-down click for more information, to have the user fill out a request for a contact, or to push the user forward to a potential sale.

Online stores use personalization to achieve a greater "conversion ratio"(i.e., the ratio of the number of visitors to the number of buyers). This might involve merchandising items based on a past purchase or a recent browsing pattern. Some products may need to be configured but allow only certain valid combinations (for instance, a person signing up for courses online may need a configurator to choose between allowable combinations of courses involving timings, prerequisites, credits needed, etc). Configuration and payment systems cross over from interaction to transaction processes.

Customer service may arise in both the interaction and transaction phases and through combinations of email, chat, and phone. After the transaction, order management personnel may be involved in sheparding the order through the transaction. Such workflows can range from simple inventory-based fulfillment to complex third-party support through international shipping, customs documents, and tariffs. Finally, delivery to the customer may involve outsourced fulfillment services, with reporting of the shipping status back to the interaction systems (both in a self-service model for checking an order status as well as live customer service help to provide that information).

In arranging the dimensions against their elements, Table 3.7 focuses on the business functionalities embedded in an e-commerce platform. A user's e-commerce experience may or may not result in a sale or a transaction. Yet, the functionalities themselves point to how each dimension may be managed to get optimum results from the perspective of both the user and the e-tailer. For each functional area, such as content, store navigation, etc., the needs of the platform are identified and discussed in greater detail below.

Hopefully, the entrepreneur should be able to use this list of required capabilities to match against either off-the-shelf software or against a 'requirements document' for development.

Meeting Content Management Needs

Every e-commerce site needs to serve content in the context of a site's primary focus. For an e-commerce store selling goods, this may be product information; for an information site delivering breaking news, it may be categorized news content; for a community, it could be information on events and activities of interest to the community. Content management systems encompass data aggregation, preparation, categorization, and management. These are covered further in Chapter 4, "The Content Stack."

Merchandising

Merchandising refers to the attractive display of content with the purpose of eliciting that all-important click. Merchandising may include the following elements:

- Featured manufacturer, brand, or product
- Category discounts or special offers
- Product bundling offers
- Discount for purchases above a price level
- Free shipping, free gift-wrapping, or other services
- Product reviews to gain customer confidence
- Clearances and bargain sales
- Gift ideas

Merchandising is an active process, not a one-time design element. Similar to a traditional store such as Macy's buying promotional merchandise, conducting seasonal marketing campaigns, changing its window displays and product arrangements within the store, it is critical for a site to appear "refreshingly different but reassuringly the same."

Effective merchandising requires an understanding of:

- Site content and aging of content.
- Inventory and cost of inventory.
- Manufacturer and supplier compulsions to trigger new product sales or dump products being phased out. These may lead to comarketing dollars.
- Customer profile and origination of customers. These are often available buried within the Web server logs of customer navigation patterns and search queries.
- Merchandising options within the site: number of locations, feasibility of change.
- Discounting options supported by the transactional model.
- Seasonality and relevance of promotion.

- Piggybacking of current offline merchandising trends.
- Benchmarking with competitive sites.

Baseline Measurements for Merchandising

1. Number of merchandised objects in home page and major pages
2. Percentage of clicks on merchandised objects as a fraction of total clicks on the page
3. Conversion ratio of click-throughs to order for merchandised products
4. Number of clicks and conversion as a function of time
5. Effectiveness of time-bound promotions versus unbound promotions
6. Merchandising effectiveness on new customers versus returning customers
7. Response rate to merchandising email campaigns
8. Merchandising effectiveness when tied into ongoing offline advertising
9. Merchandising effectiveness when piggybacking on campaigns of other online and offline retailers

Navigation

Once content is available, cleaned up, and nicely categorized, it needs to be displayed in the site. Site navigation attends to the front-end needs of display, site structure, and search at a primitive level. In other words, a site may have a wealth of content, but does it do a good job of helping the user navigate the site to get at the content he or she wants to look at? Industry jargon for this is user interface (UI) design. Simply put, it's common sense design.

Consistency in categorization and placement, availability of contextual help, search tools, simplicity, and user-oriented design principles go a long way towards making navigation easy and hassle-free.

Underlying this "outer skin" is the equally complex issue of modeling the store to support the best navigation and user experience. The platform for e-commerce needs to provide such functionality in a simple, configurable way.

Store creation used to be a homegrown process and, even today, top-line sites are based on internal development at the core. However, e-commerce software packages geared to customizable sites are increasing in popularity. Furthermore, they offer out-of-the-box integration with other software packages and services, such as to tax computation packages, personalization software, or ERP applications.

Either way, the functionality required is as follows:

- Ability to support different store designs or templates.
- Categorization of products into one or more navigation styles. The most popular ones now offer a two-dimensional drill-down, with the top navigation bar supporting the major product categories and the navigation axis on the left side supporting a drill-down.
- Simple and advanced search capability. This is a very important utility, especially in the case of extensive content. Search should be contextual as far as possible, that is, relevant to the customer location within the store environment. The product content should be cross-cataloged extensively and indexed for high speed and relevant searching. The more advanced search engines provide search based on language stems, fuzzy logic, and linguistic similarities. Refined searches enable the site to bring up content associated or related to the primary search element.
- Support for high quality interaction between the customer and the online store.
- Simple login and ordering process to facilitate queries on order status, usage of the shopping cart, etc.

Customization

The cost of customer acquisition is very high, ranging from $75 to $100 in the United States. This high cost is due in part to the rapidly expanding availability of choices. As customers hop from site to site, the bewildering variety has a mind-numbing effect with low recall of the more desirable sites. Merchants who are able to get customers to visit again are enormously advantaged. One key element to get a customer to revisit is to have a site that is conveniently arranged and customized to meet the needs of an actual customer.

The key elements of customization are account customization, content customization, and need customization.

Account Customization

With account customization, the user defines preferences associated with his or her relationship with the merchant. The user uses the browser, for example, to get a look and feel for navigational style, functionality, login mode, account access, security information, address data, notification preferences, and basic interaction terms between merchant and customer.

By providing this basic level of customization, the merchant can obtain significant information. Functional choices reveal where a merchant should add emphasis or what to target for deletion. User account information reveals geographic location as well as frequency and time of access. Repeated usage of account-based logins may identify an inclination to use the merchant as a gateway for other services, including taking customization to the next level: personalization.

Yahoo! is a good example of account customization. Starting from a preferred location for search, Yahoo! enables a stream of functional "products" to be provided through simple account customization, such as email, briefcase, personal Web site, fax service, shopping, gaming, financial services, chat, and community services. The key link in all of this is the identification in the consumer's mind of a "Yahoo! Account," wherein choices can be made. For Yahoo!, every new functional choice by a customer provides a new data point regarding the value of the customer. Amazon.com's collaborative filtering operates in the same way, providing Amazon with valuable input on customer preferences while giving the customer a starting point for online shopping, and that most valuable reference point is his or her name.

Baseline Measurements for Personalization

1. Number of customers who have accounts
2. Percentage of customers who have customized their accounts
3. Most popular account personalization elements
4. Usage history of custom features

Content Customization

At this level, the customer is deliberately narrowing the scope of available choices to abstract and thus simplify the breadth and depth of products offered by a merchant. As content explodes and choices mushroom, focus becomes very important. Consider a financial news environment. If the customer can delimit his/her exposure to the site to show the financial products of interest, then the "visual noise" of unrelated content is thankfully absent.

Thus, the account owner may want to maintain a personal portfolio of owned and interested financial positions and news associated with those; he then may wish to subscribe to a few additional services of a complementary nature. The important lesson for a merchant is that a high volume of information does not equal value.

Information on how a customer customizes content provides the merchant with a sectional view of that customer, a dimensional slice of preferences. This has significant potential value in conjunction with the corresponding account profile. Customized content that is being traversed can potentially be gainfully targeted for specific merchandising, such as new but related products and upgrades, or be used as "advertising fodder" for sales to third-party selling.

In the financial site example above, a customer selected aggressive stocks. This customer is potentially interested in option trades, which are either offered by the merchant or by a third party. Ditto, perhaps, with aggressive mutual funds. The value of content is significantly higher as it allows effective targeting, and the customer is making a deeper commitment to a particular merchant's offerings.

Baseline Measurements for Customization

1. Percentage of customers who have customized content
2. Categories that have the most demand
3. History of customized content for navigation versus selection
4. Effectiveness of merchandising and advertising inside a customized environment (click-throughs, transaction rate)
5. Transaction volume in a customized environment versus the main site (i.e., having customized the desired content, does the customer effectively use this channel or does he/she fall back to the more standard merchant offerings?)

Need Customization

At this point, the dynamic relationship between the visitor and the merchant is undergoing a substantive change. The "standard" model in most e-commerce environments is a "supply" model, wherein the merchant makes the visitor aware of the wares. This supply-based push strategy is blind to the needs of the customer. For example, a "Product of the Day" may have no relevance to 99 percent of all visitors; it is just a figment of an imagined merchandising scheme. As customers provide evidence of need, the equation can change in favor of the merchant.

Consider, for example, that a merchant is effectively able to capture a customer's prospective needs (say through a mini-poll at the end of a transaction or a survey conducted by email when the account was set up). The customer may conceivably denote an interest in specific products or product categories and may allow the merchant to target directly upon availability. If the need has been properly defined and captured (with elements of time, price, and features), the likelihood of a sale increases tremendously. Such a "service" element on the Web has enormous value, with the customer perceiving a higher level of "personal service."

A potentially lucrative area for need customization is in establishing the following registries:

- **Individual Registry**—A wish list for the individual. This is relatively simple and allows direct merchandising and marketing within the boundaries set by the customer.

- **Wedding Registry**—This is comparable to the offline wedding registries at Macy's, etc., with one important difference: in the offline world, the wedding registry may be vested with one retailer; in the online world multiple merchants may be involved to satisfy the totality of need. This may require coordination between merchants, such as an online wedding registry network that consolidates purchases and handles the interface between the gift giver, the marital couple, and the merchants. The bride and the groom, on behalf of the merchant, do online wedding registry "direct marketing." The likelihood of transaction is fairly high along with the value of the transaction and, when properly handled by the merchant, may lead to new customers. Customized offerings and "wedding registry" packages are significant attractors.

- **Gift Registry**—Here the intent is to shop for family or friends at Christmas or for birthdays. Because gift giving is an annualized ritual, it is important to understand the significance of gaining the customer's confidence in creating a gift registry. There is a parallel here to Intuit's launch of a financial and tax software package. Once customers take the trouble to provide details of their financial transactions and file a tax return, there is a very high likelihood they will reuse the same package next year, since the incremental effort is much lower. Similarly, a customer who creates a gift registry with names, addresses, birthdays, and preferences of friends and family will have a high propensity to reuse, if the first trial is successful.

With registries, the intent is to raise the customer's switching cost, making the effort to change to another vendor cumbersome, time consuming, and possibly expensive.

Baseline Measurements for Need

1. Percentage of customers who identified and customized their needs
2. Nature of need expression (products, categories, services)
3. Elements of need (time, price, features, registry services)
4. Registry depth (number of registries active, number of target customers within each registry account, level of detail available, such as email or address)
5. Usage history of need customization
6. Method of customer interaction (email, Web site, phone, chat)
7. Transaction effectiveness for specific needs identified (conversion rate, sale per order, number of items per order, effective margin)
8. Account retention

Needs Personalization

For shoppers on the Web, it is important to note that every move can be tracked, often analyzed, and increasingly utilized to derive additional activity. When a visitor enters a Web site, a "user session" is initiated, which identifies the user for all subsequent clicks on the site for that entry. The user's origination is typically known, at least at the level of an IP address. Many simple parameters can be queried, such as operating system, browser type, and version. If the user has permitted cookies (a small text file on the end user's computer that allows a Web site to track a prior visit or enable account logins), then the merchant has valuable information about the customer's tendency to return. At a basic level, every click of the user goes into a Web server log, which can be selectively peeled out to reveal sequential activity.

This record of the click-stream can be used in many ways, as illustrated in Figure 3.7.

Cost of Personalization

Personalization capabilities are fairly intricate and best acquired through third-party software rather than developed in-house. The following tasks are associated with profiling and personalization, and are available through software and services vendors:

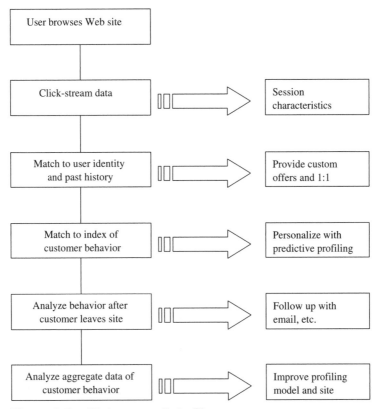

Figure 3.7 Click-stream Data Flow

- Consulting engagement to review online transaction data to understand customer-purchasing history
- Conjoint analysis to create customer behavioral maps
- Business rules to create personalized offers
- Tracking of online click-stream to provide instantaneous and delayed merchandising propositions
- Post-transaction analysis of behavior

Profiling and personalization costs may run anywhere from $250,000 to over $1 million.

Software Vendors

Datasage.com: Customer analysis, custom Web pages, email campaigns

Verbind.com: Real-time interaction, messaging, and email

Personify.com: Predictive algorithms using psychographic data

Epiphany.com: Multichannel data acquisition; structures offers and evaluates effectiveness

Needs for Configuration

Configuration allows a customer to choose from a set of options, as in the following scenarios:

- Configure complex equipment pieces together with guaranteed inter-workability, typified by Cisco's ability to self-configure networking elements.
- Choosing a build-to-order computer system for a budgetary target, such as with Dell computers. Consider the purchase of a standard issue staff computer with a budget limit of $1,500. The configurator on the Dell site allows a purchaser to configure the system for the target price while disabling selection of incompatible options either for reasons of price or technology.
- Aggregation of complete sets, such as for housing contractor work.
- Gift configurators to suggest choices constrained by a budget. For example, to purchase gifts for an extended family with known ages, interests, and a budget limit.
- Financial configurators for investment choices to meet a defined investment risk target. For example, to invest $100,000 in a variety of financial instruments (stocks, bonds, funds) to achieve a 12 percent return target at a "moderate" risk level.
- Travel configurators to achieve an "experience goal" with cost and comfort constraints. For example, a 12-day trip to Europe from the U.S. to see three countries and not exceed $5,000.

Configuration basically consists of three aspects:

1. Configuration Engine to provide the interface and help with choices
2. Product Categorization, which identifies the cross-matrix of products that can be configured together

3. Customer Tracker to provide any personalization associated with configuration for a specific customer

Cost of Configuration

Configuration products are complex to build and maintain. Similar to personalization, the configurator is best bought externally, along with suitable consulting services to set up. Costs may run from $500K to $1 million.

Software Vendors

Calico.com: Integrates configurator with quote building and customer accounts

Firepond.com: Provides an integrated e-commerce environment along with configuration

Trilogy.com: Particularly useful in large business to business environments

Selectica.com: Configurators available for various vertical market segments

Needs for Payment Systems

A variety of payment systems are used on the Internet for electronic commerce. They include standard, readily available credit cards; debit cards and ATM cards; e-wallets, which include credit cards and personal information; and cyber wallets, which consist of "virtual cash" that is stored in the customer's computer.

Credit cards systems (see Figure 3.8) are by far the most accepted in the U.S. for the following reasons:

- Universality of acceptance of Visa, MasterCard, Discover, and American Express
- Familiarity of usage in offline world
- A presumption of "consumer protection" with credit cards as opposed to newer forms of payment
- Flexibility of usage from home, office, airport, etc., versus locked in payment systems on a specific computer
- The advantage of a one-month payment float versus instant payment mechanisms

Cost of Credit Card Transactions

Typically, the online credit card transaction is viewed as a transaction without visible identification of the buyer, much like a phone authorization. Corresponding to this "higher" risk, the credit card processor charges a fee of about 50 cents, in contrast to a charge of less than five cents for a transaction through a payment slip at a credit card terminal in a retail store. Moreover, the credit card companies, such as Visa and MasterCard charge 2 to 3 percent of the transaction. The merchant, therefore, gets about 3 to 3.5 percent less than the sales order total, but receives the amount in cash in the merchant's own bank within hours of the transaction *if shipment occurs immediately.*

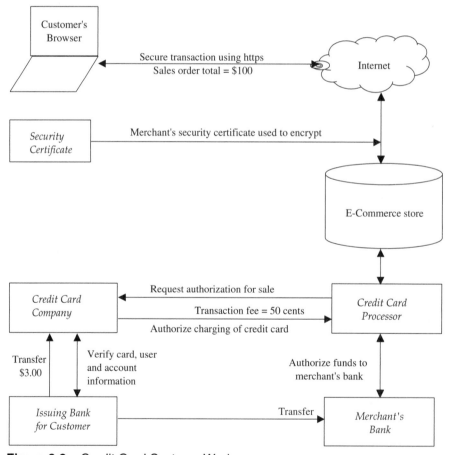

Figure 3.8   Credit Card Systems Work

Security of Payment Systems

Are credit cards safe to use on the Web? This question has vexed customers and has led to some considerable innovation on digital security systems. Credit card safety is easily divided into the following risk categories:

- **Transaction Risk:** Can the credit card revealed by the customer to the merchant be captured by a third party on the Web? Given digital encryption, the answer to this seems a confident *no*. There appears to be no case of credit card theft during "transit."
- **Theft Risk:** Merchants often store customer credit card information in their database systems. In many cases, these are poorly secured and often stored in unencrypted form. As a consequence, a hacker or a disgruntled employee potentially has the ability to capture the credit card information. Moreover, unlike the offline world where the credit card information is also vulnerable to theft (such as at a table in a restaurant, etc.), the situation in the online world is more perilous. Credit card numbers and details are usually available concurrent with customer information such as address, phone number, etc. There have been numerous break-ins into company database systems and subsequent theft of credit card information. In addition, credit card thefts in the offline world continue, which also lead to bogus online transactions.
- **Identity Risk:** The credit card industry seems almost cavalier in its distribution of credit cards with ever-increasing lines of credit. Obtaining credit cards is often trivial. It is no surprise then that identities are "stolen" from digital databases and new credit card are obtained for fraudulent use.

Online fraud using illegitimate credit cards is likely to increase. Interestingly, as noted in the article referenced above, the customer is not at risk. Usually, the customer is liable up to a maximum of $50. The merchant is liable, though! The merchant is left holding the bag when an online transaction is identified as fraudulent.

E-Wallet Systems

Electronic wallets have been much touted as the Internet technology to supplement the traditional credit card system (see Figure 3.9). While this has yet to happen, the promise of e-wallets is appreciable. In the e-wallet approach, the consumer registers with an electronic wallet system and enters personal information such as name, address, telephone number, and credit card numbers. When shopping at a merchant that supports the specific e-wallet system, the customer clicks on the e-wallet icon and authenticates him/herself. The customer is then given a choice of credit cards to use as well as any saved addresses that could serve as a 'Ship To' address for a gift. The merchant then receives this information in the shopping card environment for order completion.

E-wallets are convenient devices for the three major participants in e-commerce—the consumer, the merchant, and the e-wallet issuer. Consumers can enter personal information such as their credit card number once, avoiding the need to repeat the process each time they make a transaction, while keeping the information accessible and secure. Perhaps more significantly, because access and trust issues are always changing, the consumer can use the e-wallet as a personal digital assistant complete with tools to create and use an online address book and a reminder about important events. Similarly, the e-wallet

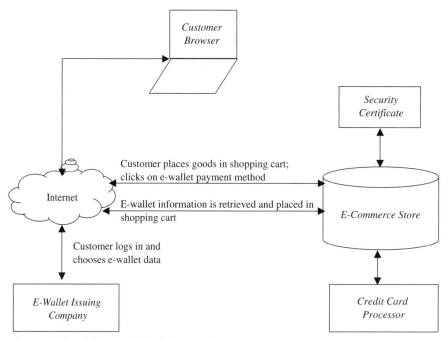

Figure 3.9 A Typical E-Wallet Implementation

can be a repository for affinity program data, such as airline mile credits and other loyalty point programs.

Merchants also benefit when some of the reasons for abandoned shopping carts are removed. E-wallets can help reduce buyers' fears of giving credit card information. Because the merchant cost is either nominal or non-existent, the overhead associated with e-wallets can be less than with credit cards, though there is some integration required to configure the e-wallet software into the hosted shopping cart.

E-wallet issuers, most likely financial service firms with other online payment mechanisms, can extend their brands to yet another transaction device. Their brands can be important in minimizing consumer resistance to another "online scheme." The downside is consumer attachment to the e-wallet versus the credit card, but when the same institution issues both, the loss is minimal.

Needs for Customer Service

The Web is often accused of being an impersonal environment. To truly deliver on its promise, it needs to improve its ability to deliver a higher level of customer service based on personalization techniques. All demands for efficiency and automation notwithstanding, it is essential that merchants tap the inherent interactivity in its various forms to make customer service more viable than a mere listing of FAQs. Many sites have corrupted this once useful capability into a meaningless mélange of trite statements that management "hopes get asked," but in no way alleviate a merchant of any responsibility to be responsive.

Usage contexts and metrics of various forms of customer service are shown in Table 3.8.

Example: E-Commerce Platform Costs for a B2C Store

Here, seen in Table 3.9, we consolidate the costs associated with creating and sustaining an e-commerce platform for an online consumer store. Also identified are vendors providing software, content, or services for the various e-commerce platform layers.

E-Commerce Enterprise Architecture

It is often forgotten that creating a Web site is not the same as creating a business. The Web site is a window to the entities that need to interact with a business. This window accepts and returns data. For a business to be successful, it needs to have systems and

Table 3.8 Customer Service Interaction Types

Type of Interaction	Usage Context	Metrics	Estimates and Cost Per Rules of Thumb
Phone	Customer calls in; likely upset; sales context high	1. Phone calls as percent of total order backlog 2. Average call length	15 minutes per call
Email	Customer query for product Customer query for status Customer complaint or feed-back	1. Inbound emails as percent of total order backlog 2. Breakdown of inbound emails	10 minutes per email Email sorting required for major sites
Live Chat	Product query	1. Live chat sessions as fraction of total user sessions 2. Conversion to ordering from live chat	10 minutes per chat session 25–50% order conversion
Letter	Invoice mailing Customer faxed order	1. Outbound letters as fraction of total orders	20 minutes per letter
Outbound Email	Order confirmation Pro-active order status Confirmation of shipment Confirmation of delight	1. Number per order 2. Number per customer database 3. Number based on third-party lists	Internal cost of 1 cent per email External cost of 5 cents per email

processes in place that can handle incoming data (such as orders) and obtain new data that represent a change in status (such as order confirmation). As the volume of interactions at the Web site grows, it becomes imperative for back-end systems to be highly efficient and automated. The business architecture for e-commerce needs to handle a fairly substantive set of interactions and functional needs between the Web-centric front-end, the internal systems, and the extended supply chain outside the company.

Table 3.9 Interplay of Cost and Time for Site Elements

E-Commerce Layer	Capital Cost	Implementation Cost	Implementation Time	Sample Vendors
Content	Increases with volume	Low to moderate	Varies by industry	Requisite, Grainger, OnDisplay, CardoNet
Navigation	Low to moderate	Low	Small	Microsoft, InterShop, Open Market, IBM
Customization	Low	Moderate to high	Weeks to months	Internal modification of code base
Merchandizing	Low	Moderate	Moderate	As above
Personalization	High	High	Months	DataSage, Epiphany, Personify, Verbind
Configuration	High	High	Months	Calico, Fire-Pond, Selectica, Trilogy
Payment	Low	Low	Small	Part of standard soft ware
Customer Service	Low to high (depends on features and integration)	Low to high	Weeks to months	LivePerson, Siebel, Oracle
Order Management	Low to high (depends on integration)	Low to high	Weeks to months	People Soft, SAP, Oracle, Microsoft, IBM,Yantra
Fulfillment	Low to high (depends on integration)	Low to high	Weeks to months	Yantra, Same-day, FedEx, UPS

The following list identifies the stakeholders and systems that may require integration in a comprehensive e-commerce environment:

- Marketing channels, (including offline and online)
- Affiliate partners (including sales leads and direct orders)
- Customers with their accounts, history, customization, and personalization
- Communications infrastructure and providers
- Content providers
- In-house development environment
- Integration with customer service and order management
- Integration with internal systems (accounting, inventory, purchasing)

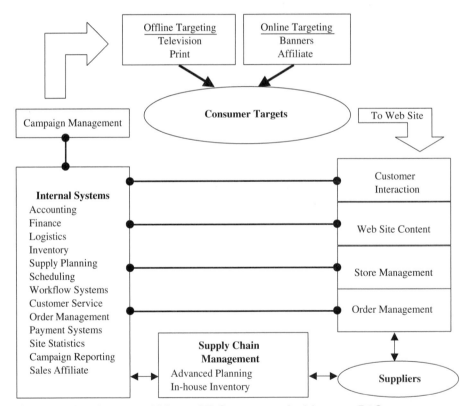

Figure 3.10   Integrated View of E-Commerce Architecture B2C

- Interface to payment systems
- Integration with suppliers
- Interface to delivery systems

Figure 3.10 takes this list and presents a road map with them in one context as an integrated e-commerce architecture for a B2C enterprise.

From our analysis of the Internet platform layer, it should be apparent that a good deal of the enabling functionality is delivered as software. There are operating systems, networking software products, applications, and a wide range of utilities. Some of these packages can be used by the merchant; others are designed for use by ASPs and the myriad number of service providers that support online commerce.

E-Commerce Software Environments

To take full advantage of an enterprise's functional needs, the e-commerce software environment needs to be flexible and capable of integration with a variety of information sources. A typical arrangement of a software environment is shown in Figure 3.11.

There is a trend away from the current preference of enabling Web store functions to operate independent of the enterprise software associated with back-office ERP applications. Traditionally, Web store applications were not geared to high volume customer transactions. For instance, in most e-commerce store environments, the orders are taken in the Web store environment. Credit card validation and authorization occurs in the Web store and the customer transaction is completed. Asynchronously, the orders are transmitted to the ERP system for further processing. These throwbacks to the batch-processing era are coming to an end as software packages not only become more robust but also become more and more interoperable.

Ten Rules for Choosing and Operating the Internet Platform

1. Design the Internet platform from the outside to the inside. Specifically, understand the external environments and their needs from the internal infrastructure. The key stakeholders are likely to be customers and customers of the

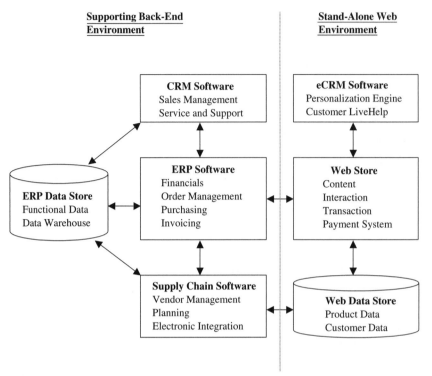

Figure 3.11   Back-End Systems and their Interface with Front-End Systems

customers, as in B2B. There are also value chain participants such as affiliates, suppliers, and service providers. Knowing stakeholder preferences can help define the internal environment.

2. Do not become a software company if your company is not in the business of selling software. Understandably, software is the platform for e-commerce. But, just as we use electricity to run factories but do not see the need to generate electricity ourselves, similarly, software development is best left to those specializing in specific offerings. Too many companies create software competencies inside the company, which are an asset in the short run and a liability in the long run. In-house software development tends to create narrow functionality and "unmaintainable" code. As much as possible, get professional software standardized to build your platform.

3. The Internet today is a whirl of change. This "acceleration" in technology evolution and redefined business processes provides new opportunities and threats. This pace of change needs a new "guerilla management" approach. Constantly review new options and re-evaluate current implementation. Example: improvements in voice-over-IP may invalidate huge investments in traditional phone-based call centers.

4. Time may be more important than money. Traditional ERP implementations took a year or two to implement. Your business may not survive a traditional ERP implementation. Focus on core needs and put together an agile team to execute a forced march deadline.

5. Look at hosted ASP solutions carefully. While this evolution, which has its roots in time-sharing, is still in its early stages, there is much to be said in favor of competent specialists maintaining the application environment. There is little to be gained by "owning the license" to software. Paying by the sip may be much better than drowning by a gulp from outright ownership.

6. Mix and match competencies to obtain best of breed. With increasing availability of fairly modular offerings, you have the flexibility of choice.

7. Your company does not have to do everything itself to achieve its business objectives. As far as possible, outsource all non-core operations. If you do not, you will have suboptimal performance in several business processes and may not be able to identify or quantify this suboptimality.

8. Limit your license/contract terms to a minimum. All outsourcing vendors will want the maximum contract period; try to limit it to a year or less. Understand clearly the consequence of contract termination on transfer of data, software, products, and procedures for doing so without disruption, as well as the flexibility of short-term office leases!

9. Worry about security continuously. Internet security violations for accessing business data environments are fairly high. There is considerable risk of business disruption, spamming, stealing customer data, placing fraudulent orders, etc. *Do not* use simple passwords, unencrypted vital information, and poorly controlled data environments. While an investment in security can be daunting, the costs of being driven out of business by inadequate security are a trade-off worth considering.

10. Ensure optimal performance and uptime. Nothing is worse than an attractive site that is also slow or non-performing in a strategic area.

Summary

In this chapter we analyzed the elements of an Internet platform required to develop a complete e-commerce environment. The Internet platform layer can be a medley of interlocking and cooperative internal and external resources, all designed to make the customer experience rich and rewarding. Alternatively, this layer can be a mélange of disconnects, excessively costly software packages, and a dysfunctional array of service providers.

At every stage of development and integration entrepreneurs and site architects are faced with make versus buy decisions. One of those decisions might suggest bringing in outside services. To have a cost-effective infrastructure design and to achieve optimal results from electronic commerce, it is necessary to have a clear view of what you want to accomplish and some baseline measurements. Having metrics to judge success or failure is important, however; without baseline measurements and objectives, metrics are meaningless. Throughout, we have listed best-of-breed software products and sites that apply sound principles covered in this chapter.

CHAPTER 4

The Content Stack

Interested in butterfly gardening? Yes, gardening designed to attract butterflies. Then go to a site managed by the North American Butterfly Association (*www.naba.org*) and you not only get focused information on how to lure any species in your area, but you can also take out a membership in the organization and even order brochures. To the butterfly enthusiast, the NABA site is sticky, a term being used more and more to describe sites that have an appeal that not only brings customers around once to smell the roses, but then draws them and their friends back to take another whiff.

In the process of coming back again and again, two things happen: selling is more likely to occur and the acquisition cost of getting a customer drops dramatically. This underlies the reasons why content is an important element in making the online experience so viable. The others are the quality of the Internet platform, community and, of course, commerce, all supported by our chosen team of service providers.

Not enough can be said about having pertinent, solid, viable, and interesting content at a Web site, even one like the butterfly site that is not specifically set up for e-commerce. The key ingredient in any well-visited site is *memorable content that is also useful*. If attractive and useful, customers stay and explore. If the content comes from someone you trust, the added credibility makes it even easier to set up a purchasing environment. If they tell their friends, you have the beginning of a community. When the friends tell friends, it explodes—all because the content provided the user with a positive experience.

For a B2B site, content is equally valuable, whether that is simple catalog listings or complex circuit diagrams for advanced semiconductors, networking architectures, or detailed case studies of how a product is implemented.

In the new economy information rules, and information is the draw and reward for a site-visit. But, with few exceptions, attempts to charge for content (or barter it away) fly in the face of one of the strongest forces on the Internet—content for free! There are many forecasts that suggest in the next 5 to 10 years virtually all content available on the Internet will be given away for free. That is too much of a generalization. What is perceived as free might be a mask for giving one form of information (personal shopping data) in return for another (insight into butterflies, for example). Is this free? By one definition, yes. By others, no.

In survey after survey of what draws customers to commerce sites, the qualities that consistently emerge as primary motivators are a blend of relevant information and a memorable experience. Information even leads navigation ease and aesthetic design, in second and third place, respectively, as desired traits in a site. In other surveys, the reason for being there is listed as entertainment, alone. The two concepts are actually linked: entertaining information (or infotainment) is relevant.

Content, however, is much more important to most e-commerce sites than its revenue potential because solid content also allows a merchant to begin the process of interaction with the customer. As this process unfolds, more information (content) allows the merchant to build a relationship with the customer. From this relationship stems loyalty and an opportunity to offer and sell products or services.

Presentation of content online is highly variable. Because there are still very few standards or conventions in the online world, diversity in content is the word of the day. This diversity, however, has bred near anarchy in how content is created, organized, and displayed, and then subsequently made available for distribution/consumption.

The important idea to get across is the need to engage and involve the visitor and then make the visit memorable enough so the person returns along with friends. Metaphors, theories, and experiments abound as to how to index, promote, and present content—and thus make the site sticky. Of this we know for sure: If content is absent, nothing good happens because the customer goes where content is.

Content Is Valuable

As we've seen and heard from one industry pundit after another, in the new economy information has value. Time and time again it is proven in the offline and online worlds that the ingredients for success are simple: having an easy-to-find and accessible location and giving visitors a reason to visit.

This means appealing to the real interests of the customer. As evidence of how powerful this can be, nothing is more personal than health. Health-related information is a leader in generating page views. There are an estimated 15,000 sites dispensing information and fulfilling orders for drugs, vitamins, supplements, and other medical products.

A white paper, "The Impact of E-commerce on Legacy Health-Care Companies" published by Cyber Dialogue, reports that close to 25 million adults sought online health care information over a one year period of time. (Cyber Dialogue, 304 Hudson Street, New York, N.Y. 10013, *www.cyberdialogue.com.*) Most online consumers start with inquiries into particular diseases (cancer being the most frequent, followed by heart disease) that affect them or those close to them. Nearly half go to health information sites to purchase specific medical products.

Content is the key element that provides the basis for interaction and/or transaction. The interaction is between the end-user or audience to whom the content is directed and the organization that assembles the content. Without viable content there is no possibility of an ongoing engagement with the customer. The end-user has to have a positive experience at the site, perhaps even be affected in a positive manner through some sensory mechanism for the content to have relevance.

In today's digital world this means using many of the strengths and capabilities that are inherent on the Internet: first and foremost, interactivity, followed by dynamic content. This may or may not encompass streaming and static video, text, and to a limited extent sound, such as music and voice. However, we have only five senses: sight, sound, touch, taste, and smell. The extent to which sight and sound can be bolstered with online techniques is important in adding stickiness to content, and thus a reason for customers to get to the site, stay there, and return.

New advances indicate the ability to project aromas in the near future. You may smell pizza when a pizza advertisement pops on your screen. Gameplay already simulates and stimulates ersatz touch and other sensations. Can digitized taste or more advanced tactile sensory creations be far behind?

This chapter focuses on the content stack, an integral part of an organization's efforts to embrace the Internet to conduct its business for commercial or non-commercial purposes. Just as a book with no matter—blank pages—is of little value, Web sites without content have little practical usefulness. E-commerce is a predictable failure if the site is minus products or information (content) presented in a compelling manner.

Content is multidimensional. It invites attention, draws comments, prompts exploration, and predicts the possibility of a return. These are of more than academic interest to online merchandisers and e-commerce startups. For one thing, content is information. Information, in turn, is power to the user or customer who has come to value the convenience afforded by the online experience.

Customers expect content to save them time, save them money, and make it convenient for them to find, filter, compare, select, and shop. Economically, content also bears the burden of a uniquely online characteristic: a higher rate of content "turns" and, therefore, a shorter shelf life. Content begins to look a lot like inventory in a high velocity retail environment where turns are a critical metric of success.

How so?

As purchases can be dynamically monitored, the catalog, too, is dynamically altered to attract buyers and keep them coming. Merchandisers have the ability to weed out sleepers and continually restock new content to reflect demand. On Web sites that have news or similarly intangible products, the old print paradigm of refreshing it to suit the edition—often once a day—may not be fast enough! Updates have to happen in real time: fast and furious.

The Nature of Content

Look closer at our daily media diet and it's easy to realize that not everything we see, read, and hear fits the same pattern. *The Wall Street Journal* appears once daily, Monday through Friday, but its interactive edition is always being updated and refreshed. Over the weekend until some time on Sunday, the printing machines lie silent and some of the journalists are probably taking it easy, with the exception of those working on the Monday edition.

On network and cable TV we are "treated" to a seemingly endless train of insipid programs and marginally updated but nonetheless repetitive news interspersed with talk shows, sitcoms, and educational fare. *The Wall Street Journal* news is as static as it appears in the day's newspaper and remains so until the next day's news supplants it as another static news in another day's newspaper. TV news, by contrast, despite the high degree of repetitiveness, is relatively dynamic when compared with a newspaper. Constantly gathered updates serve to alter the news whenever it is aired on CNN, making this news outlet and its headline news counterpart even more dynamic.

Radio comes a little closer to the online paradigm. News can be refreshed and updated on a more regular basis, but radio stations are locked into patterns called formats. News must be broadcast at certain times, weather at others, sports in their time slots, etc.

The Web introduces another wrinkle—while retaining all of the dynamic qualities of the broadcast medium, it also accepts and facilitates *your* input. That may not be true of print or broadcast content also made available online (such as magazines, newspapers, radio, and TV), but it becomes more meaningful and personal because of user interactivity.

There are three types of online content: *static, dynamic,* and *interactive.* All have a place in one context or another online supporting or participating in e-commerce. Static and dynamic content more or less follow patterns established by offline media. Interactivity is truly unique to the Internet.

A travel site, for example, could have all three— "published" or static content about travel destinations that may be relatively fixed, dynamically changing airline fares, and interactive discussion forums where users/travelers share experiences.

In the sections that follow we develop and contrast the three types of content in more detail.

Static Online Content

Normally, static content is information stored in a database, at a Web server, or on a file server to be retrieved by an online request. We often refer to static company content as brochureware.

Imagine you are going to New York and want to research weekend possibilities there. Upon logging onto the 'Net you go to the New York City Convention and Visitors Bureau's Web site. You click on "museums" and then on the link for the Museum of Modern Art (MOMA), which gives you directions on getting there, opening and closing times, and perhaps even a complete description of current and future exhibits.

The actual data may be several minutes to several days old. If MOMA's opening and closing times change with the season and the page being pulled up was not changed accordingly (it does not matter if the Visitor's Bureau was accessing the pages from MOMA or was independently maintaining it), you are likely to be looking at old and possibly erroneous information.

At the MOMA site, each piece of information is pulled up as a pre-existing page linked to a request entryway. For Web pages, the term "static HTML," which is the underlying formatting language used to present the content, denotes the kind of page being retrieved.

Static Web pages like these are often an administrative nightmare. Why? While it is relatively easy to create static Web pages, content begins to bloat as organizations get bigger. At some point, managing and maintaining content takes on greater importance than merely creating it. Also, stale content sends a strong signal to the end-user about the company owning the site—it may be as stale as its copy!

Large online stores need to ensure that their catalogs reflect the products available and the prices at which they are available. Links have to stay current and not dead-end the user with 404 errors. Changes to locations of particular content need to support previous links redirecting users to the new location. Unfortunately, dated static sites litter the information highway, with dead links and unreliable content. Examples of static content are:

- Detailed historic or other reference listings, perhaps frequently updated by research data, such as biological studies of migratory birds, butterflies, and endangered plants
- Product information posted by any manufacturer or retailer site with rarely-changing product listings
- Maps, as with Mapquest's (*www.mapquest.com*) offering of cities, towns, highways, and specific destinations
- Trade news
- Unfortunately, many of the close to three billion Web site pages still available worldwide

Dynamic Online Content

A user retrieves dynamic content on demand. In some cases, the information retrieved from the site is browsed and, in other cases, retrieved from linked environments. When a page is constructed on demand for the user, the phrase "Dynamic HTML" or DynHTML is used. Technologies such as Active Server Pages (ASP) and Java Server Pages (JSP) are also designed to deliver dynamic pages. The page is constructed automatically for each request. Once set up properly, content creation and delivery are done on the fly, immediately.

Unfortunately, without proper consideration in layout and design, such pages may also load slower than static pages. Unlike static pages, there is no swift query to a file server to pull up the appropriate file. Rather, based on specific input from the user, the system searches to put together a response specific to the input query.

A good example is the tracking system now in place at all courier companies. Say you've shipped an item by FedEx that is supposed to reach its destination in two days. Two days after you sent the package you inquire about the status of the shipment using the tracking number.

Wherever the package might be is logged in the database at FedEx and your tracking number constructs a query for the database and brings back a response via the Web that dynamically displays the progress of the shipment to its current location. The response may have been pieced together from several systems or joined from various tables in a massive database.

Information (such as a product description) is often extracted from one database, which ensures a higher likelihood of speed and accuracy.

Other examples of dynamic content are:

- Search and Find—information is retrieved for a specific request. This may be in portal environments or within a Web site, for example, doing a search on CNET for a price or feature comparison of notebook computers with a particular configuration.
- Order Status—as in the above situation involving FedEx, or perhaps Joe in marketing wants to know what happened to the departmental order for white boards and colored pens.
- Real-time inventory query—as when a supplier of side view mirrors for an automobile manufacturer has closed down owing to a strike and downstream suppliers are interested in determining if there is enough in inventory to sustain a few day's run.
- Stock quotes
- Broadcasts—movies, cartoons, such as at a Web site for kids.
- Advertising—as in banner advertisements, including highly targeted advertising that is delivered based on the context of the user. For example, a Web user who searches for Java may be served a banner ad from Sun Microsystems featuring its latest Java platform release.

- News—including content associated with politics, business, lifestyles, etc. Online news dissemination is becoming the dominant channel and, for many, the preferred medium over television, radio, and newspapers. The immediacy and dynamic nature of such content as well as the multiplicity of information on a given topic makes online news compelling. During the 2000 Presidential Election, traffic to online news sites soared while the painful recounts in Florida unfolded. You can go to a news portal or have news syndicated directly to your own personal site.

Interactive Online Content

Interactive content requires simultaneous interaction of two or more parties. While primarily text and minimally graphical today, this should rapidly expand to Voice Over IP and Video Over IP. Interactive content places higher demands on good quality connectivity between the interacting parties, which requires both high bandwidth and low latency.

Latency is the time taken for a small but significant amount of data to travel between two points on a network, usually measured in milliseconds. While the bandwidth issue may soon see dramatic improvement, latency is a more problematic issue given the global nature of the Web.

Consider, for instance, four players hitting a U.S. gaming site almost simultaneously. One of them is in the U.S., one in Europe, one in Australia, and one in Asia. Today, such a game is doomed to disaster because latencies between the U.S. and Europe are about 180 ms; from the U.S. to Australia about 300 ms, and to Asia as slow as 800 ms. The game would move in fits and starts.

What is needed for high-quality interactivity is a guaranteed latency between points of interactions. In some instances, consistent or guaranteed latency fits with a site's operating strategy: setting priorities for fast delivery of some content and allowing other material to be slower in delivery. Network providers may be able to address such needs in the future.

Examples of interactive content are:

- Chat—at merchant sites and in community environments. VerticalNet, a B2B e-commerce and community site, hosts communities in most of its 50-odd industry verticals. Users at its aerospace or water community, for instance, can chat with industry counterparts and share information, issues, problems, etc.

- Online games—against a computer, or versus other participants.
- Interactive learning—SmartPlanet.com, a division of ZDNet, hosts several online courses that are available to registered users. These include self-tutorials, workshops, and instructor-led online "classes" that use a mix of chat, emails, and whiteboards serving as the virtual counterpart to physical classrooms.
- Voice and video interaction—Net2Phone, a pioneer in IP telephony, was among the few that ushered in voice-based interaction between online remote users via the computer. This continues to evolve to include audio and video teleconferencing.

Consider the following two detailed examples that illustrate the nature of content. First, we look at a third-party content source that gathers, categorizes, and syndicates content in a focused area—health care. It interacts with many other entities – from the sources of content to the consumers of content. The second example looks at content generated by an entertainment provider. In this instance, it is itself a source and aggregator of content picked up elsewhere.

In both cases, content is packaged in a form that fulfills the needs of users and adds the dimension of partnering to their respective business models to create mutual gain.

HealthyInfo.com: An Online Health Site

HealthyInfo.com is in the medical content business. This site provides an interactive environment where content is created, collated, shared, and syndicated among various stakeholders. Note that content here is a two-way street. One site's inbound content will be someone else's outbound content.

Consumers, who form the primary target audience for the *HealthyInfo.com* Web site, contribute queries and requests for information about specific diseases, concerns, etc. In the other direction, *HealthyInfo.com* dispenses generic advice, information, and medical guidelines.

Portals and search engines refer audience members to *HealthyInfo.com* in return for outsourcing specialized health profession content. Additionally, *HealthyInfo.com* may enter into more alliances and partnerships, leveraging a mutual need for content. Such content may take the form of referrals, health news, research, cobranding, etc. These dynamics are shown in Figure 4.1.

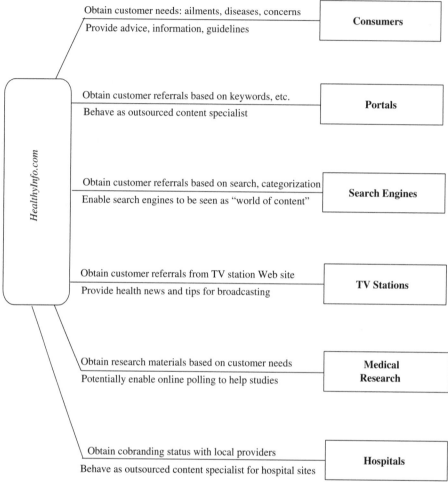

Figure 4.1   The *HealthyInfo.com* Content Stream

DigitallyEntertained.com: An Online Entertainment Site

DigitallyEntertained.com (a mythical site) is the computer equivalent of television. The company produces live-action shows such as short movies, comedy, and sitcoms. As with *HealthyInfo.com,* DigitallyEntertained.com acquires, manages, and supplies content among several entities that form its community of stakeholders.

As an online, interactive entertainment site, it seeks an enduring relationship with its core target audience, the consumer. The consumer is entertained while providing input into the provisioning of entertainment. This is similar to being in the audience of *The Today Show* and being urged to contribute through verbal and physical appreciation. Other *DigitallyEntertained.com* content includes in-house studio work, branding opportunities, sponsored advertisements, news, and interviews (see Figure 4.2).

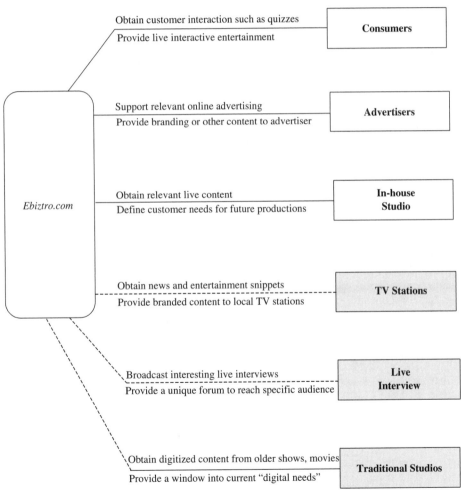

Figure 4.2 The Content Stream for *DigitallyEntertained.com*

Broadcast news sources have the expertise and the credentials to unearth and deliver news that can be traded with HealthyInfo.com or DigitallyEntertained.com in return for branded content coming out of these specialist providers of content. In each instance, content management addresses comparative advantages of their communities of interest for specific information, which the two online sites then leverage for their economic benefit and that of the portals and others referring an audience to them.

As Figures 4.1 and 4.2 show, obtaining and using content effectively is complex. Figure 4.3 stratifies content in terms of creation, distribution, and access. From content production to its final reception by the end-user, there are many different players, each with their own specific business model, involved in the content supply chain.

Collecting, categorizing, understanding, and displaying content is particularly complex and worthy of study in all its different dimensions. To understand effective content usage, we are drilling down into three aspects of content:

- Content Production—Sourcing and managing content
- Content Distribution—Taking created content and making it available to businesses that can use it on their Web sites
- Content Technology—Using prevalent industry standards, processes, and methods to handle content

Content Production

What and how content is produced is as strategic a decision as to how often it is updated. As with many other areas of concern within and without our five stacks, make versus buy decisions face every site operator. Whether content is completely "homegrown" or outsourced to professional sources, freshness of material often represents an important influence on whether the customer drops by once and never returns or becomes a loyal visitor.

Content Sources

Content can come from many sources: content from product manufacturers and marketers; financial information and news content from professional media organizations and freelancers; entertainment content; content from interactions, and content offered by third parties.

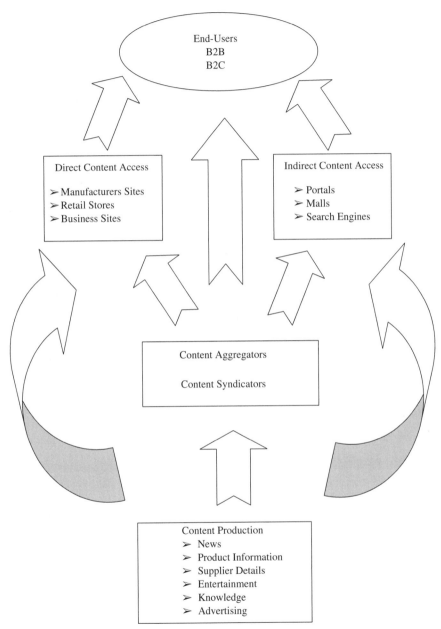

Figure 4.3 Production, Distribution, and Access of Content

Product Content

Consider the old Sears catalog. This American innovation aggregated hundreds of manufacturers, products, pricing, and availability within its pages. In aggregating content, the Sears catalog foreshadowed the birth of an industry—that of catalog merchandising.

Today, that same kind of product information from a manufacturer is integrated with expanded product specifications and case histories that include descriptions, pictures, multimedia, warranty information, etc. As we will see later in this chapter, use of this information helps generate product sales, or, at the least, comparisons.

Financial Content

Financial information encompasses stock prices, interest rates, bond yields, earnings releases, financial filings, and financial news. Content in this space is relatively easy to procure and deploy, given its relatively simple structure and standardization that existed long before Web-based information distribution came along. This industry is well organized with routine methods of flowing content into the system and then retrieving it.

Prior to Web-based interactions, stock and bond traders had private networks enabling them to stay current and to place trades. The Internet now facilitates dissemination of financial information to a much wider audience, making it possible for customers to use pager systems to receive stock alerts and cell phones to place trades.

News Content

Arguably, the Internet has changed the information business forever. Prior to widespread adoption of the Internet, offline media was *the* prominent portal of choice for sourcing, distribution, and receipt of timely and useful information. The pillars of offline news gathering and dissemination are crumbling, as now-dominant online portals such as Yahoo! and AOL emerge as information gateways of choice. With the merger of AOL and Time Warner, online and offline media giants, the landscape of content generation and dissemination takes on new meaning that only can be conjectured as this book goes to press.

The Sports Network (*www.sportsnetwork.com*) provides "real-time" "sportsstream" as content fed directly to various types of Web sites. Sports-specific content is prized by many sites because of the high degree of interest by their target audiences and buying patterns established with offline media.

As users become more comfortable with the idea of a "personal portal," they may well construct their own online versions with headline stories from *The New York Times,* the financial sections of *The Wall Street Journal,* the sports pages of *USA Today,* and the international sections from global newspapers.

Delving deeper, producers of news might not be the branded newspapers or broadcast news gathering organizations. They receive a good proportion of their underlying content from other news gathering entities such as the *Associated Press,* the non-profit entity founded in 1848 that is jointly owned by about 1500 daily newspapers. AP is increasingly selling news directly to Web sites, even though these Web sites *are not its traditional members.*

While this is a winning partnership for AP and the online news-centric sites, it leaves traditional members of the AP network out in the cold, illustrating the startling win-win-lose consequences of online commerce.

Entertainment Content

Entertainment content is generated through the following areas:

- Music: Until a couple of years ago, the Web was largely a "silent medium," as few home and office computers had sound cards and speakers. With audio systems now standard and increasing bandwidth becoming available, the Web is set to rock and roll. A case in point is *www.com,* a large producer of turnkey music for Web sites. *www.com* claims to have over 275,000 songs and digitized collections from more than 200 music stations. New standards for delivery of sound content such as vXML (voice XML) portend that the Web may soon speak and sing for you. When you are stuck in traffic, the Web may deliver your music selection from your personal site. This is clearly an explosive category, especially with the arrival of compression standards and music-centric search tools from MP3, Napster, and Gnutella. Users are now able to query the Web for music of choice and download to their systems for online or offline usage. Theoretically, rock bands may release singles directly on the Web, bypassing traditional recording studios. They already derive most of their revenues from live performances!
- Video: Traditional content such as feature films, news clips, and documentaries are making their way to the Web, initially as syndicated content. High-quality digitization and compression allow full-length feature films to be a viable download for viewing on a hybrid computer-TV device. WireBreak Entertainment, for example, streams live-action shows such as mini films and stand-up entertainment.

- Films: A delivery mechanism that is just being piloted with immense potential impact is the digitized delivery of films by studios to cinema theatres directly via high bandwidth channels. Instead of the current method of loading release prints into vans and onto airplanes, digital versions are uplinked to satellites or fed over the Internet to a private network of receiving stations. Digitized films are stored in large servers and converted back to an analog format via special projectors. Studios can save enormous costs involved in printing and distributing thousands of canisters of films worldwide. For cinema theaters, there is no inventory; and they can also make dynamic changes to schedule film screenings to be much more responsive to audience demands.

- Telephony: Other online video such as conferencing and video telephony through the Web are on the verge of becoming increasingly common. With widespread availability of digital cameras, the production of online content is becoming easier. Soon, wireless digital cameras will project content directly to subscribing Web sites. Remote participants of Web shows will join online, and even remote members of a band may be able to play together online.

- Gaming: Unlike news and magazine sites, subscription-based online entertainment sites are doing well. For example, the online sports site ESPN.com started fantasy football in 1995 and now brings in several million dollars from this and other fantasy sports. Content in these fantasy game environments is mostly interactive in the form of betting. On August 31, 2000, Sega Enterprises launched Sega Net, a multiuser gaming site that enables users to compete in video games with other players around the world. Such a positioning as an "entertainment services provider" creates a marketplace for interactive entertainment. The underlying content comes from the game, which has to be carried simultaneously and effectively throughout the world to meet interactivity needs of the players. As we saw above, an interactive global game cannot afford to be stymied by poor network performance in any part of the world! This demand created by a major game producer and literally millions of fans creates new requirements for higher performance in global networking.

Online entertainment is anticipated to grow rapidly because the tools of content acquisition are in place through syndication. Any explosion of activity is limited by international end-user connectivity only.

Interactive Content

Every customer's click and every Web page hit is information that is actionable content. Just as customers "talk" with their feet in retail environments, Web visitors talk with their clicks, leaving behind them a valuable trail of information. Such click-stream data is often used to design better Web sites, remove unused links, affect merchandising strategies, and enable personalization. Knowledge Strategies specializes in analyzing click-stream data for online retailers. Clicks on advertising banners characterize user behavior, providing feedback to designers and, hopefully, result in improved banner design and targeting.

Interactive content is abundantly available in community environments, albeit often in unstructured and unusable forms. The operator of the community has visibility into ongoing discussions, debates, and disputes. These environments are the equivalent of sampling, and they may provide a unique window into the world of the online community.

Privacy issues and site policies may strictly limit the usability of content within interactive environments; however, under suitable circumstances and guidelines, interactive content can be a good basis for customer action.

For example, a community chat session might unearth a discussion about hazards surfacing as a consequence of children playing with a recently released toy. This may spur action on the part of the online store to contact the manufacturer, who may take action to rebut, mitigate, or eliminate the danger. Discussions pertaining to hazards with a particular toy form the basis of content that gets cumulatively bigger (interaction). Its usefulness derives from highlighting potential dangers to kids, spurring action on the part of the retailer and manufacturer. Two purposes have been served in such content that results from interaction between discussion group members: community information and community action.

Third-Party Content

Content can be obtained from external parties other than news sources. It consists of:

- Solicited Opinions and Reviews: Some sites such as epinions.com and deja.com solicit consumer opinion on a variety of topics. Those providing reviews and other opinions may be paid a nominal amount.
- Expert Review: Some sites solicit professional reviews from experts on a topic to help sales in a particular store or to be resold as content.

- Professional Advice: In some cases, content in the form of professional advice is made available and publicly shared.
- Polls and Email Queries: Consumers may also be targeted with online polls and email queries seeking to understand the customer mind on needs, fashion, and moods.

Content comes in various forms depending on the category and source of content. For an e-commerce store, this may be product information. For a news site, it may be categorized news. For a community site, it could be information on events and activities.

News content traditionally was text-based, although there is increasing availability of audio and video content. Financial news is largely text and numbers. Gaming and online entertainment content deal with some software downloads, preferences, and interaction data. In any event, data for any particular purpose needs to be organized, collected, and managed.

Content Management

In the following discussion on content management there is a strong bias towards describing the process for selling products online. Content management for other areas of online commerce, such as digitized news, etc., are generally less complex, although they might be more automated.

There are four types of Content Management systems:

- Data Aggregation
- Data Preparation
- Data Categorization
- Data Management

Data Aggregation

Content may come from diverse sources, such as from different suppliers who may have a different way of describing or providing product information. Product data collection from a furniture supplier, for example, might be substantially different than from a supplier of flatware, but both might supply their offerings to the same online store.

The e-commerce environment needs to be capable of aggregating data from different source data environments. Data interaction standards have to be clearly specified in any contract between the parties to ensure a consistent basis for obtaining data. To some extent, there is recourse in classifications established by standards bodies, to be discussed later in this chapter. Such standards, however, do permit identification of products at a broad level as well as at a granular level. Moreover, standards enable a reseller of similar products from a number of manufacturers to accept data from the different manufacturers that have compatible identification schemes.

Data Preparation

Data that comes directly from some suppliers is often not very "clean," especially in these early days of e-commerce when vendors are still waking up to this new online environment. As a consequence, data can range from high-quality digital images and associated information, to paper catalogs with faxed pricing sheets. To preserve the uniform look and feel needed for minimum levels of compatibility and to provide a consistent quality of user experience, it is necessary to "prepare" the data. Data preparation may include digital enhancements, reduced image sizes, usage of a representative image for multiple products, and using alternate source data such as a particular manufacturer's information.

Data Categorization

Every e-commerce site must have a way to systematize categorization of its content structure. This establishes the "ontology" of the site. The resultant breaking down of the data to a standardized basis is called data normalization. Badly categorized data can lead to frustrated end-user experiences because visitors are led down many paths but cannot find desired products.

Consider, for example, a specific user browsing for a gift. If the store has a Gift Ideas button, then this drill-down should be productive for the visitor who unearths all products at the site that can conceivably be a gift. Indeed, it is critical for the store to create and maintain a subcategorization of products that fans out under the Gift Ideas section.

If, instead, the store shows a few "selected" products as gifts, then the opportunity for a sale may have been lost during a specific visit. Too many sites populate tons of data that are "digitally lost" because they are invisible to visitors in the context of a session.

A database of academic enrollments has data tables for instructors containing names, ID, departments, etc.; students, and courses. Each table, in its turn, has fields that capture attributes of each entity. In a similar fashion, a Web site of a store could identify its various entities (e.g., a department store Web site may have men's apparel, women's apparel, cosmetics, kitchen, furnishings, etc.) and data attributes within each. This permits data that ends up as content to be categorized and easily accessed by users.

Data Management

Retrieving, preparing, and organizing data are half the story. Much like perishable goods, data has a short life expectancy and should be rendered obsolete by new prices, availability, product updates, new images, recalls, reviews, etc. Unmanaged data becomes unusable data, and this leads to end-user frustration and anger. You've probably seen sites that show the infamous 404 "Page Not Found" errors. Data ownership by individuals in a company rather than as a departmental responsibility leads to data fragmentation and loss of maintenance.

Let's consider a company starting a product review feature on a site. If the person in charge of a specific review leaves the company, will the product review written by that person still be maintained and updated? Even more problematic are maintenance of pricing and availability information for product sales. Such information may change many times a day, depending on the volume and the sourcing mechanism. Ad hoc methods of maintaining data may result in significant user dissatisfaction.

Systematic policies for maintaining data integrity are essential for every Web site.

Content Management for E-Tailing

In this section we take a more detailed look at the complexity of selling B2C products online. Content and its inherent quality engender trust. The more content and the better it is presented, the more likely the customer is to feel comfortable with a merchant. Content is perceived as information, the disclosure of which implies more truthful and forthright business practices. Therefore, a well-conceived content strategy contributes also to brand equity.

For selling goods on the Internet, it is essential to support the product sale with information. In traditional retail, the tactile touch or visualization may provide the basis for a purchase, even though there might not be adequate product description. On the Web, the product needs to be accompanied by substantive description and often rich media content, depending on the product category.

A toaster may have one graphic, but a sofa may require multiple views and color swatches to permit selection. Obtaining rich content is not easy, as the traditional offline supply chain between manufacturers-wholesalers-distributors-retailers does not need such accompanying data for retail sales. However, in the online world, manufacturers are rapidly being pushed to assume responsibility for providing product and content online to everyone from the original sources of supply right on through to the eventual customer.

Let's take the example of an item on a shelf in the grocery store. This item possibly came out of inventory—either directly from the manufacturer or the grocery store warehouse (it does not matter for our illustration). It is displayed with a price tag that also indicates its name, size or weight, and price per unit measure. This bit of information captures several essential pieces of information for the customer, including a metric that can be used to compare substitute products (price per unit measure).

At checkout, the bar scanner retrieves the same details for the product from the database. The basis for purchase, in this instance, reveals:

1. The visual and tactile content that satisfies the customer as to the brand, looks, size, etc.
2. Print information that includes details about the name, price, and a tiny bit of comparative information (tiny because the onus is still on the consumer to use that to look at other boxes of cereal or tins of sardines close by).

That's the offline experience. Now, let's consider what is possible online.

Visual cues cannot be aided by tactile feel. Visual, therefore, has to compensate for the absence of the other and be rich in and of itself. An offline store is usually skilled at focusing customer attention inasmuch as the customer effort involved in getting there means she would still go on with the shopping despite some information scarcity or possible breakdown in customer service. She may get that box of cereal cheaper elsewhere, but says: "Why bother, I am here already."

Online, that equanimity disappears. "If I can't get the details or don't like what I see, I'll leave to another site," she says. An abundance of information usually helps, together with competitive comparisons by a neutral third party. Other factors at the site include ratings, preferably by customers themselves; support information of all kinds, information about returns and refunds, etc.

Unfortunately, content management for selling goods online is fairly complex. Data sources are often poorly organized and product manufacturers may not have the expertise to provide good quality information to support the sale of their products. In selling furniture on the Web, the following data elements are needed to complete the sale:

- Product category (Furniture: Living Room: Sofas: European: Leather)
- Product description (usually a short description and a long description)
- Supplier Stock Keeping Unit (SKU) number
- Product size
- Product weight
- Options (style variations, colors, texture)
- Product photos (multiple angles) and video (if available)
- Customer testimonials and ratings
- Competitive comparisons, preferably from a third party
- Availability (available now, manufactured on request, etc.)
- Manufacturer lead time
- Delivery time
- E-tailer pricing
- Wholesaler pricing
- Suggested retail pricing
- Warranty
- Packaging, shipping, and installation information
- Pre-sales support information
- Technical and post-sales support information
- Related products (cross-selling to complement this item)
- Returns and refund policy

While eminently desirable, it is unlikely that most manufacturers are capable or willing to provide this level of detail because it may be too expensive and time-consuming to document and/or provide information about every aspect of a product. Is the likely value of the product worth the effort? And what is the core competency of a manufacturer anyway? Make a product or produce photographs and descriptions? This is the essence of online *merchandising* and *interfacing* it with marketing—the two are different disciplines in B2C!

As evident, many high-profile online furniture e-tailers are in deep trouble, perhaps because of ineffective merchandising policies and procedures. Or, they might be deficient in understanding the market. In either or both events, display and management of content is generally weaker online than at offline furniture outlets.

Modern commerce has many layers of players involving multiple stages of production and specialized delivery. The source of this information is often invisible or unclear to the customer. Some customers may not want it; after all, we are told we want to tell time, not build a watch! At the present time, the compulsions of online commerce force the e-tailer to provide considerable levels of detail behind branded and unbranded products, especially those assembled from multiple sources. In addition, the e-tailer may need to reveal the original manufacturer, distributor, in-house staff, and any third-party product reviews.

All of this detail means content management can be expensive. Acceptance of standards for capture and display of information based on mutually accepted protocols (such as XML) can help. In the short run, the best bet is for intermediaries that want to avoid disintermediation to play the role of consolidators! Thus, manufacturers might conform to one way of reporting content information to an intermediary, and then e-tailers can get their content updates from the intermediary. More and more vertical intermediaries are rising to the challenge. The metrics listed in Table 4.1 are geared towards the e-tailer.

Content Distribution

With global connectivity, everyone can be a content producer. This is clearly a recipe for chaos in the absence of any existing means of qualifying, categorizing, aggregating, and redistribution of content.

Catering to efficiency in content distribution, a new industry termed aggregators and syndicators is emerging. Aggregators obtain content in vertical industries and provide systematic methods to obtain content within their market space. For example, an aggregator for machine tools obtains industry product data about machine tools in every subcategory and from each manufacturer. The aggregator then makes available bundled or piecemeal online catalogs.

Syndicators, on the other hand, collect submissions of content from contributors for redistribution. A freelance travel writer may provide a weekly article to a syndication company that "sells" the writer's article to many different travel sites.

Content Aggregation

The content aggregator seeks to play the important role of an infomediary in a chaotic content marketplace. There can be a problem if multiple suppliers try to interact with multiple

Table 4.1 Metrics for Content Management

Metric	Example Value	Example Cost (labor cost at $10 per hour)
Time for supplier acquisition	1 person can acquire 1 supplier per day	$80 per supplier
Number of suppliers	100	
Total time to recruit all suppliers	800 person-hours	$8,000
Time to prepare 1 SKU (prepare and categorize)	30 minutes per SKU	$5.00 per SKU
Number of SKUs per supplier (average)	200	
Total number of SKUs	20,000	
Time for all product SKUs	10,000 person-hours	$100,000
Time to maintain 1 supplier	4 hours per month	$40 per supplier per month
Total time to maintain suppliers	400 person-hours per month	$4,000 per month
Total capital time req'd	18,000 person-hours	$180K
Total monthly time req'd	400 person-hours	$4,000 per month

online retailers (Figure 4.4). In a non-aggregated marketplace, every supplier has to interact with every online retailer. More specifically, the catalog systems of every supplier have to be integrated, automated or otherwise, with the catalog systems of the online retailers.

If there are 100 suppliers that service 1,000 online stores, a total of $100 \times 1,000 = 100,000$ different integrations need to be implemented. This clearly leads to an enormous waste of time and money. The supplier is distracted with having to deal with each online store, individually. Proprietary systems of catalog updates, receipt of orders, tracking, and reporting cause delays and errors. The result is that suppliers are unable to interact with fewer

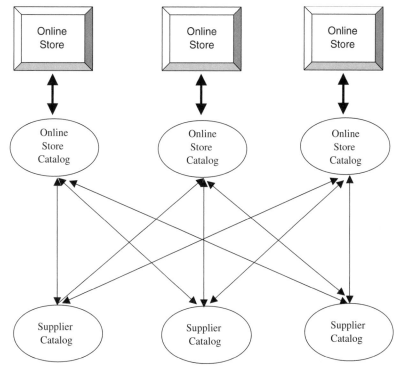

Figure 4.4 Direct Integration Between Catalog Systems of Suppliers and Online Stores

online stores than they would like and online stores carry less selection than desired by their customers. Breadth and depth of product, termed "scope" in an earlier chapter, are lost.

The aggregator as infomediary first works on the supplier side by providing a standardized process for vendors to upload content into a specified category schema. Then the aggregator builds a workflow process for orders and tracking. This bundled solution of categorized suppliers and automated workflow is then offered to the online retailer, who has a single point of integration, as illustrated in Figure 4.5. Thus, for 100 suppliers and 1,000 online stores working with an aggregator, the number of integrations involved are $100 + 1,000 = 1,100$ interactions.

This is one one-hundredth of the 100,000 integrations involved in the case of direct interaction between all the suppliers and all online stores.

Notice also, as denoted in Figure 4.5, that the online store can dispense with its own catalog system and rely solely on the catalog system of the aggregator. In such a model, when a customer clicks on a product link, the product information will be served from the catalog systems of the aggregator. Cost savings to the e-tailer are obvious.

While aggregated systems are undoubtedly efficient, are they as obvious to all merchants as a solution? There is no answer, unfortunately, because there is and always will be a bias toward not revealing sensitive information to customers or competitors, even in what is supposed to be a environment that fosters "co-opetition." The more complete the service from the aggregator, the greater the risk to the online store in value that is provided to the end customer. Online stores risk being "disintermediated" out as more power accrues to the aggregator.

Fine-grained and more tangible commercial interests of various parties can also clash. The aggregator might charge online stores a premium for turnkey provisioning of

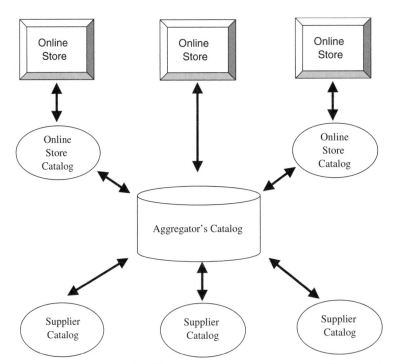

Figure 4.5   Integration Between an Aggregator, Suppliers, and Online Stores

catalogs. There could be a transaction fee, either as per-transaction or as a percentage of the sale. Also, the aggregator may charge the supplier a "finder's fee" for bringing in the transaction. Software costs, implementation costs, and maintenance costs could be tacked onto the transaction.

Despite these issues, aggregators are achieving considerable prominence, particularly in the procurement field. Often referred to as maintenance, repair, and operations (MRO) procurement, purchasers buy office supplies, nuts, bolts, tools, etc. that keep offices and plants running. Corporate expenditures for MRO procurements are estimated by many research services to be over $1.5 trillion dollars per year.

- TPN Register (*www.tpnregister.com*), a joint venture between GE Information Services and Thomas Publishing, is a comprehensive cataloging system that aggregates products from thousands of suppliers' catalogs. Suppliers are assisted in putting up electronic catalogs on the Web. Buyers then structure private catalogs with pricing and specific content that they frequently buy and the terms they want. Such a private custom catalog is often referred to as a "buy-side" catalog, typically hosted by TPN Register and accessed over the Internet. For a large corporation with qualified suppliers, such a system saves considerable expenses in the procurement process.
- Grainger.com (*www.grainger.com*) also provides an aggregated catalog from several thousand suppliers covering the MRO space.

Outside of MRO purchasing, catalog aggregators exist in many vertical industries. Examples are:

- Questlink (*www.questlink.com*) is the successor name to NetBuy, an online procurement service for the electronics industry that integrates catalogs from hundreds of suppliers.
- Cahner's Manufacturing Marketplace (*www.manufacturing.net*) is a comprehensive site for engineering professionals that provides industry catalogs for all aspects of engineering such as design, operations, services, and logistics from several thousand suppliers.
- The Plastics Network (*www.plasticsnet.com*) provides information on resins and plastics processing equipment. This network aggregates the catalogs of several hundred manufacturers for buying efficiency in this highly fragmented market.

- CommerceOne Marketsite (*www.marketsite.com*) creates a trading partner network by utilizing the supply base of Fortune 2000 companies. As the supplier base grows, the integrated catalog solution attracts smaller trading partners to draw from this supply base.

Content Syndication

Syndication is the right to rent and use, not own, proprietary content. Syndication of content resembles other forms of rental such as furniture, housing, and automobiles. There are two differences, however. First, syndication is usually associated with *intangible* intellectual property. It is, therefore, informational and has high utility or value.

Second, because of its less than physical nature, it has a *virtual* existence: it can exist everywhere simultaneously. You can "rent" or syndicate that intellectual property while someone, somewhere, has the right to enjoy the same content as you. Newspapers chanced upon this as a great tool to gain wider distribution for their news and opinion content—and charge a price for it!

Instantly, *The New York Times* did not need to publish a competing newspaper in Los Angeles. It simply syndicated its material to *The Los Angeles Times,* with suitable compensation and attribution.

On the Internet, syndication takes its virtual persona one step higher: In its digitized form, content is available everywhere to all comers—it can be updated, manipulated, juxtaposed, personalized, and made interactive in hundreds of ways. Anything that can be digitized can be syndicated.

Syndication of content is rapidly expanding into a sizable business. Jupiter predicts that online content licensing will be a $1.5 billion business in 2004. An e-commerce site may use syndicated content to achieve increased site stickiness by improving relevance and personalization in the following ways:

- Updated news about politics, events, financials
- Categorized information—such as information at a portal site, whether general purpose, travel, health, etc.
- Contextual entertainment—examining a jazz music site? How about streaming audio from Satchmo?
- Product reviews
- Tips—housekeeping, cooking, home improvement, career, etc.
- Business-specific information—commodity prices, market conditions

- Competitive updates
- Targeted search against newly collected content
- Personalized information—horoscopes, travel information, etc.
- Category-specific content such as room decoration tips, color matching, appropriate toys for children
- Product reviews for items carried with links directly to the product or products shown within syndicated content
- Personalized content based on user preferences or prior shopping behavior. For instance, if a click-stream indicates a navigation trail through furniture: sofas, chairs, dining tables, and lamps, this might indicate a new owner or someone interested in considerable changes to a home environment. A syndicated piece on household furnishings may be well received.
- Styles in vogue or emerging trends
- Entertainment content but framed within site boundaries
- Complementary content that adds value to the primary focus of the site by targeting similar demographics to stay longer ("stickiness") and to revisit
- Snippets of fun—jokes, "online cookies"
- Research materials
- Consulting services

A community site can select from several different sources of syndicated content to reflect communal interests:

- Content specific to the interests and focus of the community, such as weather for an outdoors community, travel news for a vacation community, etc.
- Personalized content within community context as revealed in sign-up data, such as interests, age, locality
- Community building content such as technology, infrastructure, intercommunity links

A B2B site can cater to the prospective needs of business partners with content that provides:

- General business news
- Specific industry news

- Custom alerts set up by participants: notification of market conditions, price of oil, unrest in the Middle East
- News about other portal players, including contract arrangements, management changes, etc.

Syndication in Action

There are three parts to syndicated content: submission, categorization, and distribution.

Content Submission. Content is created in numerous ways—from traditional news sources, magazines, online content, contracted work, etc. This content is then submitted to the syndication agent. At sites that primarily focus on content, such as newspapers and magazines or e-zines, submission by means of internal procurement or creation and categorization for Web sites are handled without necessarily revealing them as discrete steps.

Content Categorization. The syndication agent accepts each submission and categorizes the content into a suitable hierarchical structure as shown in Figure 4.6. This collection may have history, threading, and archival consequences. The structure replicates what we see in a daily newspaper: different sections focus on specific categories of news (politics, business, living, sports, etc.) with subcategories (national, international, agriculture, industry, football, baseball, etc.). Categorization brings order to the process. It also enables a user to seek out the news he or she is interested in and makes it easy to automate the insertion and updating of content.

Content Distribution. Syndicated content is now available to the buyer, namely, the Web site owner as an automated feature to the Web site. Alternatively, it can be retrieved on a daily basis. It can be woven into the context of individual Web pages, statically or dynamically. Content can also be ephemeral, such as what a booking engine serves up at a travel site. In this case, content generally resides elsewhere even if it is transparent to the user. From the perspective of the site that pays for use of the engine and associated content, it has a license to the booking engine and the result gives that site its own look and feel. From the perspective of the site that has syndicated it, it has in reality licensed retrieval of content residing at its own facilities, and provided a tool to do so.

The typical cost of a content piece ranges from $1.50 to $2.00; the cost of syndicated content to the Web site owner ranges from about $3 to $4 per item. These costs are likely to go down for generic, non-specific content and rise for highly categorized and

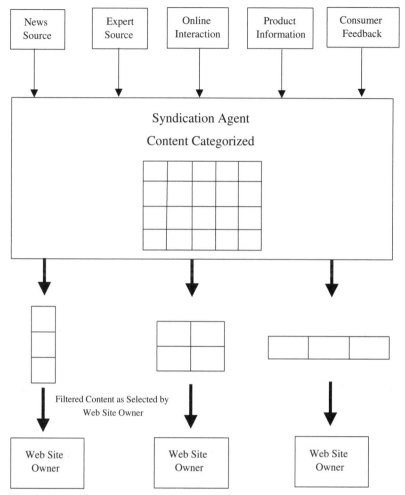

Figure 4.6 Syndication Agent Roles in Acquiring and Reselling Content

focused content. Qualification of the content is likely to occur increasingly with XML content tags as specifications are written by the content syndicators.

Modular Content

Content exists in one form or another on the Web and this environment is the quintessence of interlinked content, which is where hypertext fits in. Current search engines can indeed recover voluminous results, but they are often pointless in their abundance.

Baseline Measurement for Content Syndicators

1. Cost per content piece (paid to content creator by syndication agent)
2. Number of content categories and subcategories
3. Number of content providers
4. Number of content buyers
5. Content size per piece (average)
6. Daily aggregate content size (in gigabytes)
7. Content location: at Web site owner, at syndication agent, at edge servers
8. Content type: static, dynamic, interactive
9. Cost of content selection software and filter creation (charge to content buyer)
10. Cost per content piece (charged by syndication agent to content buyer)
11. Number of times a syndicated content can be reused on Web site
12. Cost per click on syndicated content
13. Conversion rate from syndicated content link to product purchase
14. Number of syndicated content elements on Web site
15. Increase in time spent on site by customers as a consequence of syndicated content
16. Increase in sales (in specific pages and in aggregate) due to content syndication

Merely associating keywords within content and ranking them is arcane and irrelevant, especially with the exponential growth of online content. Unfortunately, rich content of information on the Internet is not yet available in modular form, which occurs when we extract specific relevant content from the original source.

Extracting modular content can be done by tagging the original data source systematically and exhaustively. Similarly, search engine data can also be modularized for cataloging and retrieval. Thus, research reports, news stories, and online content can be modularized, tagged, and reassembled as needed. Global publishing standards for content, easily accessible in popular document editors, could allow creators of content to *"format" the documents in advance, as it is created,* for online retrieval.

Extend the idea of modular tagging to music and videos. What if audio and video segments were tagged for retrieval and maintained fully searchable indexes for user control? Some businesses, seemingly ahead of their times, were launched in 1999 to tag and retrieve streaming audio and video clips. None have survived the shakeout, though the technology, which is rudimentary at best, is still available on a license basis from its progenitors, one of which is the University of Kansas.

Consider the following two scenarios that illustrate modular content tagging:

- Business strategists in a company, looking for public information on competitor XYZ, would like results such as "XYZ in Asia business," listing all recent news relating to Asia businesses for this company. This is widely available from several sources through what many now call Business Intelligence services, like cyveillance.com.
- A medical researcher looking for references to reactions to a recently released drug would like to aggregate data from community forums on drug efficacy and side effects.
- A movie buff would like to rewind his online movie to an earlier scene where the crook stole the top-secret briefcase in a Starbucks café.
- If publishers of books were to tag content using XML (discussed below), including every section and subsection in a book, then a student's query would be able to bring back the specific subsections from several books that meet the search requirement. Today, a graduate student in engineering, looking for example applications in nonlinear differential equations, would need to access several books and consolidate the information within. Imagine if the student could search for "examples of nonlinear differential equations" and recover a result set of examples!

Content Technology

There are four aspects of content technology:

- Content Standards
- XML
- Content Management Tools
- Content Delivery

Content Standards

There is not yet a single standard for globally categorizing products and services, primarily because usage is as widely varied as the sourcing. If a toaster is offered for sale, it can be tagged differently by each supplier and then each retailer. In contrast, a global code for a toaster would enable all intermediaries in the supply chain to understand that a specific transaction, such as a purchase requisition, is uniquely for a toaster. The offline equivalent is a bar code. The Granada Research white paper, "Using the UN/SPSC: Why Coding and Classifying Products is Critical to Success in Strategic Procurement," clearly lays out the case for standards in codifying products and services. (Granada Research, El Granada, CA 94108, *www. granadaresearch.com.*)

The key benefits of product and service content standards are:

- Standard codes help automate the supply chain process. This facilitates electronic cataloging and enables transactional efficiency along the supply chain.
- Internet tools and languages adapt well to standardized codes. Web sites are able to bring up products based on search requests or category links using standard product codes. Thus, instead of searching on a text keyword "toaster," the search engine searches on a digital numeric key 51-21-22-13, identifying a toaster. This identifier is more likely to produce consistent and valid search results.
- Tagging techniques using XML facilitate data exchange between buyers and sellers. XML data sheets with product tags can be handled in an automated fashion using programmed workflow logic. Thus, an order for a toaster with product tag 51-21-22-13 can be processed per established business rules.
- A hierarchical product standard then allows for easier Web site navigation. For instance, a logical structure would allow a drill down from: Appliance to Kitchen to Electrical to Toaster.
- Vendors throughout the supply chain from manufacturers to wholesalers and distributors can participate more easily in global marketplaces using standardized product definitions. In contrast, today each supplier has internal SKU numbers associated with their own inventory control and a manufacturer's ID, which is typically unique. Every buyer-seller transaction typically requires tagging and retagging, because in just about every industry there is no consistency in product

definition. All this effort and cost can be saved with industry-accepted standardized product tags.

- Standardized codes facilitate forecasting and analysis. For example, today there is no simple way to answer the question: How many toasters were sold last week in the United States? Reporting on a standardized basis will enable such analysis to produce efficiencies throughout the entire supply chain.
- For enterprises, requisitioning and purchasing processes achieve greater efficiency when there is a uniform basis for aggregating, collating, and responding to different department needs. If the product code for a toaster were universal, then consolidation of toaster purchases would be easy, saving all departments time and money.

The available standards that can be implemented are:

- Uniform Code Council (UCC): uses a product identification code along with bar coding.
- European Article Number (EAN): same as UCC for product identification.
- U.S. Standard Industrial Classification (SIC): a hierarchical system for product and service classification.
- United Nations Standard Product and Service Code (UN/SPSC): an emerging standard based on a merger of the United Nation's Common Coding System (UNCCS) and Dun & Bradstreet's Standard Products and Services Code (SPSC).
- Universal Description, Discovery, and Integration (UDDI) is a specification for distributed Web-based information registries. A series of white papers describing this unique Web service is located at *www.uddi.org*.

The UN/SPSC schema is particularly noteworthy and may be well positioned to create the most comprehensive global standard for product classification. This covers entire industry segments for products and commodities. In this system, a five-level hierarchical system designates Segment: Family: Class: Commodity: Business Function. Two digits represent each hierarchical level, leading to ten digits if all levels are used. As an example, "Pen refills" would be categorized as UN/SPSC 44-12-19-03 based on:

Segment:	44	Office Equipment
Family:	12	Office Supplies
Class:	19	Ink and Lead Refills
Commodity:	03	Pen Refills

The hierarchical roll-up to a number that can be digitized to the Office Supplies family or the Office Equipment Segment is reflected in this example. Further information about the UN/SPSC categorization schema may be obtained from *www.unspsc.org*.

XML: Facilitating Information Exchange

The dominant global standard for exchange of information prior to Web-based commerce was EDI (Electronic Data Interchange). EDI has had a long run as a mainstay for data interactions in high-volume environments, particularly manufacturing and supply chain integration. By necessity, EDI achieved "standardization" around X12 in the U.S., and as the EDIFACT global standard under the auspices of the United Nations.

EDI, which was sponsored by a network of enablers including software providers, integrators, and value-added-network (VAN) operators, called for rigid global standards and a complex mechanism of encoding and decoding data for specific transactions. This resulted in significant costs to engage and deploy an EDI solution, making it useful only in high-data-volume environments. EDI is not practical for small and medium businesses, except those forced to participate as an EDI-enabled supplier to a larger EDI-centric manufacturing house. General Motors has the market clout to specify that a hub cap maker be EDI-enabled to participate in the automotive manufacturing supply chain.

EDI does not make sense because it is expensive to enable and maintain. Furthermore, it requires a complementary EDI initiative on the part of every other partner. A small hardware store cannot independently decide to "go EDI" unless the vast majority of its suppliers are compliant with its version of EDI. Thus, efficient, standards-based data interchange is far from the norm for the vast majority of global businesses.

A new player, in the form of the eXtensible Markup Language (XML), is gaining wide acceptance. XML provides a framework for dynamic interchange of data relating to content creation and interpretation. XML data can be self-describing, both in content as well as the actions to be taken with the data. Furthermore, XML is fundamentally *extensible,* allowing it to be morphed according to the needs and compulsions of any interacting parties. With XML, all businesses, big and small, are empowered to interact effectively.

Advantages of XML for content management can be summarized as follows:

- **Adaptability to the Web:** XML is designed to work on the Web using standardized HTTP and associated security protocols. The infrastructure built to support HTML readily adapts to the exchange of "intelligent" data that XML carries.
- **XML Popularity:** XML is becoming the defacto information interchange language on the Web. There is support from every major constituency for XML interaction: software companies including database, applications, and ERP providers; commerce application vendors and supply chain participants. Even traditional EDI vendors "see the light" and are rapidly providing EDI-to-XML (converters/interfaces) solutions and offering to convert older EDI customers to the XML data interchange model.
- **Easy Content Definition:** XML allows parties to exchange content by tagging data in XML. The dominant prior model for data exchange was EDI. In contrast, XML allows two parties to interchange information seamlessly and easily.
- **Content Structure Definition:** By its extensible tag facility, XML allows data to be properly structured and represented. The structured data can be easily read and understood, both visually and in automated contexts. The optional usage of a DTD (Document Text Definition) attached to a XML data file makes the content more specific for usage by multiple parties.
- **Content Standards:** Unlike inflexible EDI, XML is making numerous vertical standards for many specific industries and contexts. Several industry standards are evolving around XML, such as the Open Trading Protocol (OTP) for e-commerce, Mathematical Markup Language (MML) for mathematics, and Open Financial Exchange (OFX) for the finance industry. There are several others.
- **XML Extensibility:** Beyond the core XML language architecture, significant advances are underway to layer additional functionality, that is to build an XML technology stack, which is discussed below.
- **Auto Indexing:** With structure comes the notion of data indexing and cataloging. It is relatively easy to take structured data and enable the population of indexed

repositories and catalog systems. This allows easy retrieval and manipulation of data and content. What if a vendor sends a new product catalog using XML? The associated DTD would define the vendor, the product hierarchy, and the product detail. Automated scripts then read this XML product catalog, access the specific vendor's information in the database, and add, modify, or delete product information. The result? A vendor catalog update process accomplished in a matter of minutes instead of a week or more!

XML Jargon

XML, eXtensible Markup Language, which is defined by the World Wide Web Consortium (W3C), is built on several elements:

- XSLT—the XML Stylesheet Language Transformation lets the user convert XML documents between different schemas.
- DTD—the Document Definition Language is a rule sheet used to interpret an XML document.
- XSDL—the XML Schema Definition Language supports schema validation more so than that provided through DTD.
- XSL—the eXtensible Stylesheet Language (a potential replacement for HTML, though XHTML appears to be a contender for this honor) lets the user format XML documents for a browser.
- XQL—the eXtensible Query Language allows users to search through XML documents.
- RDF—the Resource Definition Framework lets the user structure Web site content for other purposes (such as searches, queries, reading by spiders and bots, etc.).

In Table 4.2, there is a considerable amount of information on the rate of adoption and adherents to the various XML schemas presented by various industry groups. Figure 4.7, which follows the table, provides a diagrammatical overview of the various points at which XML can be instrumental in facilitating data and content exchange in one of today's fastest moving environments, one that integrates wireless WAP functionality with standard online.

Table 4.2 XML Industry Initiatives

XML Initiative	Primary Players	Applicability
cXML (*www.ariba.com*)	Software standard propa gated by Ariba, and support- ed by some soft- ware vendors.	Largely oriented for procurement applications in B2B interactions for content and transactions. Provides simple DTDs.
xCBL (*www.commerceone. com*)	Standard proposed by CommerceOne; support by some soft- ware and suppliers.	Provides a foundation for business transactions.
BizTalk (*www.biztalk.org*)	Microsoft and many other software pro- viders.	Business framework for document exchange. Strong support for standardized XML schemas.
tpaXML (*www.harbinger.com*)	Proposed by Harbinger as an XML standard.	TPA (Trading Partner Agreement) and tpaXML focuses on the electronic contract between partners such as terms, condi- tions, roles, communication, se- curity, and rules.
XML/EDI	EDI vendors.	Industry approach to represent EDI transactions using XML. This allows EDI vendors to utilize EDI processing infrastructure to send and receive XML or EDI documents.
XML, XSL, XHTML,etc. (*www.w3c.org*)	W3C Consortium of uni- versities, companies, and organizations.	Global standards body focusing on improving and enhancing the usability of the Web.
ebXML UN/ CEFACT and OASIS	United Nations and the Organization for Ad- vancement for Struc- tured Information Standards (OASIS)	Standards for consistent global in- terchange of documents. Provide a framework roughly similar to the EDIFACT standard for EDI.
eCo (*www.commercenet. net*)	Nonprofit organization with substantial in- dustry participation.	Defining interoperability between multiple XML standards. Empha- sis on registration and self-de claration of intended business functionality.

(continued)

Table 4.2 XML Industry Initiatives (*continued*)

XML Initiative	Primary Players	Applicability
RosettaNet	Consortium of computer-centric companies, such as Compaq, IBM, etc.	Defining interaction basis for process and interaction. Published PIP (Partner Interface Process) documents.
OAG Open Applications Group	Non-profit consortium of software vendors, system integrators, and other organizations.	Focusing on business and application integration.
OFX Open Financial Exchange	Founded by CheckFree, Intuit, and Microsoft.	Standards for exchange of data between financial institutions.
aecXML	International Alliance for Interoperability (IAI).	Focused on project management and business communications for architectural, engineering, and construction industries.
vXML	New standard for voice proposed by telecommunication companies.	Integration of Web and voice.
SML, MML, etc.	Vertical Market Makers.	Emerging standards for each vertical such as in steel (Steel Markup Language), etc.

Content Management Tools

Standardized methods of content management are bringing forth a host of vendors offering tools and services in this space. These catalog management tools typically offer the following functionality:

- Enable systematic categorizations and subcategorizations
- Adapt to industry data formats if available (UN/SPIC for instance)
- Provide a method to insert content into the system (forms, standard templates, content entry screens)
- Map content based on rules
- Provide inbound and outbound translation engines

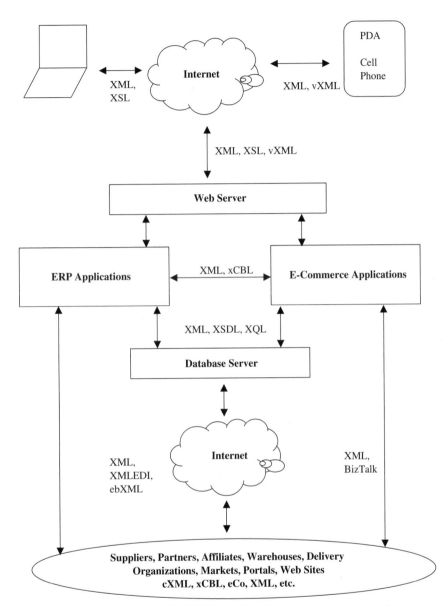

Figure 4.7 Illustration of XML Usage for E-Commerce Interactions

- Aggregate and integrate catalogs
- Provide permission-based access to catalog data
- Participate as an engine in the product display process
- Provide external interfaces for interaction to other existing standards such as EDI

Some prominent content management tool developers are Cadabra, CardoNet, Cohera Systems, OnDisplay, Poet Software, Requisite Technologies, Vignette, and WebMethods. These content management tools can be expensive. A typical model consists of combinations of the software component (license fee of from $50,000 to over $500,000), an implementation fee depending on complexity ($50,000 to $250,000) and an annual maintenance fee (typically 15 to 20 percent of the license fee). The Content Service Provider model, where the content resides in external servers, has monthly service fees based on the number of interacting partners (such as $10,000 to $50,000 per month).

Content Delivery

Content delivery methodology depends on the source and type of content. This issue is very important because it may drive network design, bandwidth requisitioned, co-location needs or outsourcing for delivery. Early in this chapter we discussed the several different possible sources of content—manufacturer/retailer, interaction, third party, entertainment, and news.

Imagine a store like Wal-Mart on the Web with millions of SKUs covering hundreds of thousands of products, each with its own attributes, date of manufacture, and price. Imagine that all this content is to be acquired from thousands of manufacturers where available (and created internally where not). That's only the half of it. You've also got to contend with content produced according to different standards. Representing content source and type in the aggregate magnifies problems of volume, site management, and user experience.

The following sections describe delivery mechanisms that are viable from the perspective of technology and management of processes.

Content Delivered Directly from Site to Consumer

In this case the content resides on the site and is served directly to the consumer of content. This is sufficient when content size is small and the content is fully contained within the site.

Baselines for Measurement:

- Number of concurrent users (at peak time)
- Average amount of bandwidth used per customer
- Average session time

From the above baseline statistics it should be possible to determine the bandwidth that needs to be provisioned.

Content Delivered from Secondary Source

In some cases, content is not owned by the site on which it resides; rather, it is linked in from a secondary source. Examples are stock charts, portals aggregating content links, malls with independent stores, and supplier-side catalog systems. Here, the page to the customer is assembled directly from the primary site and the secondary site, and the difference between the two may be transparent to the end user. There are comparable statistics required to develop a baseline for measurement as with content delivered from a primary source.

Baselines for Measurement:

- Number of concurrent users (at peak time)
- Average amount of bandwidth used per customer *from own site*
- Average session time

Content Delivered by Content Delivery Servers

A particularly elegant solution for heavy content dissemination is the use of "edge servers" for content delivery as seen in Figure 4.8. These third-party services, like Akamai, Digital Island, and Inktomi, work as follows: heavy bandwidth content is stored in servers located at the "edges" of the Web, globally. When a user requests a page, the "light" content is delivered from the site owner and the "heavy" content is provided by the edge server closest to the user. Edge servers are updated with content, typically based on the first request of a user from that vicinity.

This solution is an attractive option as distinct from co-located hosting to maximize bandwidth. With the latter, the bandwidth is acquired at the point of co-location (for example, co-location, at major data centers). However, end users are all over the Internet and quite likely all over the world! High availability of bandwidth from a co-location

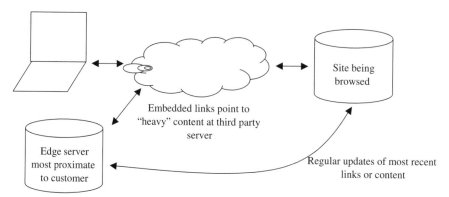

Site being browsed

Embedded links point to "heavy" content at third party server

Edge server most proximate to customer

Regular updates of most recent links or content

Figure 4.8 Illustrating Content Delivery from Distributed Edge Servers

facility does not necessarily guarantee good performance at the edges of the network. In contrast, the content delivery servers at the edge of the network can provide good bandwidth and low latency to enable higher quality site performance. Figure 4.8 shows how edge servers help reduce latency, maximize bandwidth, and provide faster response times for an e-commerce site.

Baselines for Measurement:

- Number of concurrent users (at peak time)
- Average amount of bandwidth used per customer *from own site*
- Average session time
- Amount of bandwidth provided by content delivery servers

Top 10 Questions for Evaluating Content Appropriateness

1) Does it fit the personality of the site?
2) Does the content contribute to profitability (some is costly if purchased from another source)?
3) Does the content and its source bolster credibility, fostering trust on the part of the customer?

4) Are all sources of content credible, lending luster to the site?

5) If content is also the product, who owns it and who is responsible for the source, quality, and maintainability?

6) Are there ethical or other social pressures that govern the type of content (gun control, substance abuse, political views, hate, sexuality, etc.) and how does it cut against or go with the grain of society and the customer population?

7) Is the content self-supporting, that is, can the content be clearly and cleanly separated from the commerce segment to be a strong, credible contributor to your venture's brand?

8) What controls do you have over downstream uses of the content when in a partnership deal with another licensee for sharing?

9) Is the content fresh, interesting, and interactive?

10) Is the content relevant enough to the customer that it brings the customer and the customer's friends back to the site?

Summary

In this chapter we focused on the essential ingredient of the Internet: content. Content is the core of every Internet business. Choices in content sourcing, management, and technology can be critical ingredients to the success or failure of an enterprise. Outsourced services for content are numerous and, indeed, all content can be outsourced. We addressed the nature of content and its usage, including sources of content and specifically what it takes to create one's own content catalog. The alternatives of serving up aggregated and syndicated content from Content Service Providers were also examined and related to non-production purchasing and vertical industry marketplaces.

Content technology and standards issues, which currently remain in a state of flux, were highlighted, with special emphasis on the role of XML as a powerful new technology to reconcile varying data and content standards. XML has many variants, and Table 4.2 depicted them.

Finally, delivery technology was related to the efficient distribution of content to the end user.

The question then is whether such an enterprise with fully outsourced content has successfully created other value, such as in services or processes, to remain viable. For example, it is easy to create an online mall with outsourced content from other online players. But what sustaining value does such a mall have that ensures customer loyalty? At the other end of the scale, not utilizing any outsourced services for content may lead to enormous capital costs in content provisioning and may create an island of content that cannot be maintained. As in other parts of the e-commerce stack, judicious choices need to be made between creating value and outsourcing value.

CHAPTER 5

The Community Stack

People connecting with others is part of human history, dating back to our tribal origins. It is also a time-honored marketing technique, because from interaction a community emerges. Communities are exploding on the 'Net for social interaction and to conduct business.

Forming online communities predates the World Wide Web. For instance, The Well created an online bulletin board system (BBS) when it was formed in 1985. This BBS is now on the Web, boasting several thousand paid-for subscribers participating in hundreds of discussion groups.

AOL took communities mainstream in the early 1990s with chat rooms and buddy lists, which created an interactive community environment. Immediate key metrics AOL found in hosting a community site were greater time spent per visit and increased stickiness to the site.

Chat in a chatroom is content on the fly. Chat is more than a virtual bar like the one in the TV series, *Cheers,* where people of a like mind share views and experiences. Chat is the third most popular activity on the Internet after information searches and email. Many business sites integrate chat to create a sense of community by stimulating a dialog with and between customers.

In many industries, the offline counterpart is the user group. Trade shows are communities that rotate location, exhibit member wares, and provide intellectual presentations to contribute to the community's body of knowledge.

The following characteristics, in the main, form the broad social basis of a community, whether offline or online:

- A cooperative framework where members share an identity and even adopt some common language and rituals (the mere act of signing on to a chatroom is a ritual experience)
- Members group and delimit interest around explicit or implicit boundaries associated with their shared interests and values (members of the North American Butterfly Association would be mortified at the thought of a pesticide used in their garden!)
- Communities can be isolated and become identifiable often because they have places where members gather (their online and offline addresses are symbolic in their own rights/rites)
- In more cohesive communities, membership is relatively stable over time (some online chatrooms have a longevity that transcends the Web itself) because there is rule-based governance
- There is often an environment of risks and rewards to being a member

The reasons for joining a community are as varied as the people who join. The tighter the sense of community, the more likely there is to be bonding between members and the sponsoring organization. Communities can build customer loyalty, which reduces acquisition cost and improves customer service. Thus, the tighter the range of interests, the more predictable the affect when e-commerce arises out of the community.

Broadly speaking, communities form around common interests, there are frequent interactions among the members, they share content, and there is often an ability to conduct transactions between members. As noted in Chapter 2, "The Five Stack E-Commerce Model," each element is powerful in its own right.

Elements of a Community

- **Common Interests:** Members share a particular interest that is either narrowly or broadly focused, depending on member needs. Communities grow only when there are motivated founders and team leaders who maintain the DNA for the community.
- **Frequent Interactions:** When shared interests combine with regular contact, communities start to take off. Online at first we had BBS', which still exist but are mostly limited to text-based threaded discussions.

- **Shared Content:** As memberships increase and interactions accelerate, shared content evolves into a dynamic, and often valuable, database. Web-based communities often excel in organizing needs around specific information, resources, searchable indexes, cataloged content, and threaded communication trails. Community members are rewarded with a personal library in the area of interest and are granted access to specialized resources (e.g., the other community members).

- **Transactional Power:** As purchasing potential increases in a community, it becomes attractive as a venue for vendors willing to supply goods and services. Some sell at "community-negotiated" prices for product categories that do not necessarily relate to the community's specific focus. In other instances, vendors cater to the specific and often narrow interests of the community. Team leaders play a critical role in enabling such transactional features because they recognize and extract suitable benefits from vendors on behalf of the community.

Some common threads usually run through the members, and what drives membership in the online and offline worlds is comparable: antidote to boredom, anxiety fulfillment, human contact, and subsequent bonding with those who hold similar values (the ice is naturally broken when members share common interests . . . there are no wallflowers).

The most popular chat destinations focus on the topics most likely to elicit controversy, but members are highly supportive of others while they avoid "flaming" members. Break this unwritten rule and all pretenses of civility are likely to fall by the wayside.

Civility already exists in most B2B environments. "It is unbusinesslike to . . ." (readers, you can fill in the blanks based on your particular community of interest) in a particular business environment. To break unwritten rules in a B2B environment risks losing business, ostracism, or worse.

Many communities found that their environments could be self-policing. The membership often evolved codes of conduct and the moral weight of a majority would drive the occasional disruptive radical out of the community by overt hostility or ostracism. Such community-based policing was convenient to site management because they could stay above the fray in most cases. Internecine online battles sometimes encouraged additional participation and stickiness.

In fact, a significant aspect of communities is that of silent participation, where the postings and interactions of some are watched, assimilated, and utilized by a silent many.

This is called lurking, a term many use in chat rooms. For example, in car buying communities such as Edmunds, there is a significant silent membership, which reads the comments of the community to gain knowledge for a better deal, but never contributes to the discussion.

In the offline world, it is hard to hide your identity without elaborate means, but in the online world, a member of a community can elude the scrutiny of others by using an anonymous "handle." The screen pseudonym allows one to be more vocal and even irresponsible while being totally honest. In fact, chat rooms allow participants to escape from their current self and be anyone they want to be. Some chatters use the anonymity as a means to express their real selves, "safely," while others are free to explore and even test different personas.

The Target Audience

Merchants need to make some decisions about the target audience—who is to be attracted and who will come. The latter point cannot be overlooked or over-estimated. Knowing the demographics of who you want and what you want them to accomplish helps establish the framework for the community. Here and now content or experiences provide the adrenaline rush of immediacy that attracts younger audiences. Older groups tend to go for longer copy and more thoughtful sites where the continuity of thought is posted for all to see. Extended conversations on a topic geared to seniors can often run for weeks or more.

What is important is the ongoing involvement by individuals and members with a site, however it can be maintained. Many sites use a variety of techniques to sustain interest. They bring in celebrity guests and tie them to content. Others pose questions in the body of their content and provide a hotlink to a Web seminar or chatroom so the dialog can continue or even begin. Taking this idea to the ultimate, the savvy merchant can even stimulate a dialog between customer and customer support personnel to create a bond of mutual trust between company and customer.

If the merchant can engage the customer in a dialog—or have surrogates begin the dialog—a major step toward customer and merchant meeting in the marketplace can result. Right now, the online shopping world is largely impersonal. There are no counters to lean over, no clerks to send to a storeroom, no customers to compete with for the last item in the bargain bin.

Enabling Interactivity

In the online world, analogous activities are emerging to just about every other offline technique for bringing people together. With technology in place and stickiness fostered by membership and content, the commercialization of communities is in full swing.

Gooey from the company of the same name *(www.gooey.com)* and Third Voice *(www.thirdvoice.com)* are two products Web masters can acquire and install at their sites to create dialog sessions around content much like two shoppers in a supermarket aisle can comment on cake mixes.

Gooey allows members of the community to download free versions of its software that replicates the chat experience. Users then surf around and when they encounter others with Gooey software, a dialog about the site or its offerings can begin. Gooey operates on the principle that there are enough "others" out there with the software to engage in a dialog. So far, this is not the case, despite the allure of finding fellow travelers at various sites. Too much self-starting initiative is required of the user community for this solution to be in widespread use.

Third Voice is similar in that surfers have a downloaded piece of software. Third Voice users can leave a post-it style note on a site when they are there for others with the same product. These electronic post-it notes are only visible to those with Third Voice linked to their browsers. In theory, users who have comments about the site or the merchant's offering will leave a trace in the form of the sticky note for others. Those who leave provocative notes with compelling thoughts and their email address encourage the dialog to continue away from the site. There is a downside for the Web master: there is not control over who says what and when because Third Voice users are totally independent of the site.

A way to "force" the dialog is to create an online seminar or other Web-event to engage the customer. We often attend offline seminars hosted by "altruistic" firms selling everything from tax services and financial counsel to overstocked and end-of-season merchandise.

In addition to being cost-effective, the well-managed Web-based seminar is also highly focused. Only those with an interest usually sign up. If the content is well handled, there are also opportunities to download the entire body of information to each prospect. Of course, the same strictures apply in Web-based event management as in other forms of content: make it relevant and memorable.

Putting on a Web-based event is usually a draw that engages someone and then, if done right, builds a community and a following. The good seminars bring visitors back time and again. The Web-based seminar is a cost-effective alternative to holding a meeting at a hotel and hoping guests arrive. The problem with the hotel venue is obvious—it is a time drain. However, if the company establishes an online seminar and invites either a targeted or general list, the cost is relatively low and the potential payback high in involvement and, more importantly, sales.

At first, the Web-based seminars required visitors to use both the computer and the telephone. Those with a dial-up connection had problems participating interactively. Lately, with good voice technologies being designed in, it is possible for anyone with a decent sound card and set of speakers to tune in and participate with video and audio, simultaneously. Another advantage to holding an online seminar is that it is scalable. From small numbers on up through hundreds can be engaged, each not knowing how many others are participating.

But there are also other online services and software products that can be used to create communities of interest. Software such as iChat and eShare permit more widespread deployment of community environments. Topica *(www.topica.com)* and WebEx *(www.webex.com)* are online services that can help set up and maintain dialogs about topics created for a particular purpose.

WebEx, as just one example of an online collaboration tool, has a set of customization options that allow an organization to create its own space for dialog between cohorts with access rights. When fully employed, these services improve productivity by linking users in far-flung locations and often from different organizations into browser-based ad hoc groups. Content links include joint browsing target sites, document and presentation sharing, white boarding, and even editing a letter. A higher-for-fee service also incorporates video and VOIP teleconferencing. There are several payment options, including a free version and increasingly sophisticated services at escalating fees for organizations.

Monetizing Membership

Communities are inherently focused on single topics, such as ParentSoup, Women.com, GeoCities' neighborhoods, etc. Web sites realize that to leverage or monetize membership, community members are identifiable and thus are ideal targets for online advertising.

As a consequence of engaging in highly-focused dialogs, a member of a community today can expect that participation in an online chat room ultimately can produce a highly specific advertisement geared to him or her. Such targeting opportunities help maintain relatively higher advertising rates in community environments as compared to lower rates in other less-differentiated situations.

Some sites, such as *ParentSoup.com* went the sponsorship route, giving specific vendors such as Procter & Gamble and Sony the right to host a section of a community site. Others provided online real estate for targeted advertising, initially based on the community charter.

Even more interestingly, community sites discovered that members were often willing to pay membership fees to belong to a community that was right on target. Although often nominal, the willingness of a member to pay fees attests to value perceived. Much as in offline membership organizations like Costco and REI, a nominal membership fee promotes a higher degree of loyalty, which might not be obtained if the service were free. To put it another way, there is some basis to believe that "membership fee" community sites are likely to do better than "membership free" community sites.

Community: The Four Dimensions

Communities can be organized along essentially four dimensions: Identification, Interaction, Content, and Transactions. Communities exist in consumer settings as well as business settings, and may or may not explicitly harbor a commercial orientation. Increasingly, however, the power of aggregation, focused profile, and stability of membership illuminate their commercial attractiveness. Figure 5.1 shows the value in each of the four dimensions.

Identification

The primary organizing basis for a community is a sense of identity with other members of the community, an implicit understanding that participants are gathered for mutual benefit and would need to share, contribute, and gain as appropriate. This subtle and implicit bonding is powerful because we know it focuses the audience and fosters interactions. In such a milieu, members are often willing to disclose details about themselves with more specificity than in non-community environments.

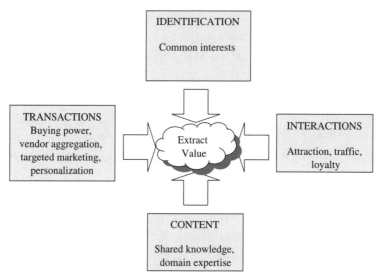

Figure 5.1   Value Extraction in a Community

Members at GolfWeb are willing to share details of their golf game such as handicap, years of participation, play frequency, and strengths and weaknesses of their game. The implicit understanding here is that such detail about their identity enhances their value in the community and provides them with a benefit.

Similarly, in business communities, identification of one's company with the various interests of the community lends itself naturally to roles such as vendor, leader, organizer, etc. Thus, in a community on steel trading, a buyer of steel that identifies itself in the forums on steel quality, pricing, and trade issues, finds itself in the industrial limelight for relatively little effort. However, steel buyers, especially in the "used" metals market (scrap), are notoriously secretive about their buying or selling intentions! There is a bias towards secrecy that actually inhibits the formation of community in this very example. The old-boy networks that exist in some industries are offline communities that are finding it hard to go online because it opens up their secret society to outsiders until someone figures out a way to make attraction useful for them!

Interaction

Interests of consumer communities are generally focused on lifestyle issues, support issues, professional issues, family issues, hobbies, etc. In a business environment, they may cater to skill-based, function-based, or issue-based needs. These interests are fostered and enlivened online by the presence of a moderator or team leader. Frequent interactions illustrate the second dimension of communities. Communities evolve on the basis of initial attractiveness, growing traffic, and established loyalty. The stability of a community cannot be ensured until a measure of loyalty is achieved and that takes time, effort, and constant fine-tuning to get it just right.

In the world of electronic commerce, the community-building nature is most evident at auction sites. eBay is even using peer pressure to enforce appropriate behavior, including economic appropriateness, with its rating system.

Mutually rewarding relationships are a by-product of community building. When the mutually rewarding relationship is with a company, its products, or management, loyalty results—one of the desired experiences for the merchant. From loyalty comes recruitment by one customer, and then more customers, and the network effect becomes real.

In the online world, enabling interaction within a community can reinforce social and economic foundations (such as the demographics, size of membership, cooperation, etc.) and bring added value to it. The following features identify some of an online community's technological base:

- threaded discussion—enables a sequenced discussion of a specific issue
- conferencing systems—allows multiple parties to interact concurrently
- categorization—much like street signs, allows easy navigation
- archive—facilitates a system of storing value within a community
- search and retrieve—finds value within community content
- links and cross-references—provides a means to validate and substantiate points of discussion

Content

The third dimension of a community is the accumulation of contributed content whose volume and rate of growth is directly proportional to member interaction. Because cohesive communities are focused in nature, member-generated content is valuable inasmuch as it articulates the community's shared knowledge and domain expertise. It is not unlike having many experts under one roof. This content becomes especially valuable when the community becomes sophisticated enough to organize, archive, and make it available in its entirety to any and all interested in it. Both common interests and frequent interactions are the impetus for the rapid aggregation of content, and at some point the content becomes the hub around which the whole community revolves.

Content in a community comes from the following:

- Membership profile—enables searching and finding members with any desired profile. Example: List all members in the steel community who have interests in exporting steel to Venezuela.
- Categories of interest—allows members to focus and enables community organizers to add materials here for reference. Example: Edmunds.com has categories on different types of cars, with detailed information on each model.
- Discussion forums—creates online interactive content that can be cross-linked and indexed.
- Expert content—community Web sites often recruit freelance experts to provide content, moderate discussions, and respond to community inquiries.
- Vendor content—such content from vendors is usually free and adds to community value, although it may be biased in the vendor's favor. Example: a community for moms may have content on "summer styles" from a manufacturer of children's clothes.

In ParentSoup.com *(www.parentsoup.com)*, content was at one time structured around:

- Features: Back to school, pen pals, focus on sleep
- Communities: Prepregnancy, expecting parents, parents of babies, parents of toddlers, parents of school-age children, parents of teens
- Video content: Teens and cars, dads and drugs
- Expert content: OB/GYN, breastfeeding, pediatrics, children's health, etc.
- Content du jour: Articles on kids, adoption, etc.

Online business communities are more than recreation or ad hoc collections of surfers, coalescing around special interests. Members often benefit from proactive participation. Content in chat rooms and forums sometimes comes from members who take it upon themselves to collate and contribute information, provide advice, and establish standards of online debate. Many standards organizations function well in this context.

Members who contribute content tend to return to see the reaction of their community to their contribution. This engenders further interaction, thereby spinning the web of content at this community to create stickiness.

For Web site management, active member participation reduces the cost of creating and maintaining content. Volunteer leaders quickly crop up with the approval of both management and the membership (and are even paid), but only through the psychic reward of being recognized for their expertise. For their part, Web site management often has to walk a tightrope with such unpaid online leaders who, to some extent legitimately, take credit for the success of forums that they lead.

Along with the wanted come the unwanted. That's the nature of the online world. With the unwanted comes the desire by many to exercise some level of control, either in terms of access or over content.

Transactions

Finally, a community brings value from leveraging its transactional power. A successful community aggregates power that is focused on an issue. Its popularity generates critical mass and loyalty, active contribution, and significant content base. From an e-commerce perspective, such a community holds enormous potential to create value. In B2C, customer acquisition is a tedious and expensive area of business, often representing as much as 70 percent or more of marketing expenditure. It involves targeting, attracting, and retaining, all of which, in a sense, are in place in a successful community!

With transactions, the community becomes monetized for value. The principal ways are:

- Membership—Typically monthly dues, although free communities are still the norm. Strong vertical communities charge for membership, particularly in business.
- Advertising—Given a good coherent audience, with statistics to back up user behavior, communities are able to charge top dollar for banner advertisements, sponsorships, etc.
- Vendor Slotting—For similar reasons as above, communities can hawk slots (i.e., fixed advertising or preferential placement in listings) in highly visible community areas.

- Transaction Revenue—In return for providing potential customers to vendors, communities may collect a piece of the transaction as commission or as micro-payments. Revenue generating capabilities of a community are discussed further in the following section.

Assets and Key Drivers

The following represents some of the assets that drive site growth and the means by which they can do so:

- Member base and usage profiles
  - Membership has mass and focus. Vertical communities may lack mass but make up for it in an extraordinary focus on some issue that forms the *raison d'etre* for the community. A generic community, on the other hand, must demonstrate breadth of membership to survive.
  - Usage profiles are hard currency in today's commercial environment.
- Transaction-friendly community organization
  - Online communities can exist outside of the market environment. Increasingly, however, communities are beginning to wake up to the value of their member-ships. Communities can leverage their memberships by creating an environ-ment that provides an implied sanction for buying and selling.
  - Communities are too loose to recognize anything on their own . . . it takes lead-ership to monetize a community.
- Content
  - Why does one join AOL or pick Yahoo! as the portal of choice? As we saw in Chapter 4, "The Content Stack," relevant content is aggregated at one place. People crave content, but they crave convenience more. Combine convenience with superior content, aggregated and integrated in one place, and you have another basic element of a successful community.
- Ability and willingness to exert aggregated member power
- Managed profiling (discussed in greater detail in Chapter 6, "The Commerce Stack")

- Declarative profile—what members declare themselves to be
- Associative profile—mapping of an online visitor to categories of consumer behavior; for example, a member might get slotted into a profile category as white male, mid 30s, high income bracket
- Transactive profile—actual purchasing behavior of a member
- Click-stream profile—trail of clicks on each visit
- Advertisers—its role in communities comes from two qualities
  - creating awareness and, thereby, the basis to seek more information
  - revenue generation
- Vendors—communities attract vendors because they see a potential market and vendors are attractive to members because they reduce search costs
- Database marketing
- Active filtering
- Group services (vendor/product offerings, lead generation, value redistribution, etc.)

Characteristics of Online Communities

Industry experts agree that the four major components of an online community are content, members, vendors, and advertisers:

- Content Attractiveness is the starting point and it brings old and new members alike to the site, which in turn leads to new member content.
- Member Loyalty then produces greater time on site and increasing interaction and, in the better instances, proselytizing among members as well as recruiting— the network effect.
- Member Profiles become measurable from increased knowledge about members, which forms the basis for targeted content, advertising, and commerce.
- Transactions are then possible because elements of trust and cohesion are built around the three above qualities, and this in turn attracts new vendors and advertisers.

Essentially, a community site creator triggers off a set of reactions by creating content and attracting a set of members. Paucity of content may often spur members to create new content or find another site that meets their needs. Furthermore, interaction among members creates content that could be mined, categorized, and refined. As membership grows, this attracts vendors, who make commerce offerings available, and create new content. This spurs increased membership and sustained interaction among members. The growing page views attract advertisers, who may be willing to pay for advertising in selective environments of the community site.

In Table 5.1 we associate the key entities in an online community with metrics to measure their relative importance.

Making these relationships more dynamic in a community site between the various entities is captured in Figure 5.2.

Table 5.1   Community Entities and Associated Metrics

Entity	*Metrics*
Content	Core content created by site owner (development cost)
	Content subscribed from syndication (syndication cost)
	Content gained through members (free or rationalization cost)
	Content obtained from vendors (free)
Members	Number of members
	Number of visits per month per member
	Time spent per visit
	Amount of interaction with other members
	Content contributed to site
	Rate of member attrition
	Number of new members per month
	Rate of new membership (visitor conversion rate)
	Membership cost
	Membership profile and detail
Vendors	Number of vendors
	Cost of vendor slot (depends on number of members and type of members)
	Number of commerce transactions
	Commissions provided to site owner
	Vendor partnerships (co-branding, private label, etc)
Advertisers	Advertising rate based on page views and membership profile
	Click-through rate and any associated revenue share

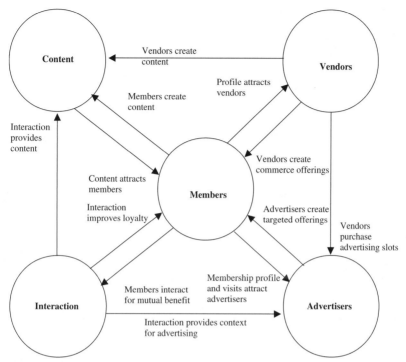

Figure 5.2 Dynamic Interactions between Community Entities

Consider how a community gets formed and how it extracts potential value. A felt need, such as by novice parents who log onto *ParentSoup.com,* is the starting point that initially may get expressed as a query to one or more persons, perhaps on a bulletin board. This exchange evolves as a series of postings and emails, slowly grows to include more interested people, more responses, more information, then gathering momentum becomes self-generating. The increased activity is aided and, in its turn, affected, by its organization and moderation. Word-of-mouth publicity adds another spin, generating traffic. Increasing activity, growing attraction, and willingness by participants to share their knowledge rapidly expands the pool of contributed content, reinforcing its attractiveness to new members.

At this point of maturation, there is critical mass, visibility (and high order of word-of-mouth publicity), stable membership of loyal participants, and a repository of invaluable shared knowledge. In the following steps that exemplify again the network effect, evolution to a mature community starts with prospective need, is followed by an initial exchange through mass communication, and becomes a mature organization, as shown in Figure 5.3.

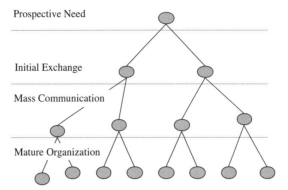

Figure 5.3   Stages in Community Evolution

Growth to maturation presents the organizer of the community with an opportunity to extract value buried within. This embedded value is in the form of aggregation: aggregated audience, aggregated content, and aggregated specialization. The large assemblage of active members represents both buying power and a concentrated market for vendors. Aggregated content is knowledge and expertise that can be formatted, indexed, and harnessed in multiple ways. Specialization—in the form of the primary focus of the community—represents a self-identified target market for vendors and advertisers in that space.

Online communities are successful when they meet the primary goal of satisfying a need around which a particular community is centered. In this respect, the community's transactional power is a derivative of its focus. In evaluating a community's underlying value to vendors (and its ability to unlock this value), its transactional power must be considered. The community's attraction to potential vendors of products and services lies in its size, quality of membership, and trajectory of growth. Communities that hit upon some vein of popular interest or support—for example, senior citizen issues, baby boomer issues, teen issues—and successfully tap into this vein are likely to see exponential growth rates in memberships.

Indeed, this is why highly-focused Web initiatives (such as the motleyfool.com, wine.com and women.com, to name a few) appear to hold their own while sometimes larger, better-pedigreed initiatives flounder.

Community Models and Transactional Power

The transactional power of successful communities arises from the two types of communities that can fall under the *member-benefit model* and the *community-focus model.* In the former, the critical mass of a community enables it to leverage buying power and negotiate community-favored prices. With the community-focus model, vendors take advantage of a niche target market where they can offer appropriate products and services.

The distinction plays off the horizontal breadth of the member-benefit model versus the vertical depth of the community-focus model.

Member-Benefit Model

This model of community resembles a co-op or a commissary. The particular intent or focus of the community is stickiness. Its importance arises from large buying power that enables the community to obtain negotiated prices for a variety of goods or services. The prices are generally lower than retail or some other value is higher. The best, however, are not necessarily judged by providing the lowest price for a given product.

An example of this model offline is Costco. Costco uses its large buying power to secure low prices for its members. In exchange for receiving a low per unit cost, the customer "agrees" to accept higher quantities of products, commonly called bulking.

Another example is the Automobile Association of America (AAA) that offers negotiated pricing on a variety of services for its members, ranging from car insurance to discounted rates on cruises, hotel and car rental rates, travelers' checks, and reduced commissions on foreign currency conversions.

On the Web, AOL comes closest to resembling such a community. Membership is large, about 35 million in the U.S., and represents a surprisingly loyal one despite the monthly dues in the face of falling (or even zero) Internet access costs from competition. AOL itself recognizes the inestimable value of its community and has used it to extract the most favorable terms from advertisers and vendors.

Yahoo!, likewise, is turning into a portal community, one that represents the portal of choice for millions of users. While it does not draw revenue from membership subscriptions, Yahoo! shrewdly leverages its early entry, rapid growth, and high popularity to propel itself to a unique position of a financially sound Internet juggernaut. Unlike AOL, however, it has used its fundamentally different model and visible brand to expand rapidly abroad, facilitating communities that are at once global and local.

AOL, Yahoo!, and other examples of online communities are not exact replicas of the offline models. News content, stock quotes and portfolio tracking, maps, and the aggregated shopping experience that are made possible are all benefits that users avail themselves of thanks to the size and strength of the AOL and Yahoo! communities.

VolumeBuy and Procurenet both operate as buying cooperatives for aggregated members. These two sites are closer to the Costco model without, perhaps, the onus of taking down large quantities. In the B2B environment, there are hundreds of member-benefit sites that convert content and transaction power into viable businesses.

Member-Benefit Model characteristics are as follows:

- Large and growing community membership base (critical mass)
- Loyal membership
- Attractive member profile
- Value delivered that is often economic

Community-Focus Model

In this model, the community's principal focus revolves around specific industry issues and vendors align themselves with content. For instance, a community may be constructed around alternative health issues (e.g., *www.drweil.com)*. Such a site presents an opportunity for vendors in that space to provide goods and services like supplements, herbs, diet programs, aerobics and yoga classes, acupuncture, etc.

Community-focus vendors have the advantage of directly addressing a clientele that conforms to its own values, thus saving on bulk mailing and scattershot marketing that typify offline community building efforts. These online communities focus on a well-defined and often narrow specialty, and what they lack in sheer size they make up in loyal membership and unwavering commitment.

The following are the principal characteristics of companies that operate online to this model:

- Large and growing community membership base (critical mass)
- Loyal membership
- Attractive member profile
- Vertical depth
- Focused membership allowing targeted marketing

Both the member-benefit model and the community-focus model of community organization can extract value for its members by leveraging the above characteristics.

Cost Structures of Online Communities

Active online communities with an eye to leveraging transactional power have costs not unlike other organizations that incur expense in the provision of services. As communities expand, the marginal costs generally tend to fall over time. In the following five sections, we examine the important components of cost incurred in managing such a community. Those five sections are:

- Technology Infrastructure and Administration
- Member Acquisition
- Vendor Acquisition
- Data Acquisition
- Content Acquisition and Development

Technology Infrastructure and Administration

Online communities predate the commercial Internet, and trace their origins to dial-up bulletin boards and Usenet groups that involved simple postings. At one level, they were often just threaded discussions on specific topics, but the underlying technology was more than simple at the time. Recently, they expanded into multithreaded discussions that are moderated, archived, indexed and linked; they also provide search tools and are password-protected. The technology infrastructure and its maintenance to support all of these represent a cost that rises as memberships grow.

These costs are:

- Cost of computers/servers
- Network connection costs
- Software (database, messaging, bulletin boards, transactional, etc.)
- Community Web site development
- Maintenance (hardware/OS, network, Web administration, database administration)
- Transaction facilitation
- Scaling

How much do technology-related issues affect the cost structure of a community enterprise? The sad tale of boo.com is enlightening. Fashion is a community built on fads, glitter, and being trendy. Boo tried to incorporate these community traits and others into its site as a high-end fashion retailer. In an attempt to be unique in the fashion community, boo.com flamed out.

The London-based e-tailer of high fashion sportswear and accessories made management decisions about company strategy that turned out to be completely out-of-sync with technological reality. Boo had neither a solid technological infrastructure nor the kind of customers to appreciate the company's intentions. Sophisticated animation, plug-ins, features designed for broadband access, all suggest that Boo's management had ambitions that exceeded their abilities to incorporate technology.

Server crashes were common occurrences because of heavy demands from online and immediate currency conversion to support sales. Security did not scale. Community-building efforts were also hampered, creating more dissatisfied customers.

The story is worth telling because two kinds of errors appear to characterize many a startup venture (community or not) with reasonably adequate capital (boo.com's was an excessive $300 million plus)—technology focus and business focus. Intense technology focus to the detriment of understanding whether high technology alone is enough to get the customers is a problem that has afflicted many a technology company. Most times, it is simple ignorance and at other times hubris.

Not to be overlooked and equally fatal is management's failure to recognize or appreciate the *minutiae* of technical challenges that could hobble aggressive deadlines and rollouts. Aggressive rollouts encourage unrealistic expectations, especially of people removed from the day-to-day grind of bolting together a technological infrastructure. It is almost a given in this environment to incur programming glitches, slip-ups in testing, wayward schedules, and out-of-control expense, many of which can scuttle even the least ambitious efforts to gain an elusive first mover advantage.

Member Acquisition

Acquisition of members is possibly the most important cost incurred by a community during its existence. There is cost in acquisition even if a community has no commercial intent or desire to incorporate transactional processes. Those with a commercial orientation have more of an incentive to assiduously seek new members, thereby increasing the costs. The following, which are equally marketing-and infrastructure-oriented, are representative cost items:

- Advertising (media, direct mail)
- Marketing
- New member processing
- Member database (contact info, user cost tracking info, click-trail info)

Estimates run into the millions on marketing costs needed to establish a venture and then brand it. The higher the profile desired, the higher the marketing costs.

Vendor Acquisition

Lately, many Internet business models emphasize community identity. These businesses, to a large degree, base their revenue forecasts on advertisements, partner fees, and commissions from transactions. For this reason, such commercially focused communities have large vendor acquisition costs.

In one sense, "new" communities—such as *www.women.com* and *www.wine.com*—are different from earlier generations when community meant just a meeting place. With the new sites, the pressure to earn revenue has many of them struggling with the well-known chicken-and-egg problem: attract both members and vendors, often simultaneously, and achieve breakeven volumes.

As many startups breathlessly tout their potential for revenue growth, vendor acquisition is another significant cost they have to assume until the attractiveness of the size and profile of community membership has vendors lining up at the door. It is unlikely, however, that vendors can be acquired the same way as members—via advertising in several media outlets alone.

For vendors to be interested, such communities have to demonstrate potential, forecast growth, and opportunity. Much of this will come from market research. Vendors may also be lined up by means of charter affiliations that are costless to them (free ad space, no fees, etc.). Another possibility is to tap into content created or acquired by a community site that can be tied to vendor products or services, such as:

- Advertising and marketing
- Market research

- Charter vendor placement (affiliate)
- Content tie-ins
- Vendor database

Data Acquisition

Data acquisition is sometimes implicit in the member acquisition process, yet represents a cost nevertheless. It is often overlooked as well. Data acquisition requires the use and manipulation of data gathered from members that reside in the database. Following are the elements:

- Data categorization and administration
- Data mining to analyze and discern patterns (details about what content is being looked at by members, aggregate reconstruction of member access to site, traffic through type of links, vendor advertisement effectiveness, etc.)
- Reporting and "packaging" for sale to buyers of profiles
- Analysts

Content Acquisition and Development

Content, as we know, assumes great importance in the community structure to the point where new membership and the extent of interaction between members begin to revolve around it. This is the stage of maturation for the community when it becomes most attractive to partners and vendors alike.

Reaching this stage, however, is anything but easy, as is evident from the struggles of countless so-called community Web sites targeting often obscure interests. Unlike earlier experiments in building virtual communities (such as The Well, which went on to gain cultlike status), today's sites are constantly mindful of the need for working capital as well as ongoing revenue generation.

Start-up capital is channeled towards rapid acquisition and/or development of content in an attempt to collapse the time to maturation. The hope is to amass critical content and attract "eyeballs." Content acquisition has these cost components:

- Content syndication
- Content hosting
- Content development and publishing

These costs are by no means comprehensive and are shown here only to illustrate those that a community organizer is likely to confront. Other cost elements are specific to the type of structure being constructed, strategies to develop an audience, and even the nature of the community and interest area targeted. Table 5.2 summarizes the various cost elements and documents metrics to go with each.

Table 5.2 Cost Structure and Metrics

Cost Type	Cost Elements	Metrics
Technology Infrastructure and Administration	Cost of computers/servers Network connection costs Software (database, messaging, BBS, transactional, etc.) Community Web site development Maintenance (hardware/OS, network, and database administrators) Transaction facilitation	Server Cost Per Capita = Total cost of servers/total number of users Network nodes per thousand users = Total number of nodes/total number of users Member efficiency (percent) = (Total number of online users/total number of registered members) *100 Maintenance Per Capita = Total maintenance cost/total number of users Admin. ratio = Number of administrators/total number of users
Member Acquisition	Advertising (media, direct mail) Marketing New member processing	Member conversion = Number of new members/number of unique non-member visitors Member acquisition ratio = Total cost to acquire members/total number of new members Advertising efficiency ratio = Total advertising cost/total number of new members Marketing efficiency ratio = Total marketing cost/total number of new members Media outlet efficiency ratio = Total cost per outlet/total number of new members secured from the outlet

(continued)

Table 5.2   Cost Structure and Metrics (*continued*)

Cost Type	Cost Elements	Metrics
		Processing efficiency (percent) = (Cost of processing new member/cost of administration per member) * 100
Vendor Acquisition	Advertising and marketing Market research Charter vendor placement Content tie-ins	Interaction time. Costs to acquire vendors are part of business development, an amorphous area in companies. Integration effort. Programming time at $50/hour $\times$ # of hours estimated for content integration
Data Acquisition	Data categorization and administration Data mining to analyze and discern patterns Reporting and "packaging" for sale to buyers of profiles Analysts	Software costs for logging and maintaining data Software costs for mining community information Various ASPs and consulting services provide these services at widely varying rates.
Content Acquisition and Development	Content syndication Content hosting Content development and publishing	Chapter 4, "The Content Stack," outlines some metrics you can apply

Revenue Structures of Online Communities

While the costs are many, the avenues for earning revenue are, unfortunately, few and mostly untested. An excellent example, once again, is the spectacular failure of Boo. Boo burned through at least $125 million and finally came crashing down despite big name funding from JP Morgan, Bain, and Benetton.

Beautyscene, another fashion and beauty e-tailer, folded in April 2000, eight months after launch. Dr. Koop *(www.drkoop.com),* a health-content company, is another high-profile e-tailer with a gloomy prognosis.

Boo and Beautyscene had at least two other similarities beyond playing in the *haute couture* space. They succeeded in generating enormous hype and managed to spend extravagantly without commensurate revenue. Dr. Koop appears headed down the same path despite fading vital signs.

Beyond a tale of woe, the failing Internet sites are testimony to the ravages brought about because of unproven revenue models and cost structures that defied the rosiest of expectations. One may recognize in many such sites the basis for a community. Dr.Koop focused on health care content, thus drawing hordes of visitors eager for more information. IVillage, a community for women includes message boards and self-help advice. The company had nearly six million unique visitors in March 2000, and first quarter revenues were $20 million even as losses exceeded $25 million.

For many of them, traffic is not a problem; revenue and cost structures are. Below, we examine some of the revenue models in use that support online communities. Bear in mind, the first two do not require direct financial participation by members, while the last one does. Ads and transaction payments, on the surface, seem like passive income while revenue from membership subscriptions could create some tension between the host of the community and its membership.

The model of choice should be dictated by what the site is designed to accomplish and what is most tolerable to members. Some members are adverse to any level of commercialization, which invalidates the appearance of ads or e-commerce transactions while at the site, and in their community. Other communities might feel their time is more precious than their money and they are willing to pay for the privilege of using the site if it provides a level of convenience.

From a member perspective, there is a one-to-one relationship between member and community, and the latter has to be compelling for a member to be prepared to pay at any level to be a part of the online community. The relationship is with the community, not vendors. This reasoning cracks when we consider B2B communities; however, communities in this space have business procurement activities embedded in them and it is difficult to say if member benefit accrues from community activities or from procurement offerings.

Advertising Model

There are two ways to monetize traffic in an advertising type model: outright sale of space on a Web site and through sponsorships.

Space Sales Model

Many Internet companies today expect revenue from advertising to be an integral, even primary, part of their revenue models. In every case, they expect results similar to how traditional media like print, radio, and television derive revenues: by selling space or time based on audience.

Basing a business model on advertising, and advertising alone, is generally a bad idea for all but the main portal sites. There is not enough revenue available based on today's limitations on traffic, ad formats, and advertisers willing to invest in Web sites. Most of the advertising online at high traffic sites is from a fairly small number of advertisers, and most of them are online businesses or offline businesses with an online presence.

At an Internet site, community or otherwise, advertisers rent space on a Web page and pay according to the position. The role of advertisements on community Web sites is generally accepted to be different from the role they play, for instance, in print media. Advertisements in online communities direct customers to the environment where, in simulating member interactivity within the community, they hook the customer.

Communities have focused interests and like-minded members, so contextual advertisements with clear benefits go beyond merely stimulating an impulse to secure a sale. By advertising in a particular community, there is an implied endorsement from the community sponsors or host.

Before selling ad space on a community site, the following factors need to be considered:

- Benefit to potential customers: members/customers tolerate the presence of ads at "their" site if they perceive some value in exchange. Are advertisers on a health site, for example, sponsoring the presence of an expert to share knowledge and answer questions? Is a resource being made available that could be of use, such as a financial calculator or a retirement planning toolkit on a financial community site?
- Context: in terms of relevance to the Web page content and member use of the site. Example: a calendar, a world clock, and a temperature table for various locations at a travel community site
- Ad type (banner, slotting, preferential): an advertisement can appear in any of several places in the small real estate controlled by the browser. The options are

banner, slotting and preferential. An advertiser may insist on a persistent position; say, top right every single time a page is brought up. As with real estate, location is all important and the ad type has a bearing on the rate a community (or any Web site) can charge, along with other factors such as qualified traffic, number of unique visitors, impressions, etc.

- Placement (top, bottom, left, right, etc): again, as with ad type, the choices are few and dictated by the realizable browser size
- Size in pixels: the most often used measurement

In Chapter 7, "Pricing Models on the Web," we present a more complete discussion of the primary advertising revenue models.

Sponsorships

The sponsor model relies on securing a partner to defray the cost of a particular operation at a site in return for advertising. Alternatively, the sponsor could secure sponsorship status by paying for a prominent ad location. In communities, for instance, a sponsor could "host" a particular channel, as on AOL, in return for prominent placement in the channel and other advertising/style considerations. On AOL, this can be extremely expensive, perhaps more expensive than the revenue-generating capacity of the community!

Another example is that of Vitamin Shoppe, a sponsor on Dr. Weil's community alternative health care Web site, which is more focused and certainly a lot less expensive for an alternative medicine community. A community for amateur gardeners, for example, may be sponsored in whole or in part by those associated with the garden industry—equipment manufacturers, seed companies, nurseries, garden stores, chemical companies, and so on. A photography community may choose to have its "channels" sponsored by film manufacturers, camera manufacturers, and other equipment manufacturers.

The difficulty in securing a sponsorship at a community site lies in the appearance of a sellout to vested interests that could be perceived as less than benign to the interests of that community.

Transaction Fee Model

Transaction fees prevail in a wide range of community-site environments. If the site has weaker than acceptable traffic, it might seek revenue on a variety of bases, but mostly as a percentage of sales. This may be most viable when a community is starting up or its demographics and other member characteristics are not sufficiently attractive to a vendor. In this case, the community cannot insist on payment by impressions or payment for click-throughs. The merchant says, "show me the money, and I will pay," but only for transactions completed.

There is greater risk in a transaction fee model because the community gets no revenue for anything other than its ability to convert traffic to a purchase. This may conceivably cause a community to drive members towards the vendors, dulling the promised luster of an impartial community Web site focused on a theme.

A community not immediately subject to the strains of accounting for expenses may see transaction fee-based revenues as better than nothing and continue to improve its site and its traffic by its membership. This is weak because marketplaces operate by this same model, and most communities are not designed to monetize their membership in the same way.

Subscription Model

There are two types of subscriptions: those from members and those from vendors. The first requires a commitment from the membership once it sees value from being at the site. The other requires vendors to see the site in the same light as they would if they were an advertising vehicle or a site on which they want to sell a product. The site must generate viable and measurable traffic.

Member Subscriptions

A member subscription community model imposes a fee on members for participation. This is akin to subscribing to a magazine or an e-zine or becoming a Costco member. *The Wall Street Journal's* Interactive Edition has a subscription of about $29 yearly (for print edition subscribers) to have online access to news and other content generated by their paper.

Similarly, some communities charge for membership. The Well is a pioneer in this regard and many subscribers have memberships that span the life of this site from when it was a bulletin board.

Siliconinvestor.com, an investment content and chat community, charges about $60 for six months; most of its members see invaluable benefit from belonging to it and using it to guide their investment decisions.

By far, the most well-known model of member subscription-based delivery is AOL, though some argue that the subscription is indeed solely for the community features it provides and not AOL's complementary role as an ISP.

The pure subscription model, though, has not exhibited much traction in community environments. For the majority of communities, it seems to be a secondary revenue source, though in other areas it does show promise, requiring deep pockets and high-powered marketing.

The member subscription model is not without direct implications for both advertising and transaction fee revenue. The danger is real as users resist community membership fees and would likely keep away from the site, resulting in fewer members and, thus, weakening its ability to attract advertisers.

Vendor Subscriptions (Sponsorships)

A counterpart to the member subscription model is the vendor subscription model. This has noticeable gains, especially in B2B communities and marketplaces. Unlike a community member, a vendor has a relationship not with the community as a whole but with its members individually. The vendor prefers those members that are stronger and/or more actionable to those who are passive and less likely to be of influence.

Seen in this light, the relationship of a vendor is one-to-many, that is, each vendor is able to target and potentially has access *selectively* to many users or members. Given such a relationship, a vendor then has an incentive to pay a subscription to be able to participate in the community.

A variation on subscription, which is somewhat passive, is the more active role that ensues from sponsorship, which is presented in Chapter 8, "Customer Acquisition Models for E-Commerce."

Content Hosting Model

Communities that have sufficient published content that is either member-generated or from other sources that are proprietary to them can merchandise this asset elsewhere. Typically, such content is specialized in nature and any other community operating in the same or a similar space faces high costs to publish and maintain it themselves.

Such content publishing piggybacks on a community site that has acquired excellent recognition and a solid membership. This provides the stronger site with a revenue stream from those on the lookout for good, applicable content.

An example of this is *www.rockhounds.com,* a community of rock and mineral enthusiasts. Rockhounds hosts content provided by *Rock and Gem Magazine,* such as articles and features. This content can be acquired in whole or in part by non-competing sites, and in return there is cross-linking that sends members of the second site to *rockhounds.com.*

The following are some of the considerations in generating revenue from the content hosting model:

- Community focus (the more specialized, the better)
- Existence of published content that does not have wide circulation. Most hobbies have a newsletter or publication that caters to the specific niche interest. Only a few of them, however, have an extensive base of relatively well-off individuals taking to the hobby, such as photography. For the majority of hobbyists—as with rock collections, oil lamps, rare books, marine clocks, etc.—the hobby may have publications with very limited subscriptions. In such cases, a community represents a low-cost delivery mechanism to its circulation.
- Popularity of community among its focus or target population
- Depth and growth of membership
- Attractiveness to a publisher as an additional channel

Top 10 Rules for Setting up Online Communities

1. Focus Narrowly—The rationale for a community needs to be evident by virtue of its name, its targeting, its content, and its online conduct. If the community is too broadly based, such as focusing to all men, then it might not attract membership. On the other hand, too narrow of a focus may make the membership too small to sustain a commercial site.

2. Have Base Content Ready—A person navigating into a community site will expect to see sufficient content for entertainment or education. If there is no perception of depth, a would-be community member may deem the site immature and leave. For example, the expectation of a visitor to Edmunds.com is to

see valuable information on every car in the current model year. Participation in online forums requires satisfactory content.

3. Provide Structured Navigation—Community members tend to spend more time on their preferred sites than the average visitor to a Web site. As such, navigation should be easy, friendly, and obvious to engage them the first time and sustain them until visiting becomes routine.

4. Provide Customization Capability—An online community is the equivalent of a living room, a bar, or a conference room. Allow the community member to organize that space by providing the ability to customize their version of the community site.

5. Create and Moderate Forums—Communities need to hum with activity or they will wither away. To ensure this buzz, community management needs to create online forums, seed the debate, and moderate proceedings.

6. Allow Leaders to Evolve—It is healthy for a community to identify leaders within itself. This buildup of relationships and interaction fosters fidelity to an online community.

7. Create Reasonable Rules—Part of the membership sign-up process should be a commitment to adhere to prescribed rules and codes of conduct. Rule breakers are inevitable; keep the rules clear and the vast majority of the community in agreement to weaken the affect of the rule breakers.

8. Keep Advertising Non-Intrusive—and in the proper context of the site (if non-commercial, don't use it—and this is a rule accepted by many sites). Advertising should not intrude on the interactive nature of chat-based online communities. Pop-up banner ads can be annoying in the midst of an online chat. Slotted advertisements and contextual banners may be more reasonable.

9. Keep Pace with Technology—but not at the expense of usability. Online communities need to apply the technologies that facilitate communication and interaction. This means investing in interactive chat, audio and video online using IP streaming, sharing of applications, white-boarding and conferencing, wireless interfaces, voice-based browsing, gaming interface devices, and performance enhancement technologies when necessary . . . but always in keeping with the context of the site and its revenue generating capacity.

10. Keep an Eye on the Bottom Line—Revenue models in online communities are relatively weak. Given the need for a selective, vertical focus, there may be limited carrying capacity from membership subscriptions, advertising, and transaction opportunities. Growth in traffic increases cost but may not proportionately increase revenue. A good understanding of the metrics of revenue generation is essential for success.

Summary

In conclusion, consumer and business communities are a sustainable basis for providing enduring value and enabling commerce. Communities are often beguiling in their simplicity of purpose, of organization, and of management. Yet, they are complex organizations that deceive those who take it lightly.

A successful community brings all of the entities together—members, content, vendors, advertisers, and the sum total of their interaction. This is a powerful, potent mix that has to be just "right" for the community to take off in a self-sustaining way.

The process of self-selection into a community yields a stable membership base. Enlightened self-interest provides for continuing participation. The presence of a profiled membership brings on commerce. This may cause friction among the members, and some may quit in the face of creeping commercialization and loss of privacy. Even otherwise successful communities cannot be too sure about the fickleness of its members. Where communities are able to navigate their transformation and manage the dynamic interactions of the various entities successfully, they still have to contend with how to leverage their underlying value.

Understanding and unlocking hidden value is more art than science and has to balance the relative weights of community content, identity, interaction, and transactions. Online communities have one inherent advantage—their global reach and the commitment to participation by "true-believers."

Technology plays an important role in facilitating membership participation and interaction. Such features as providing threaded discussions, archives, search tools, cross-referencing, and conferencing make it attractive to users new and old and easier for moderators to manage.

As communities become more commercially oriented, the standard metrics by which all commercial organizations are measured take over. The underlying cost and revenue structures of communities have to be clearly understood, the areas of greatest costs identified, and the particular business model with the highest potential for earning revenue put in place.

Unfortunately, there is no single silver bullet. It is difficult at best in putting this all together. Why does The Well, with its particular model, continue to thrive in its second decade in the face of competition from really deep pockets? How did Yahoo! get to where it is today, while others like Lycos and Alta Vista did not? We may never truly know. One thing we can say with some certainty: Online communities may be expected to replicate and enhance offline communities, providing a powerful environment for online commerce.

Online communities, however, also represent one of the riskier aspects of e-commerce. Communities perform a vital role in enabling interaction, providing education and facilitating transactions. Unlike a physical community, such as a small town or a social club, barriers to exit in an electronic community are small to non-existent.

Membership retention and loyalty are difficult issues. Without a strong and robust following, the ability to obtain advertising or transactional revenues is poor. In summary, few communities are able to sustain themselves successfully as viable and profitable online entities without some form of sponsorship from a commercial or non-profit institution.

CHAPTER 6

The Commerce Stack

E-commerce today exhibits a dizzying variety of models that continue to proliferate, evolve, and morph into a wide range of businesses. Variations on the once "pure play" businesses more often than not complicate understanding of their e-commerce foundations. It seems that just about everyone, including the authors of this book, has a different definition of what constitutes a business model. Corporate hype, media enthusiasm, and absence of a consistent vocabulary are making the subject confusing at best, obtuse at the least.

Marketplace models, which are primarily B2B in common parlance, are a case in point. They are now contaminated with what are essentially price determination mechanisms. Compounding the definition problem, marketplace, hub, and digital exchanges are often used indiscriminately and interchangeably to describe the same thing.

The need, clearly, is for an analytical study of the world of e-commerce and its basic foundations to provide a commonly accepted definition of what constitutes the commerce model and how it is supported.

The commerce layer can be analyzed in a variety of ways: the broad context of the business such as B2B or B2C, sale of products versus services, revenue source, type of transaction (fixed price, auctions, barter), etc. In this chapter, we dissect e-commerce in terms of the parties to the interaction, the offerings available, and the environment necessary to enable the interactions. In the following chapter, we look at the pricing structures that are possible.

In a macro way, there are four different ways to describe a business to separate and define a business model:

1. Definition of the customer and, specifically, those that are targeted to be served profitably
2. How value is captured in the form of revenue and profitability
3. Differentiation in the market and what the distinctive competence of the enterprise is
4. Scope of operations, or the activities performed

As is evident, global terms like B2B and B2C are too broad and define very little. They are convenient, however, in isolating and discriminating between gross markets. Defining a customer is always good practice, and is an excellent strategic view. In electronic commerce, which is still relatively immature, that can vary between being too granular or narrow and not granular enough. Thus, using customer definition as a subset of another element is required, but is to be avoided in establishing a framework for a business model.

How a company differentiates itself in the marketplace is also too narrow and better left to be a driver in marketing. Also, the company definition of its own uniqueness or how the venture operates might be too restrictive. If we were to define Amazon as a bookseller or the offline Nordstrom's as an apparel firm, we would seriously misapply labels.

The E-Commerce Environment

We divide the e-commerce environment for delivery of goods and services into three parts: stores, marketplaces, and ecosystems, as shown in Figure 6.1. In each of these e-commerce environments, there are also three primary types of players: buyers, sellers, and intermediaries. Surrounding these primary participants are others who make up the value chain for the company, endorsers that influence customer buying decisions, and the community at large.

E-commerce stores were the first to spring up on the Internet. They were relatively simple to set up and operate. With few intermediaries involved, a merchant could set up a shop on the Internet and wait for customers to roll in.

Those were the good old days. They lasted a few short months. The hardest part of running an e-commerce store, and perhaps the most expensive part as well, is acquiring customers. Amazon.com, among others, is still spending heavily on the various disciplines that make up their customer-acquisition effort. Many other e-commerce stores put them-

Figure 6.1 E-commerce Environments

selves out of business in desperate attempts to build traffic and brand their offerings long before revenue was generated.

The e-commerce store is the electronic equivalent to a brick-and-mortar retail store: customers walk in, browse, and purchase. An e-commerce store can be B2B or B2C, serving business customers as Cisco Systems does, or retail customers such as Amazon.com.

The location of inventory has enormous implications for the cost of acquiring it—warehousing costs, promise to the customer, payments to suppliers, fulfillment to the customer, and the inevitable handling of returns. Stores, then, must be further categorized into three business types, all based on location of inventory. The three inventory-centric stores: *inventory stores, drop-ship stores,* and *portal stores,* are shown in Figure 6.2. Their operations are described later in this chapter.

The *inventory store* normally builds inventory of the products in-house. This replicates the traditional retail model, where inventory acquisitions are made based on a prediction of customer consumption.

The *drop-ship store* is more typically found online or in catalog operations, and is facilitated by advances in automation and communications between businesses. Thus, a store can take an order from a customer and then have the order "drop-shipped" directly from a supplier.

Figure 6.2 Store Models

A *portal store* acts as an agent to the actual merchant of record, and passes the order through in exchange for a commission.

A marketplace is an aggregation of buyers or sellers. For instance, a mall is a marketplace with an aggregation of sellers. In contrast, a co-op (such as for groceries) is a membership-based aggregation of buyers who utilize buying power to negotiate preferential prices from sellers. An e-commerce marketplace aggregates content and brings together buyers and sellers with the purpose of mediating exchange of information or transactions between them.

Marketplaces, like airports for airlines, are single "points of call," environments that provide a complete range of services to a large number of passengers. A buyer-centric marketplace aggregates buyers and secures advantages reflected in economies of scale, better pricing from group buying power, and lower transaction costs. A seller-centric marketplace likewise aggregates sellers who benefit from consolidation of power in a fragmented supplier market. A neutral marketplace favors neither buyer nor seller, but facilitates the interactions and the transactions.

Figure 6.3 shows the breakdown of marketplaces into buy-side, neutral, and sell-side hubs.

Finally, the e-commerce ecosystem represents a business environment with a multitude of interlinked players, all of whom share a common infrastructure. This ecosystem includes many trading partners, logistics companies, banks, credit agencies, and so forth. Such an environment provides for the facilities and relationships needed to sustain a continuum of transactions or interactivity.

An ecosystem may cross industries, and can be global in scope and reach as well. An essential requirement for an e-commerce ecosystem to exist is for there to be a partici-

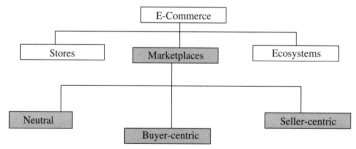

Figure 6.3   Marketplaces

pant that can provide the infrastructure, enable technology, integrate services, and recruit partners. This host can be buyer-centric, seller-centric, or neutral. In the case of Covisint, a buyer-centric marketplace in the automobile industry, the host operates with as much neutrality as possible, but when supported and funded by three major automakers, it is relatively clear where the influence resides.

Let's examine each element in the e-commerce environment in a little greater detail.

Stores

As noted above, a store is an e-commerce environment where an owner can offer goods or services to a potential customer. Stores are further classified by where ownership and management of the inventory resides.

The primary parties to any interaction are the storeowner, the consumer and, when required, the holder of inventory. There may be intermediaries involved (such as a payment facilitator, or an escrow service), but their roles complement the merchant-customer relationship, adding value or efficiency where needed.

These stores are similar to their retail counterparts that also provide products or services. As we know, most brick-and-mortar stores are rapidly creating online environments that complement the offline brand. Sometimes they are faithful to each other and use the same name, Barnesandnoble.com, alternatively bn.com; often they are slightly different, but related, such as BlueLight.com for K-mart. Distinct new online brands evolved in the last few years to compete with each other and with offline counterparts. The new online branded stores are searching for new methods of customer acquisition, customer service, and fulfillment to differentiate them from online and offline competitors.

Table 6.1 captures some general functional considerations for e-commerce stores.

Inventory Stores
The inventory store model is illustrated in Figure 6.4

The inventory store duplicates the typical retail model online. A retail store has store displays, with its counterpart online being catalogs. "Boxed" items are those unopened products a customer can pay for and take away. The boxed items are moving inventory that takes up most of the space in a retail store.

In addition, a retail store may or may not have additional inventory, either on the premises or in a separate warehouse. What a customer sees in the Web site catalog, the

Table 6.1   General Structure for E-Commerce Stores

Function	Detail
E-Commerce Role	Provide a store
Participants	Merchant, customers
Offerings	Goods and services
Infrastructure	• Self-hosted or co-located at an ISP • Electronic catalog of goods/services • Order processing • Customer service • Direct fulfillment • Warehouse in the case of inventory stores • Payment processing as part of infrastructure
Customer Acquisition	• Directly to store • Through affiliate networks • Through embedding in search engines • Other marketing and marketing communications processes, too
Role of Intermediary	• May use intermediaries for customer acquisition • No intermediaries for transaction processing • May use intermediaries for fulfillment
Pricing Models	• Usually fixed price • Optional use of auction format, particularly for clearance items • Services and complex product sales may use a Request for Quote process
Revenue Breakout	• Cost of goods/service • Marketing cost • Internal operations/administration • Inventory/warehouse/returns • Shipping • Profit
Examples	Consumer storefront: Amazon.com Business storefront: Cisco Connection Online Consumer service: etrade.com Business service: fedex.com

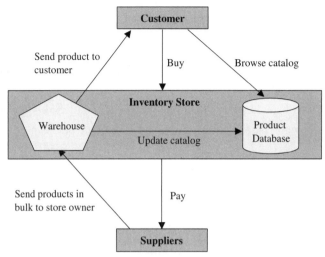

Figure 6.4 Inventory Stores

inventory store version online, is held as inventory at one or more locations for immediate shipment.

Implications for inventory stores are:

- **Inventory Cost:** The storeowner has to purchase goods ahead of the customer purchasing cycle. Storeowners are invoiced, and the payment may be due ahead of the product's purchase by the customer.
- **Shipping Cost:** The storeowner in most cases is responsible for shipping costs from suppliers to the store's warehouse.
- **Interaction Costs:** Typically, these are the traditional distributor-store supply chain costs for bulk acquisition.
- **Holding Cost:** The cost of holding inventory depends on the inventory turns that are achieved (an inventory turn is a strategic metric for retailers, and it reflects the number of times the inventory is replenished in a specific time frame, such as a year).
- **Shrinkage Cost:** Most warehouses suffer from "shrinkage" when inventory is lost either due to mishandling or theft.
- **Liquidation Cost:** Since demand cannot be accurately predicted, it is likely that goods will need to be liquidated below cost at the end of a buying season.

- **Revenue Models:**
  - Direct sale of goods to customer
  - Merchandising allowance revenue from brand manufacturer
- **Revenue Recognition:** The revenue can be recognized as soon as the goods leave the warehouse for the customer.
- **Cash Flow:** In an inventory store, cost of goods and inventory are accrued ahead of customer purchase, and cash flow is adverse to the merchant.

Since the early days of e-commerce, e-tailers wanted to create online stores with inventory. Implicitly, the idea of click-and-buy e-commerce suggests instant shipment of product. Certainly, if the online stores intend to compete directly with offline retail stores where a customer browses and buys, the requirement for express shipment ("will ship within 24 hours") is very important.

To a large extent, Amazon.com set the stage with its promise and execution of quick and easy online commerce, with shipping by any means selected by the customer. The financial reality of an online inventory model is, in truth, brutal. Many merchants are often driven out of business trying to meet these expectations.

The problem here is quite simple: To attract customers, online stores need to offer a substantive selection of products. Furthermore, the nature of demand is extremely uneven, and customers are store-hopping with the click of a mouse.

Finally, the supply chain for many online stores is still primitive, leading to large time delays for restocking of inventory. As a consequence, during heavy buying periods such as during the winter holidays, some online stores deplete their inventories of hot items and face complaints of being unresponsive to customers. Some of these issues have legal implications, mandated in the Federal Trade Commission's (FTC) Mail and Telephone Order rule.

The net result is that inventory stores have an ever-narrower range of choices: either stock deep and run the financial risk of excess inventory, or stock shallow and face the ire of customers and the strong hand of the FTC when the item desired is out of stock. In either case, the consequence to the company bottom line is adverse.

Planning for an e-commerce inventory-driven store is difficult. Even Amazon.com with its cash resources finds it difficult and expensive to maintain consistent inventory levels. Ideally, a store might utilize just-in-time (JIT) inventory, as illustrated in Figure 6.5.

In JIT, the company forecasts initial demand for a product and stocks the store accordingly. Then the e-tailer identifies the "inventory reorder level," which is the quan-

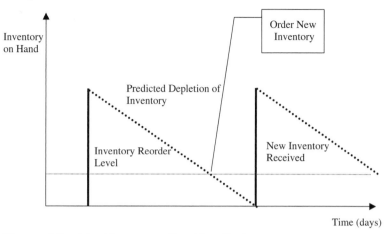

Figure 6.5 Ideal Inventory Stocking Cycle

tity at which the store should ask its supplier to restock the product. This level is determined by two considerations: the number of days over which stock runs out given a predicted demand, or by the number of days it takes the supplier to stock and restock the product given an order. Figure 6.5 depicts the gyrations a business experiences where restocking occurs exactly when supply runs out.

Accurate execution rarely happens. In reality, there is either little or no planning. Inventory stocking is ad hoc, or demand is so uneven that planning cannot keep pace. Note that supply stocking times and product demand vary enormously by specific product and industry. Therefore, few stores have the luxury of specifying restocking on a uniform criterion across all products, while others are at the mercy of exogenous forces totally out of their control and ability to forecast.

One way to alleviate this situation is to establish reorder processes based on the supplier's restocking capability, as illustrated in Figure 6.6. In this case, the inventory reorder level is based on the time required by the supplier to restock a particular product. When the targeted inventory count is reached, new stock should be ordered. There is a risk that the inventory could run out before the new stock is received. However, there is also a definitive commitment date when the product will be received, which can be conveyed to the customer. Conversely, there is also a possibility that the inventory is not run down by the time new stock is received, which affects inventory carrying costs.

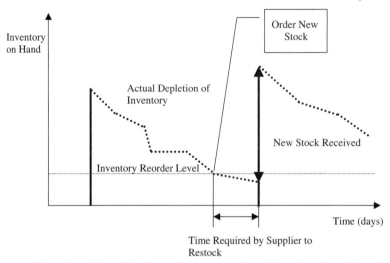

Figure 6.6 Inventory Stocking Cycle Based on Supplier Stocking Time

New inventory management systems tied into Enterprise Resource Planning (ERP) systems are scaled to meet the needs of small businesses as well as large. These systems can help automate inventory replenishment cycles.

Drop-Ship Stores

In the drop-ship method shown in Figure 6.7, the store does not maintain a warehouse or on-site inventory. Instead, the store relies on the inventory of its suppliers. Many dealers and department stores in the offline retail world today have barcode tracking mechanisms linked to the checkout counter that enables automatic inventory replenishment notification to their manufacturers or wholesale distributors when supplies on the shelves run low.

The stores themselves may not carry inventory beyond what's on the shelves and perhaps a small local inventory. The online variation extends the concept: not only do the stores not carry inventory but, true to their virtual nature, customer purchases are merely notifications to suppliers to ship. In other words, a purchase triggers a ship order to the appropriate supplier who, in fact, carries the inventory.

The implications for drop-ship stores are:

- **Inventory Cost:** Typically none. Some suppliers or distributors may ask for the minimum quantities to be reserved.

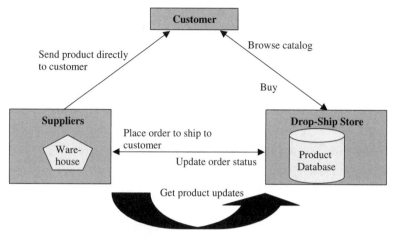

Figure 6.7 Drop-ship Stores

- **Shipping Cost:** The storeowner is billed by the supplier for the cost of shipment to the customer, which the storeowner may charge back to the customer.
- **Interaction Costs:** The cost of interacting with the suppliers in this model is higher, since the supplier needs to provide information to update the catalog including inventory information. Also, it takes effort or automation to obtain shipping confirmation from the suppliers, and there is also package tracking.
- **Holding Cost:** There is no holding cost.
- **Shrinkage Cost:** There is no shrinkage cost.
- **Liquidation Cost:** There is no liquidation cost.
- **Revenue Model:**
  - Sale of goods to customer
  - Merchandising allowance revenue from brand manufacturer along with some cross-advertising
- **Revenue Recognition:** Revenue can only be recognized when goods are shipped from the warehouse of the supplier to the customer. This is often later than that for the inventory model.
- **Cash Flow:** In a drop-ship store, the cost of goods is incurred after the customer purchase. The supplier may provide an additional float based on the payment terms. Cash flow, therefore, is favorable to the merchant.

As is obvious, a notable risk in the drop-ship store model is the inability to control shipment. In a drop-ship store, a delivery promise made to the customer is based on a shipment commitment made by the product supplier (which could be either a manufacturer or distributor).

In some cases, the drop-ship store may verify the supplier's inventory, either on a nightly basis or dynamically at the time of a customer order. Sadly, however, the norm is to accept the customer order based on a supplier's general promise of availability. This leads to the situation where the customer now has an expectation of receipt of goods, yet the merchant has little ability to ensure that the customer expectation is fulfilled.

Portal Stores

Portal stores aggregate products provided by different merchants but serve only to direct transactions to the appropriate merchant. Potential customers coming to such a store are, in effect, "passed through" to the merchant-of-choice. Early implementations of this model suffered from a loss of stickiness because the portal lost the customer once he/she passed through to a merchant site.

Today, most implementations retain customer presence by either encapsulating the merchant site within its own (that is, a merchant site bordered by a portal site) or by opening a new window for the merchant site. In the latter case, a customer then closes the window after browsing/transacting at the merchant site and returns to the portal store.

Portal store merchants have an obligation to ensure the accuracy of the product content and availability. Typically, the branding is that of the merchant. The portal store has a revenue model consisting of slotting fees for preferential location, advertising/merchandising allowances, hosting charges, and transaction fees, as shown in Figure 6.8.

The implications for portal stores are:

- **Inventory Cost:** None; however, the merchant participating in the portal store may have inventory costs.
- **Shipping Cost:** None; however, the merchant fulfilling the transaction may have shipping costs.
- **Interaction Costs:** There is appreciable cost in enabling participating merchants to maintain their individual product catalogs. In aggregating such merchant catalogs, the portal store facilitates availability of an aggregated product catalog, which provides the content value associated with a shopping portal. This allows

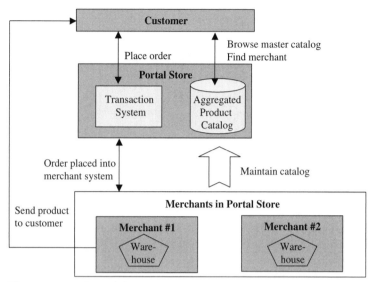

Figure 6.8 Portal Stores

the portal to provide structured ways to find the product needed, such as with category navigation, brand navigation, search functions, and price comparisons. Additional interactions may include information to update the catalog, including inventory information, and to obtain shipping confirmation from the merchants.

- **Holding Cost:** There is no holding cost to the portal.
- **Shrinkage Cost:** There is no shrinkage cost to the portal.
- **Liquidation Cost:** There is no liquidation cost to the portal.
- **Revenue Model:**
  - Advertising from merchants
  - Slotting fees for positioning merchants advantageously
  - Merchandising fees to position merchants contextually
  - Hosting fees to maintain catalog
  - Transaction fees for each order (either fixed amount or percent of transaction)
- **Revenue Recognition:** This is subject to the particular transactional risk carried by the merchant and the accounting standards established in each country.
- **Cash Flow:** In a portal store, cash flow is dependant on the revenue model selected and its relative weight; for example, slotting fees and advertising might

be dependent on the merchant's cash flow. Hosting fees are often on a monthly basis, and transaction fees will arise with volume.

Role of Offline Retailers

In the excitement over online potentialities, established values of offline stores went through a period when they were excessively marginalized, and then, when the dot com shakeout occurred, they rebounded. Offline stores have evolved over several decades and offer significant customer benefits. To paraphrase Mark Twain, "predictions of their demise are overstated." In Table 6.2, the advantages and disadvantages of both online and offline stores are contrasted.

Baseline for Store Measurement

1. Number of products/service categories
2. Total number of products offered
3. Method of creating and updating content
4. Unit cost of creating a new SKU
5. Unit cost of updating an existing SKU (price updated, content updated)
6. Capital cost to create an e-commerce store (proprietary, licensed, or hosted)
7. Operating cost to maintain e-commerce environment (monthly running cost)
8. Channels of sales (online, offline, phone, wireless)
9. Customer acquisition cost
10. Number of orders serviced by a customer service representative per day
11. Number of orders serviced by fulfillment service representatives per day
12. Number of orders shipped per day
13. Instant Ship Ratio = New Orders Today / Orders Shipped Today
14. Open Order Ratio = New Orders / Total Open Orders
15. Returns Ratio = Orders Returned / Total Open Orders
16. Cancel Ratio = Orders Cancelled / Total Open Orders
17. Gross Product or service margin
18. Inventory acquisition cost
19. Inventory holding cost
20. Shipping Cost Ratio = Shipping Cost / Sales Price of Goods
21. Average operational cost per order
22. Net product or service margin
23. Time (months) to positive cash flow
24. Time (months) to operational break-even
25. Time (months) to profitability

Table 6.2 Online Versus Offline: Benefits and Drawbacks

Function	Offline Store	Online Stores
Customer Acquisition	• Geographically limited with small stores having a customer acquisition radius of about 5 miles, branded, stores about 15 miles and malls about 25 miles. • Most dominant customer acquisition is through local advertising, predominantly yellow pages, newspaper, radio, television, direct or "unsolicited mail," and physical presence at major intersections or in malls. • Targeting efficiency is extremely poor; the "walk-through" from a newspaper advertisement may be fractions of one percent. • High reliance on "local" branding, "store" branding or "mall" branding, or through chain store or franchise affiliation.	• Geographically unlimited in principle. Realistic boundaries may be "statewide" for tax reasons, national for customs/shipping reasons, or regional for trade reasons (such as the European Union or NAFTA boundaries). • Most dominant customer acquisition is through online and offline advertising, embedding in search engines, presence in online malls, presence in affiliate environments, and direct email marketing. Some success with traditional media have been reported, notably radio. • Targeting efficiency may vary widely depending on type of customer acquisition. This is discussed further in a subsequent chapter. • Currently very few dominant online brands, leading to price-based competition.
Customer Service	• May vary widely from the "neighborly" greeting of a local merchant to the impersonal indifference at the megastores. • Customer service is available on demand. • Even when available, customer service may be unable to help due to poor training.	• The dominant focus of most online stores has been efficiency, often meaning "no customer service" or "self service." This is often a barrier to increased customer adoption of e-commerce. • Customer service may be available in other forms: online chat, email, and custom response. The efficiency or lack of it in these systems varies widely depending on the tools and user sophistication. These are still at an early, evolutionary stage and do not yet match the ability of direct human interaction to resolve issues.

(continued)

Table 6.2   Online Versus Offline: Benefits and Drawbacks (*continued*)

Function	Offline Store	Online Stores
		• Online customer service can draw upon considerable data to resolve specific issues: availability, policies, logistics, case history, etc.
Content Presentation	• A department, sections, racks, shelves. • Customer can touch, feel, and often try out product.	• Structured navigation through departments and categories. • Content detail, close-ups, reviews.
Availability	• Typically available on site. • Limited product set and options. • As a general principle, some do operate without inventory that they sell by reference, such as accessories not usually available: "What we do not have, we do not sell." • High inventory costs to maintain a sufficiently large selection of products.	• Larger product set and options. • General principle: "We have it, but it may take time." • JIT inventory model to match anticipated customer needs and expectations. • Products may not be available at online store's warehouse. • Use of back-orders to resolve lack of inventory. • Could also be third-party products —(sourced from other suppliers).
Order Management	• Transaction completed at counter. • Multiple payment methods. • Transaction security is presumed; actual security may be locally compromised. • Transaction time could range from 5 to 30 minutes. • Most stores cannot "recognize" a repeat customer.	• Transaction completed at shopping cart. • Transaction time could range from <1 to 5 minutes. • Most stores can identify a repeat customer leading to stored customer information; easier ordering and suitable rewards. • Limited payment methods. • Transaction security is mostly secure; potential for fraud or theft of stored credit information remains high.
Fulfillment	• Customer typically gets the goods immediately. • Shipping to other destinations not very convenient; most stores do not handle the shipment process.	• Easy to get shipments to other locations. • Easy to set up "personal registry" of addresses. • Customer typically has to wait for goods to be delivered.

(*continued*)

Table 6.2 Online Versus Offline: Benefits and Drawbacks (*continued*)

Function	Offline Store	Online Stores
Returns	• Can be easy to return merchandise back to store depending on store policies. • Third-party returns (i.e., returns of gifts) can be as easy as returns by the purchaser.	• Customer typically has to go through elaborate steps to return merchandise: RMA process, packing, shipping, credit block on shipped product and resolution. • Third-party returns are very difficult.
Exchange	• Can be easy to exchange merchandise at same store. • May not entail a secondary transaction.	• An exchange is the equivalent of a return plus a new purchase.
Liquidation/ Clearance	• These are huddled away in the back to minimize impact to potential new sales.	• Can be effectively merchandized with minimal impact to new sales.

The Hybrid Store of the Future

It is clear from Table 6.2 that both offline and online stores have distinct advantages and disadvantages. In B2C environments, offline stores—individual mom-and-pop, "category killers" (such as Home Depot and Toys R Us), and multidestination stores—and malls have roles to play in the context of shopping needs, entertainment needs, and town-redevelopment efforts.

Mom-and-pop stores are at risk of disappearing from America with the advent of malls, category killers, and large, multidestination stores run by chains or franchises. The economics of the latter have generally overwhelmed the viability of the small owner-operated stores, particularly in areas with a high density of population. In places where they survive, they have done so either because large stores have little to profit from a presence (isolated rural communities, for instance) or because they have turned into specialized stores targeting niche consumers.

Trader Joe's is a closely held, California-based, specialized brick-and-mortar grocery chain that continues to expand, targeting affluent, knowledgeable consumers in up-market urban areas. Typically, stores are one-tenth or less of traditional chain grocery stores while their offerings are unique and diverse, sourced from around the world.

Another trend that has to some extent re-energized small store entrepreneurship is town redevelopment, which creates an ambience for tourism, maximizes foot traffic, and thereby increases tax revenues from commerce. Annapolis, Maryland, Burlington, Vermont, Portland, Oregon, and Ithaca, New York all typify this trend to recreate old world Americana in a new and stylish fashion. In many instances, the so-called small store is but a large, branded store masquerading as a small one.

These examples serve to illustrate that offline commerce is not fading away in the face of any onslaught by their online brethren. Even with all the advantages of efficiency, availability, and price, online stores are handicapped when it comes to providing an environment for entertainment, and *non-specific* impulse shopping.

The initial euphoria over online stores, driven largely by some of their inherently perceived advantages—absence of investment in physical infrastructure or retail space, inventory-less retailing, lower costs of establishment, etc.—are giving way to skepticism and investor impatience at the lack of profits. Four principal factors have accounted for this:

- Attempts to achieve instant brand recognition and implanting brand attributes in the marketplace are expensive, especially as e-tailers race to secure market share and mind share in a fraction of the time their offline counterparts have.
- Lower costs of online retailing are proving to be illusory—expansion (in the number of market categories, channels) entails large investments in technology and, ironically, in brick-and-mortar warehouses to rapidly service customers.
- E-tailers are realizing they have singularly underestimated customer acquisition and retention.
- As online commerce begins to mature, it is becoming evident that offline retailers, with their considerable brand equity and deep pockets, are in a strong position and are now best positioned to benefit from the flux in the markets.

Successful online stores are integrating with the offline in creative ways to give birth to "hybrid" stores that draw upon each other's strengths in equal measure. The hybrid "bricks and clicks" store encompasses the benefits of the online and offline models while mitigating the problems, as listed in Table 6.3.

Table 6.3 The Hybrid Store: Benefits from Convergence of Online and Offline

Customer Acquisition	❏ Online stores affiliated to a physical presence ❏ Coordinated online and offline marketing ❏ Integrated customer loyalty programs ❏ Online kiosks for customer registration/log-in, quick search, browsing, and redirection to actual location within offline store
Customer Service	❏ Integrated customer service: help desk, email, chat, and live interaction with the local offline customer service representative ❏ Kiosk-based self-servicing
Content Presentation	❏ Online stores with complete content ❏ Local stores have samples of all online content, including swatches for variations ❏ Local retail store with flat panel displays for showcasing online content navigable through simple options screens ❏ Price matching, display, etc.
Availability	❏ All online content available from warehouses or local stores ❏ Local stores tune inventory to market conditions
Order Management	❏ Products can be ordered offline or online ❏ Kiosk-based checkout and purchase with integrated bar code reader, shopping cart, and payment methods ❏ Credit cards and smart cards used in the online and offline store for customer self-service ❏ Offline store also supports cash and other payment instruments (traveler's checks, coupons, etc.)
Fulfillment	❏ Customer can have product shipped ❏ Customer can pick up product from local store
Returns	❏ Customer can return product to local store or to warehouse
Exchange	❏ Customer can exchange product at local store
Liquidation/Clearance	❏ Liquidations and clearance section at retail store showcase same items at the online store, or vice versa

Marketplaces

Marketplaces bring buyers and sellers together and, as a rule, optimize several aspects of the buyer-seller relationship. Marketplaces are often called exchanges in the e-commerce literature (we are staying clear of this nomenclature because it often confuses a business model associated with a grouping of buyers and sellers with the dynamic pricing model associated with exchanges). Buyers and buying groups constitute one side of the purchasing process. Buyers come to an online marketplace to obtain a good price, product, and supplier diversity. They also want a one-stop shopping experience that eliminates the hassle of sourcing from multiple vendors and the higher transaction costs that it entails.

Sourcing through online marketplaces provides more effective procurement by organizations that leverage the full functionality of services that intermediaries offer. These take the form of back-end integration with enterprise financial systems, order visibility through the full cycle of order placement through delivery, enforcement of business rules and spend limits, workflow functionality, paperless invoicing, and end-user empowerment.

Supplier participation in online marketplaces is affected by the nature of supplier relations engendered by the purchasing process, pricing, negotiation, and technological links into buyer systems. Supplier acceptance of online marketplaces hinges essentially on five aspects:

- Scope for enlarging the customer base by using the marketplace as an addition to their regular marketing channels and increase revenue
- Ability to retain contractual relationships with existing customers
- Pricing forums and nature of negotiation to determine price, availability of goods, and their delivery
- Settlement terms
- Standardized interfaces to corporate back-end systems

Suppliers sometimes perceive there are threats from sharing online space with their competitors. Suppliers often see threats from price erosion because of an environment that allows comparison shopping, open bidding, and the like. In addition to channel conflict, suppliers also fear losing special relationships with their important customers and the ability to continue prenegotiated contract purchasing.

Both issues are serious enough to impair liquidity and growth of the marketplace. Liquidity and transaction volume are directly related to each other. At the same time, depending on the nature of the market, transaction volume distributes benefits in an asymmetric fashion, that is, an increase in the number of suppliers, for instance, does not necessarily benefit an individual supplier.

The benefits largely accrue to the buying community. Ironically, suppliers themselves are moving away from marketplaces hosted by single suppliers because these impose a burden on buyers to conduct more search and comparisons with other suppliers.

Marketplaces are suffering from the same forces of shakeout as those hitting the rest of the B2B environment. Many buying and selling exchanges are emerging, often as a defensive measure to prevent a third party from doing so in their industry.

Dana, Delphi Automotive Systems, Eaton, Motorola, and Valeo are teaming to potentially offer a competing front to the Covisint initiative of GM, Ford, and Chrysler. Similarly, Alcoa, Kaiser Aluminum, and many other significant metals producers are planning to launch MetalSpectrum as an exchange for specialty metal products. Another industry initiative by Abbot Laboratories, Baxter International, GE Medical Systems, Johnson & Johnson, and Medtronic is designed to set up a medical supplies exchange that competes with Medibuy and Neoforma.

Exchanges, or marketplaces, can be quite partisan in nature, depending on the parties creating them. While all exchanges match buyers and sellers, there is sometimes a vested interest reflecting a consolidation of power, and one can distinguish between buyer and seller centricity in each. The distinction arises from its source of aggregation: buyer-centric environments bring together buyers to bid for identical products from multiple providers, thereby forcing competition among sellers. Seller-centric sites, on the other hand, consolidate supplier offers and allow buyers to bid competitively to secure the transaction.

Buyer-Centricity

Buy-side exchanges are usually the initiatives of large buyers and generally enforce participation by suppliers who risk losing vendor status. In a buyer exchange, multiple sellers are qualified and admitted into the club. They submit their product content for posting in their respective categories. They also submit business rules regarding the conditions under which they would like to be notified (see Figure 6.9)

When a buyer requests a product quote or a request for proposal (RFP), the exchange forwards the request to the corresponding qualified sellers. At the simplest

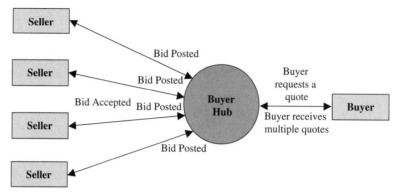

Figure 6.9   Transactional Perspective for a Buyer-Centric Exchange

response level, the sellers could participate with a single fixed bid. The exchange can then consolidate all responses and present them to the buyer for a decision.

More complex models can include an auction format with the seller identity masked. This will lead to a reverse auction scenario with downward pricing pressure exerted on the sellers. Also viable is a negotiating format where the top few qualified sellers negotiate with the buyer, leading to a final winner.

Automobile companies such as Ford and General Motors, for instance, are organizing to move their purchasing operations from EDI-based proprietary systems operating on private networks to Internet-based solutions. Covisint, formed by the Big Three auto manufacturers, is attempting to conduct all of its supplier purchases using this buy-side exchange. This ambitious undertaking consolidates the Tier 1, Tier 2, and Tier 3 suppliers of the Big Three automotive companies into a massive supplier marketplace. This has raised issues of excessive buying power consolidation and its consequences on suppliers. As of the end of 2000, the FTC ruled that Covisint was okay.

For the buyer, such an exchange has several advantages. The exchange serves as a single point for obtaining multiple bids, allows for prequalification of suppliers, and provides transactional security by enabling the marketplace to be a broker. Buyers may also enjoy significant gains from the price pressure on sellers and from supplier's ratings compiled by the exchange.

Sellers, meanwhile, are not quite left out in the cold. Sure, a buyer exchange holds attractive benefits for buyers; yet, there would be no buyer exchange if no supplier chose to join. Suppliers choose to come on board because they see benefits for themselves as well. These benefits include: perceiving the exchange as a new channel for customer acquisition, the fact that acquisition cost may be lower than traditional channels, and visibility into competitor pricing by virtue of a transparent bidding process.

The structure of a buyer-centric exchange is described in Table 6.5.

Table 6.5 Structure for Buyer-Centric Exchange

Function	*Detail*
E-Commerce Role	Provide a one-stop location for buyers to request qualified bids from a number of suppliers
Participants	Buyers, sellers
Offerings	Goods and services
Infrastructure	• The exchange maintains an electronic catalog of goods/ services • Transaction processing
Customer Acquisition	• Advertising • Through affiliate networks • Through embedding in search engines • Offline ad/marketing
Role of Intermediary	• Seller aggregation • Collection of request for quote (RFQ) • Relay of RFQ to qualified sellers • Presentation of responses to buyer • Provide buyer-seller contact or facilitate transaction • Seller and buyer account history
Pricing Models	• Usually single lowest bid • Potential use of reverse auction model • Potential for negotiated pricing
Revenue Breakup	• Cost of goods/service to buyer • Transaction fee or commission
Examples	Small business procurement: VolumeBuy.com Medical Supplies: medibuy.com Food Service Industry: instill.com Business service: Biztro.com

Seller-Centricity

A seller exchange has a supplier(s) or distributor(s) on one side inviting bids for offerings on the other. They can also aggregate a multitude of suppliers. These are markets for commodities in fragmented markets, small- and medium-sized suppliers, thinly traded one-off products, anchor company products, and services or maintenance, repair, and operations (MRO) purchases. They typically feature content aggregation, purchasing rules, order requisition, workflow management, and back-end integration into financial systems, payment, and fulfillment (see Figure 6.10).

Aggregating suppliers offer buyers a single place to engage in corporate buying while offering the benefits of lower transaction costs, optimized corporate procurement systems, workflow management, systems integration, and negotiated contract settlements to suppliers.

Seller exchanges show promise as environments for reverse auctions, although there is no requirement that they work only in auction formats. The most prominent example of a seller-centric marketplace is Priceline.com. In this model, an airline makes available an offer to Priceline (say, a round trip ticket from Boston to San Francisco for a particular date and time). Based on this offer, Priceline creates a "reserve price" with a markup. This information is stored in Priceline's database and is not visible to users.

Potential customers interested in traveling from Boston to San Francisco are now encouraged to "Name Your Price," using Priceline's patented method. This buyer bid is then compared to the "reserve price" and the ticket is purchased against a credit card if the buyer bid meets or exceeds the "reserve price."

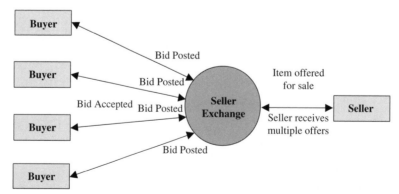

Figure 6.10 Transactional Perspective for a Seller-Centric Exchange

Technically, this transaction is not a "reverse auction," although it is sometimes popularly perceived to be so. In the business space, Freemarkets Online runs a seller exchange for industrial parts and components. This is operated in a reverse auction model, where buyers post bids against an initial reserve price set by the supplier.

Characteristics of Exchanges

Liquidity from the buy-side implicitly solves the chicken-and-egg problem associated with online marketplaces—buyers wait to join until sufficient suppliers are onboard; the latter, likewise, would like to see a large enough market for their goods to consider signing up. Once they do participate, they derive benefit from:

- Advanced search capability to identify complex products
- Catalog of products, descriptions, pictures and designs, availability, price
- Supplier directory
- Delivery options
- Order consolidation
- Negotiated purchasing
- Delivery status
- Notification
- Reordering
- Returns
- Consolidated and itemized reporting
- Participation with their peers and competitors

Typically, there are a number of inefficiencies such as in searching for products and suppliers and in conducting transactions. Products need to be compared across suppliers; for this, information has to exist in a form that enables apples-to-apples comparisons. Information on pricing, especially in dynamic markets such as energy, needs to be real time. Visibility into inventory allows buyers to optimize their purchases. Buyers also need to have information on the status of their orders and expected delivery. Supplier aggregation in fragmented markets and provision of value added services also promote buyer liquidity in the market.

Online marketplaces can eliminate existing paper-based processes (order requisition, approval, order placement, billing, invoicing, delivery, and payment) by means of automation and integration with buyer systems. This reduces cost, substantially improves efficiency, and draws in buyers.

Buyers and sellers participate in online exchanges, each to gain in different ways. The respective perspectives of buyers and sellers are detailed in Tables 6.6 and 6.7.

Vertical and Horizontal Exchanges

Vertical exchanges are based on specific industry contexts such as SciQuest for life sciences, Metalsite for steel, Enron for energy purchases, and PlasticsNet.com for plastics. While over a thousand marketplaces have been created, many were closing their virtual doors into 2001, and there are still only a few cases of financial success.

Table 6.6   Buyer Perspective in an Online Marketplace

Attribute	The Problems	The Solution
Search	Takes too long, complex products, incomplete in fragmented markets	Complex search tools, supplier aggregation
Pricing	Uncompetitive prices, incomplete and unreliable in dynamic settings	Greater competition, real-time pricing
Supplier Trustworthiness	Management of suppliers—need to discriminate between quality suppliers and order fulfillment	Supplier prequalification, escrow, insurance
Purchase Orders	Inefficient processes—paperwork, authorization, spend limits	Automation, approval workflow
Fulfillment	Order status, delivery date, slippages	Order acknowledgment, status updates, shipment tracking
Inventory	Lack of visibility into buyer and supplier inventory	Integration into buyer and supplier inventory systems
Reordering	Time to duplicate earlier order	Inventory visibility, automatic replenishment

Table 6.7 Supplier Perspective in an Online Marketplace

Attribute	The Problems	The Solution
Channel Conflict	Sale through online marketplace may adversely affect sales through other regular channels	Possibility of reaching new customers and expanding markets
Price Erosion	Information transparency and larger supplier availability could depress price and result in commoditization and customer migration	Online marketplace could provide for relationship marketing, branding
Transaction Anonymity	Supplier preference for anonymity to move excess or unsold goods without affecting regular pricing for regular customers	Is an issue mostly with commodity markets; such marketplaces can provide for anonymous transactions
Prenegotiated Contracts	Supplier fears about online marketplaces precluding prenegotiated or fixed price contracts to supply, which are hallmarks of B2B	Online marketplace can facilitate contractual relationships on the basis of price, quality, quantity, delivery, and inventory
Buyer Trustworthiness	Need to discriminate between buyers, ability to pay, and on-time payment	Advisory services to minimize risk

Key considerations for the formation of a successful vertical exchange are:

- Critical mass of buyers and sellers, which leads to liquidity.
- Many vertical marketplaces wither if there is a buyer-seller mismatch or key industry players are not present.
- Significant industry expertise by the marketplace operator.
- A good competitive marketplace without an industry giant controlling the market and implicitly controlling the price.
- Effective representation of the buy-sell potential. Many vertical marketplaces generate sales leads, with no follow up. Eventually the marketplace falls into disuse.
- Effective automation of bids, RFPs, RFQs, and other trading mechanisms.

Baseline Measurements for Exchanges

Listed below are some baseline measurements that can assist operators of buyer and seller exchanges in establishing a framework for metrics:

1. Number of product categories
2. Number of suppliers
3. Average number of prospective buyers (per day)
4. Average number of RFQs/RFPs generated per day
5. Average number of suppliers asked to respond to an RFQ or RFP
6. Average response ratio (percent of notified suppliers who respond)
7. Price spread statistics on bid
8. Percent of requestors who accept bid
9. Pricing efficiency = Hub Price/Retail Price
10. Total transactional volume (in dollars and orders)
11. Conversion ratio = Orders/Total Quotes Requested
12. Average value per order
13. Average revenue per transaction to buyer hub
14. Supplier growth rate
15. Customer growth rate

Horizontal exchanges focus on providing standard business functionality across multiple industries. Examples of horizontal exchanges are: MRO.com for maintenance, repair, and operations procurement; transportation.com for matching shippers of goods to available trucking capacity, and Employease.com for employee benefits administration.

Key considerations for a horizontal exchange are:

- Detailed understanding and capability of the horizontal marketplace. For example, Employease.com should be able to provide employee benefit solutions in every state.
- Ability to provide custom solutions to vertical marketplaces. Employease.com should be able to provide solutions for white-collar workers, factory workers, temporary labor, farm labor, etc.
- High degree of efficiency achieved through scale and scope to leverage entry into multiple markets through cost and time savings to the end users.

Pricing on Exchanges

Pricing on an exchange can take many forms depending on the model implemented or the source of power inherent in its type (i.e., concentrated in a buyer or seller). A marketplace may have a fixed price model, implement a barter form of exchange, represent one of several types of auctions, or be the basis of a dynamic price determination model. Any or more than one type could also be represented within an exchange, also as a negotiated pricing mechanism, which is a form of fixed price arrived at by negotiation between the buyer and seller.

An exchange brings buyers and sellers together, but the efficiency of the market is a reflection of the method of price determination. A negotiated price, for instance, may be the method of choice between a large buyer and seller where bought goods are not commodities.

The same marketplace may offer an auction format for disposal of used equipment or perishable commodities. The particular revenue model(s) chosen by the exchange can be independent of how the price is determined. In general, an exchange may utilize all the identified methods of price determination, namely, fixed price, negotiated price, auctions, barter, or dynamic pricing. Typical pricing in exchanges consists of fees ranging from 0.5 percent upward to 15 percent of the transaction.

Ecosystems

In an ecosystem, the entire business chain is integrated to encompass demand aggregation, supply chain integration, payments, and fulfillment. Once this is achieved, such an ecosystem will become richer over time, with new suppliers, partners, and intermediaries joining in. Figure 6.11 shows the three major member groups of an ecosystem: buyers, sellers, and intermediaries.

The Value Stack

To build membership within the ecosystem, value in participation needs to be perceived by all members. In general, this is a chicken-and-egg issue relating to the number of partici-

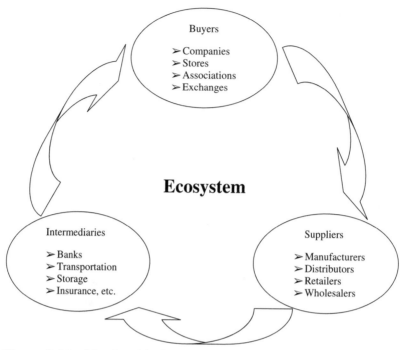

Figure 6.11   Membership Structure for an Ecosystem

pant buyers and sellers (when there are few buyers, there is little incentive for sellers to participate; when there are few sellers, buyers are not inclined to join). However, whoever creates the ecosystem can build value and inspire membership, establishing a value stack.

In Figure 6.12, we show an example of an ecosystem value stack for its constituent members. The ecosystem model is self-sustaining to a large degree: buyers within the community generate the orders, suppliers accept the orders, and intermediaries facilitate the transaction. The value stack is split into the following elements:

1. **Custom Business Interface**

   The ecosystem allows each of its members to customize its interface in the ecosystems. This may range from simple selection from standardized templates for buyers, sellers, and intermediaries to elaborate Web design consulting. Of growing importance is the need for language customization. In a

Custom Business Interface
Custom Web site design
Multilingual switching

Account Services
Maintenance of account
Rights administration for individual users
History and reports
Fees for ecosystem services

Community Services
Customized news subscription
Participation in forums of interest
Expert panels, online seminars
Digital reference library

Transaction Services
Review, post or accept bids, RFPs, RFQs
Review orders
Review order status
Check payment status and history
Create workflow for partners and employees
Create and manage transaction documents

Catalog Services
Loading products for sellers including
  categorization, graphics, and descriptions
Catalog updates for pricing and availability

Business Services
Payment methods and links to partner banks
Taxes services, automation, and reporting
Customs services for regulations, duties
Logistics planning functions and partners
Inspection services through approved agents
Escrow services for transaction integrity
Trans-shipment and warehousing partners
Insurance for goods, services, and transport
Translation of documents
Legal Services

Technology Services
Hosting of content and community
Integration within ecosystem
Support external interfaces to ecosystem
Standards evolution and maintenance

Figure 6.12 Ecosystem Value Stack for Buyers, Sellers, and Partners

global marketplace with buyers and sellers in different countries, it becomes important to allow the front end to be presented in the language of choice.

2. **Account Services**

Account administration services encompass the issues of the member's interaction with the ecosystem and its management. Typically, a member company has the right to add or delete users from its own ranks and assign rights to what they can do within the system. For example, only some designated users may have the right to place orders, and only the company's controller may have the right to release funds for purchase of goods and services. Other account service issues may deal with account history and fees payable to the ecosystem.

3. **Community Services**

The creation and maintenance of a variety of community services becomes very important in an ecosystem. Such a community will need to be the online equivalent of newspapers, trade journals, conferences, seminars, meetings, and water fountain discussions. This can be achieved through a combination of members selecting themselves into industry categories and choosing to receive customized news, engage in online forums, and participate in online meetings. It is up to the ecosystem operator to maintain the level of professional discourse by establishing standards and bringing in outside experts to provide enhanced value. For example, a forum on international trade may have a monthly expert seminar dealing with the World Trade Order or the consequence of a declining Euro.

4. **Transaction Services**

These services get to the heart of the value—the facilitation of posting and accepting orders for goods and services. Buyers need to have a facility to create orders, RFPs, and RFQs. Sellers have to be able to accept orders, respond to leads, and convert them into firm orders. Intermediaries need to be able to accept service requests, such as determination of transport or insurance costs, the availability of warehousing space, or the creation of letters of credit. Members should be able to review their account histories, such as by vendor, by season, by region, and so on. An important aspect of online commerce is the need to create workflows to facilitate the transaction. Such workflows may be internal to a company (for example: purchasing approval workflow is marked to the controller) or to external intermediaries (such as to legal counsel to review a purchase contract before final approval). Closely connected to workflow management is document management with the capability for document authentication, digital verification, versioning, and security.

5. **Catalog Services**

The ecosystem must support catalog services that are significantly more extensive than those for a store or an exchange. With a multiplicity of suppliers in broad industry categories, there is a requirement to support standard products and services categorization such as the United Nations Standards Products and Services Code (UNSPSC) or the Standard Industry Classification (SIC) code. Shipment of goods across international boundaries also requires rationalization with the harmonized tariff code structure. Such requirements push up the costs and time associated with integrating new members into the system, often requiring members to carry extensive internal work to categorize their offerings.

6. **Business Services**

A variety of business services need to be supported to facilitate transactions. Buyer and seller banks may need to be involved for large transactions relating to credit guarantees and letters of credit. International transactions may require intermediaries for customs processing and for tax accounting. Logistics planning, trans-shipment, and warehousing intermediaries may be needed for complex multimodal movement of goods. Escrow and bonding agents may be required in some cases. Finally, document translation services and miscellaneous legal services may be needed in international order flows.

7. **Technology Services**

The entire ecosystem needs to be supported by a robust technology services stack. This stack must deal with content and community hosting, and integration of data within the ecosystem. It needs to support external interfaces to the ecosystem for data import and export from its members. Finally, it needs to maintain standards for products and processes in the ecosystem and ensure other issues of integrity for the system.

Do such comprehensive ecosystems exist today? The answer is: not yet; however, here are some evolving versions:

CommerceOne

With its MarketSite™ implementation, CommerceOne wants to create a global marketplace by integrating regional marketplaces in North America, Europe, and Asia. CommerceOne builds and operates marketplaces for BellSouth, Singapore Telecom, and NTT DoCoMo. A typical MarketSite implementation may cost upwards of $2 million to implement. CommerceOne's intent is to weave all the disparate marketplaces into a Global Trading Web, with common standards.

Ariba Commerce Platform

Ariba, founded in 1996, is well positioned to play a significant role in the global e-commerce marketplace. In clear contrast to CommerceOne, Ariba's focus is on software enablement for its customers, and staying neutral, without aligning itself to any major players. This positioning appears to be successful, with almost 100 marketplaces in operation with Ariba's technology, compared to about 30 for CommerceOne (as of year's end 2000).

Summary

This chapter brings structural order to understanding the e-commerce world. The subject of e-commerce is so much a part of our lives and a rational discussion so necessary today that it calls for a simple, cogent framework to see all the pieces. This is no easy task as e-commerce now envelops our very interaction with the world. This will only become more so in the years to come.

In this chapter, we sought to understand and discuss e-commerce in three vertical segments—stores, exchanges, and ecosystems. Online stores are rather like retail stores and represent the earliest form of "pure play" commerce activities on the Web. Stores can exist as inventory stores, drop-ship stores, and portal stores. The distinctions were seen primarily in the form of access, ordering, shipment, payment, and delivery. Inventory stores own the inventory and, therefore, incur costs prior to reporting revenue. Drop-ship stores outsource inventory or have the manufacturers directly ship them to customers, while portal stores are like online malls that provide access to individual stores.

Exchanges are marketplaces that were discussed in terms of their method of organization: buyer exchanges, seller exchanges, horizontal exchanges, or vertical exchanges. Each type of exchange was examined in terms of the benefits offered to buyers and sellers and the pricing mechanisms they enabled. While exchanges have proliferated, only a few have succeeded. Buyer exchanges are attractive to buyers as they force sellers to compete to secure the purchase. This price competition has many suppliers scared to participate in exchanges, for it erodes pricing advantages established in offline channels. Exchanges face an uncertain future and much like the business-to-consumer (B2C) marketplace shakeout, experienced a wave of failures and consolidations. In spite of the heady promises of billions of dollars in B2B transactions through exchanges, the story so far is relatively poor. Rarely do any have even a significant percentage of their industries' revenue.

Ecosystems are marketplaces that create a complete environment for business transactions. Ecosystems go beyond merely connecting a buyer and a seller; they set up the infrastructure of services that facilitate the transaction, if necessary, on a global basis. Auxiliary services in global trade may include tax, customs, logistics, and legal services. At the present time, there are no outstanding examples of fully functional ecosystems that provide global integration, but evolutionary pressure to establishing one or more certainly exists.

Pricing Models on the Web

Supply chains evolved from the earliest days of commerce when caravans would travel throughout the known world exchanging one product for another. In some cultures, trading was an art form and a means of exchanging goods for local cash or for another commodity.

Because of the highly diverse nature of civilization and the equally dispersed distribution of raw materials, trade evolved, paced by advances in transportation and communications. Throughout the history of commerce, there are thousands of accounts of creative and ingenious methods by which traders circumvented physical, economic, and even cultural barriers to shape one commodity into useful goods and services and then establish a value through price or exchange of one finished product for another through barter.

One past analogous event that could be a precursor to today's electronic commerce emerged from caravans operated by Muslims who often used a technique called "the silent trade."

Into the 15th century, Muslim traders carried goods produced in the Middle East and Asia to Morocco, a major jumping off point for Europe that was used to tap into the riches of southern Africa. They would then move south, encountering primitive cultures along the Atlantic shores of Africa. At specially designated sites, traders would arrange goods and commodities in piles, then retreat out of sight. Local tribes who mined gold and other precious metals came to the shore and piled their gold alongside the desired product.

The natives would retreat, as had the Muslims. Then it was the Muslims' turn to approach the piles of gold and goods and either accept the offering or reduce their product to a size commensurate with their expectation. The traders then retired from view, and the process would continue on until equity was achieved.

In today's digital world we find that process tedious. It still resembles, however, our current reliance on intermediaries between producer and consumer. Ingenuity, paced by improved communications and faster transportation, is helping erode barriers to "closing the deal." Each time a distribution channel becomes dysfunctional because expenses are added to the price from too many hands, poor communications, or physical impediments, a new approach arises and goods and services once again flow to the customer with more efficiency (competitive prices and marketable quality).

Before the Industrial Revolution, the flow of attractively priced goods was simple because small shops catered to local people they knew by name and face. Manufacturers and farmers also produced locally and either sold direct or to a limited number of shops. Only a limited number of goods were available—a thimbleful of spices, metal works, and weapons—and they were sold through mediators/distributors, the forerunners of today's intermediaries in a complex supply chain.

In the early 1900s the maturation of the Industrial Revolution and the creation of mass production techniques set the stage for changes in mass marketing. Efficient production of volumes of goods created cumbersome mechanisms for distribution of goods. The addition of mediators, while inefficient, was more efficient than a manufacturer trying to go direct.

More often than not, technology dictated some of those innovations in trade. With the emergence of the Internet we now have a means to add more value to the supply chain. Throughout time, as new processes and techniques such as e-commerce come along, one facet of business remains the same: Producers of goods desire to get their products/services to consumers in as efficient a manner as possible *and realize the most attractive price for doing so.*

Pricing

One of the most profound impacts of the Web is in *pricing*, both in the rejuvenation of old pricing and distribution models and the creation of new ones. Pricing is a complex topic influenced by a host of factors, such as context of need, point of access, technology, availability of information, role of intermediary, if any, and demand-supply imbalance. The

Internet allows many of these factors to intervene directly or subtly between the buyer and the seller, producing interesting variants in the pricing process.

In this chapter, we analyze the different pricing models that e-commerce enables or works within. There are practices in the offline retail world that translate directly to online, and others that do not. This is particularly relevant because the offline retail world and most of B2B is stuck largely with a standardized, fixed price model that has its origins over 150 years ago and is the prevailing method in most developed countries. Such rigidity of pricing excludes other business models that might be advantageous to both buyer and seller.

The fixed price model, and its evil twin, flat rates, are now so much a part of the Internet that breaking their grip could be difficult in some business sectors. Fixed price is more likely to be found in the product community; flat rate pricing is a phenomenon we see every day in the service community, notably among ISPs. In fixed price, the buyer pays the same price for the same product as every other buyer does.

In flat rate pricing, which is even older than fixed price, buyers pay a set amount for a service, though some may get more or less service than others. In other words, the less frequent user ends up subsidizing the more frequent user.

AOL, Netcom, and others introduced flat rates of $19.95 for monthly ISP services in the early days of the Internet in what was thought to be a move toward democratization of the online fee model. Firmly entrenched fixed price scenarios are being tested by Priceline and others who are tinkering with variations in auctions, specifically in the name-your-price areas. Both fixed price and flat rates are vulnerable for what they are and what they are not, which is the subject of this chapter.

Online B2C pricing is destined to come in different hues, depending on the customer, the merchant, and the context of sale—as it often is in B2B! Pricing flexibility may provide for rapid movement of inventory, enable volume discounts, or facilitate sales by removing customer objections. Movement on any of these fronts could spell the end for "static pricing," much like Ford's original offering of a single color for an automobile, namely black, which faded because of market pressures.

As we enter the third millennium, different business models, paced by technological changes, can alter the pricing mix that saddles online commerce. As we note throughout this book, online business ventures must be viewed and understood as pieces in the overall commerce machine. They are not isolated parts. Pricing issues affect both online and offline situations, and the distinction between these situations is becoming less and less clear.

To a browser, online shopping is distinctly different than driving to a store. However, consider when a customer places an online pricing query for a gift, while driving down the freeway. Based on the result of the query, let's hypothesize that her response to the responding stores is, "I will buy this toy if your price is less than $100." Depending on which store responds, she commits to the merchant and then takes an appropriate freeway exit to pick up the gift-wrapped toy. In this situation, the store dynamically over-rides its retail price to attract an online customer.

No discussion of online or offline pricing can occur in a vacuum. In this chapter, we also discuss the nature of markets and identify the validity of different pricing models on those various markets. We also contrast offline pricing to available online pricing models. The objective here is to raise the possibility of alternate pricing models, finding a home in offline situations as they merge with online commerce. Finally, we look at each pricing model and illustrate how demand affects price.

The Nature of Markets and Determination of Pricing

We categorize markets under the following four categories (from the perspective of buyer and seller):

- **Controlled Markets:** Neither the buyer nor seller has much control, as the prices are set by a third party. This arises when a third party, such as the government, has control in setting minimum and maximum prices of scarce goods, or regulating the price of utilities so that a social good may be achieved.
- **Monopolistic/Oligopolistic Markets:** Here, sellers have all the power and the buyer mostly has the option not to purchase. These markets may arise due to concentration of supply in the hands of one or more producers, which arise when there is overwhelming market superiority, like Microsoft; or a government restricts competition, which happens in developing countries to protect local industries. Another "sanctioned" instance very close to the online world is in how the communications industry is regulated: two or three cellular providers are licensed in a region, one or two cable TV firms are granted franchises in a community, and a small (and ever shrinking) number of telephone services are authorized by a postal service (Europe) or FCC (U.S.).

- **Competitive Markets:** In such markets, the buyer has more power and may exercise it in many ways. Consumers may reward emerging merchants, may or may not be faithful to brands, and may look for alternate channels to achieve pricing advantages. The current online world is responsible for significant growth in these markets.
- **Efficient Markets:** This constitutes a "nirvana," which is mutually beneficial to buyers and sellers. Pricing varies dynamically, driven by demand and supply imbalances and not to information inequity or channel isolation. In this theoretical world, all merchants and customers have equal access to each other, and this access is predicated on the power of the information infrastructure. The downside of efficient markets? Commoditization of any offering sold in an efficient market.

In Figure 7.1, you can see the interplay of buyer and seller power.

The following pricing mechanisms exist in one form or another in these four different markets:

- Fixed Price—Seller fixes price and buyer pays that price
- Name Your Price—Buyer names a price and seller accepts or rejects

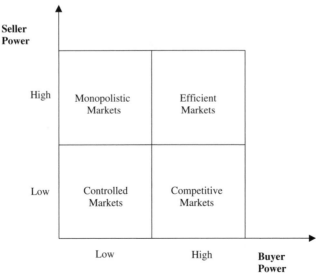

Figure 7.1 Categorization of Markets

- Negotiated Price—Buyer and seller interact to reach a mutual agreement
- Auctions—Price set by competitive bidding. These can be either "Seller's Auctions," where multiple buyers compete with each other, or "Buyer's Auctions," where multiple sellers compete to acquire an order
- Barter—Indirect pricing in the form of exchange of goods or services
- Dynamic Exchanges—A bid/ask system that dynamically moderates prices

Fixed price, as noted above, is the most common form of pricing that we see daily on the shelves of retail stores. However, fixed pricing has not always held such a dominant sway in the sale of goods and services. In many countries, particularly those less developed, it is quite common encountering other pricing mechanisms such as haggling (a form of negotiated purchasing) and bartering (exchange of goods or services).

In offline retail, control resides with the seller, whose price pressure comes almost solely from neighboring competition. There are a few instances of price definition by the buyer, as in government contracts, where sealed bids are opened. Negotiated pricing for services, particularly in single buyer-single seller situations, is quite common.

Auctions in the offline world are popular in specialized environments where there can be an aggregation of buyers. Typical examples are for antiques, cars, cattle, broadcast rights, etc.

Barter trade is still quite common globally, even among nations. For instance, Russia might sell oil in return for food grain.

Finally, dynamic exchanges are most visible in the financial markets, as in the pricing of stocks and bonds.

In all these different variants, price is determined by who has the *relative power* in the transaction, the buyer or the seller. As seller power increases, price tends to rise. Conversely, as buyer power increases, prices fall. The online buyer may find the same product at different price levels, depending on the context established between the buyer and seller.

If the buyer enters an online mall of a specific merchant, the seller is in control and fixed price may be the norm. If the buyer goes to a shopping engine, then comparative pricing may force pricing pressure and a better price, putting the buyer *and* an infomediary in power. If the buyer participates in a buying consortium, which may or may not be set up as a reverse auction, participating merchants may compete on price for a guaranteed volume of sale, a model followed by many B2B buyers and sellers.

The online world, in a very complementary way, provides buyers and sellers with a new environment where even anonymously they can "level the playing field" and *almost* eliminate the power struggle between the parties. With information and technology, buyers are better armed to extract preferential pricing under the right circumstances.

Customer efficiency arises in these new markets from the rapid and accurate spread of information: Customers can reduce their search costs and connect quickly with the best vendor. The result of this consumer efficiency is more rapidly expanding global markets.

In general, the stock market is considered to be a model of efficiency, with dynamically set prices governed by demand and supply of stocks for a given company. The underlying presumption here is that the information is equitably available to the parties. This notion of efficiency is questionable, because the individual investor is rarely on the same information playing field as the manager of a multibillion dollar stock fund!

For these various pricing models, relative buyer and seller power translates into pricing pressures, as shown in Figure 7.2.

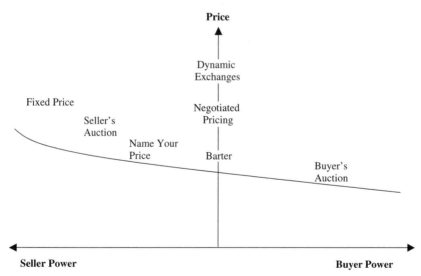

Figure 7.2 Price Variation Relative to Buyer and Seller Power for Different Transaction Models

Not all pricing models may be applicable to every buyer-seller interaction. Table 7.1 suggests suitable pricing models for three distinct market types: business-to-business, business-to-consumer, and consumer-to-consumer.

As a side note, any business looking for distinctive competence in the market should explore any and all of these pricing models, but should not let price, per se, be the sole factor for competitive advantage. It is far better to stress value and have a pricing mechanism support it than curry favor with customers solely on the basis of the lowest price. As we see time and time again, low price leadership is ephemeral and costly.

Table 7.1 shows three business environments and the likelihood of their applicability to various transaction mechanisms.

In Table 7.1, only a few pricing mechanisms are considered "unlikely," which suggests that there is still a tremendous opportunity for expansion of different pricing mechanisms to e-commerce, rather than blindly transposing offline selling mechanisms online.

Table 7.2 brings to life many variations on fixed pricing and flat fees in our three different market environments, B2B, B2C, and C2C. Note that there is a standard and accepted pricing model followed by some that are on the horizon that may or may not have enough traction to be applied by whomever has market power—buyer or seller!

In these cases, the difficult part is not the technology associated with enabling alternate pricing mechanisms. More often, it has to do with the complexity of formulating and administering policies associated with multiple pricing mechanisms. Offline retail might have a simple fixed price system in place, with items tagged by price. If the store has an online outlet that provides an alternate pricing system where the "Name Your Price" alternative is enabled, that merchant needs business rules to handle both pricing mechanisms.

In the section that follows, we present the seven primary transaction types and show their relationship to pricing online.

Fixed Price

This is the most common pricing model in the offline retail world, particularly in the developed countries, and has achieved dominant status over the last half of the twentieth

Table 7.1 B2B, B2C, and C2C Pricing

	Business–to-Business	*Business–to-Consumer*	*Consumer–to-Consumer*
Fixed Price	The common form of pricing online and offline	Most common form of pricing for both retail and e-commerce	Found rarely, and usually on classi - fied posting sites such as Yahoo!
Name Your Price	Viable in supplier situations; not common so far in e-commerce	Patented by *Priceline.com;* most prevalent in travel	Not common, but can be a variant on classified and auction sales
Seller Auctions	Commonly found, particularly for inventory disposal	Increasingly common on many merchant sites	Common on sites such as eBay, Yahoo! auctions
Buyer Auctions	Large scale buyer-side aggregation, such as at commodities-based exchanges	Tentative emergence of buyer aggregations are arising at *Volumebuy.com* and *Freemarkets.com*	Unlikely
Negotiated	Common in the offline world, and being explored in extranets and through personal exchanges via email	Uncommon but may be viable for purchase of expensive goods	Viable with suitable negotiating work flow
Barter	Enormous scope exists in this space but needs a trusted intermediary	Unlikely	Not common now but viable as a component of Name Your Price (in barter terms for goods or service)
Dynamic Exchange	Growing number of commodities achieving dynamic pricing through exchanges	Theoretically viable under large-scale consumer aggregation for highly standardized goods	Unlikely

Table 7.2 Pricing Mechanisms by Market Environment

Marketplace	Examples	Typical Pricing Mechanisms	Additional Viable Pricing Mechanisms
B2C: Auto Service	Auto repair, painting	Fixed Price	Name Your Price Negotiated
B2C: Retail Store	Furniture, clothes, fashion goods	Fixed Price	Name Your Price Seller Auctions Negotiated
B2B: Human Services	Implementation, Consulting, Maintenance, Operations, Testing	Fixed Price Negotiated	Name Your Price Barter
B2B: OEM Manufacturer	Computer power supply, monitors, machinery components	Fixed Price Negotiated	Seller Auctions Name Your Price
C2C: Human Services	Services such as gardening, child care, etc.	Fixed Price	Name Your Price Negotiated Barter
C2C: Classifieds	Used goods sale	Fixed Price Seller Auctions	Name Your Price Negotiated

century. The fixed pricing model is biased towards the seller. The buyer of goods is disadvantaged for the following reasons:

- Lack of information on seller's margin, inventory, or cost of inventory
- Potential lack of information on alternative offerings due to constraints of geography or time
- Lack of buyer aggregation to request a consideration for "aggregated bulk purchasing" for a lower price

This pricing model is not efficient online or offline because it moderates the transaction on the basis of a single dimension, namely price, for each prospective customer. The seller has an illusory advantage in each specific transaction, which is shown in Figure 7.3.

Offline, fixed pricing makes sense for the following reasons:

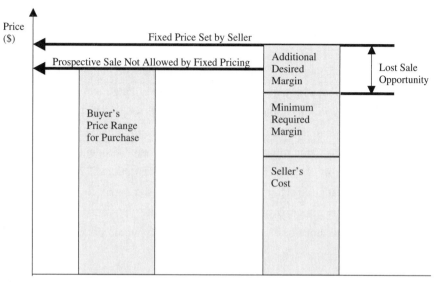

Figure 7.3 Lost Sale Opportunity with Fixed Pricing Mechanism

- Uniform pricing (as at a grocery store) requires no seller-buyer interaction on price; this minimizes floor personnel required to handle customer interactions, which produces operational efficiencies for store management.
- There are very few means to relate in-store price to alternate marginally cheaper offerings by competitors. The most popular is unit pricing at grocery stores.
- Sales obtained are on seller's terms and this often preserves desired product margins.
- Fixed published prices produce price stability in markets for packaged groceries and many travel services. In other words, all merchants tend to offer relatively the same prices in a geographical area. Price wars affect all adversely.

However, as shown in Figure 7.3, there is tremendous potential for lost sales. Sellers withhold an acceptable price range to protect a "desired additional margin." Fixed pricing is under a severe threat in the e-commerce world because:

- Prospective buyers have the ability to search competitively on prices offered by various sellers for the same merchandise.

- Given product standardization and the choice of trustworthy (brand power!) sellers, customer preference to a seller at a higher price is unlikely (unless the brand and service justify it).
- Online customers are increasingly aware of their newfound power to influence price and are demanding more favorable alternate pricing models.
- With the proliferation of online merchants, fixed price models have to coexist with other models. In such a coexistence, the fixed price likely becomes a reserve price, as in the auction model. Then the competition has immediate market information to alter its pricing. If one merchant prices an item at $279.99, a competitor can pick up that price electronically and offer the same item for less. The new breed of software pricing robots is helping consumers automate price comparisons on a continuous basis, putting additional pressure on price-sensitive merchants.

Name Your Price (Bid/Ask)

In this model, the seller invites the buyer to ask and "name your price" and the seller then responds with a bid implying acceptance or rejection of that offer from a buyer. This model is an improvement on the fixed price model because the buyer has an opportunity to indicate additional points of negotiation, namely, time and availability: "I am *now* ready to buy *if you have the item* and it can be sold to me at this price." The seller retains discretion of accepting or passing on the selling opportunity, and weighs the offer against desirability of the customer and margin.

Figure 7.4 shows how the "Name Your Price" model plays out in the real world with the interplay of bid/ask on margin.

This was the basis for Priceline's patent on its model. Originally introduced for airline fares, Priceline worked as follows: When the customer named an offer price, the software model looked up a database of airline flights for the proposed travel and reviewed the prices quoted by each airline to Priceline. This was done on a nightly basis, not in real time. Priceline then accepted or rejected the customer offer by reviewing each valid airline price against the customer offer.

Priceline has since extended this model to other hospitality services, including hotels, rental cars, vacation tours, etc. In all cases, the model remains the same for Price-

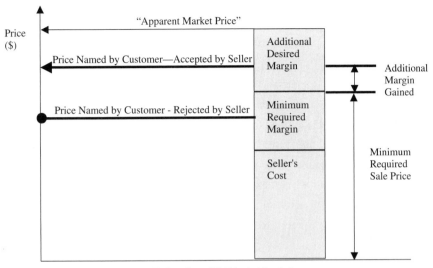

Figure 7.4 "Name Your Price," or Bid/Ask Model

line, which obtains prices from vendors who establish the minimum reserve price for the product.

The "Name Your Price" model is favorable to the seller and adverse to the buyer in the following ways:

- Buyer has no knowledge of seller's reserve prices
- Buyer may be ignorant or desperate, and may propose prices higher than necessary
- Process is cumbersome and inefficient for the buyer, forcing multiple trials
- Buyer loses any collective bargaining power
- Seller can block out availability of products from the open market and force buyers to compete under adverse circumstances. As an illustration, consider that all seats for a sports event start out openly available, and then 50 percent are "presold" or "preallocated" to a "Name your Price" merchant. In the latter case, there is then a possibility that a "perception of scarcity" could force higher prices above what the "full price" vendor intended. The second vendor extracts profits from subsequent buyers in the "Name Your Price" model. Offline this is called scalping.

Negotiated Pricing

Negotiated pricing in the offline world occurs in many contexts:

- Open market environments (farmers' markets, trade fairs, garage sales)
- Supply constrained situations (limited inventory, excess inventory, clearance)
- Selective demand situations (required volume, sequenced demand)
- Multidimensional purchases (product purchase is linked to support, delivery schedule, other sidebar deals, which is a crucial part of B2B—it's called terms and conditions and it can make or break many a multimillion dollar sale)
- Trial purchases (limited trial, early product testing—a.k.a. sampling, beta testing)
- Strategic relationship between buyer and seller, most often seen in B2B

Negotiating pricing is often a dance. Buyer and seller alternate with lower or higher bids as they seek an equilibrium point between supply and demand at that moment. This process is illustrated in Figure 7.5.

Often, pricing negotiations are multidimensional, involving price and other variables such as when the seller proposes a price, conditionally: "If you take 1,000 units, I might be able to give you a 10 percent break on price." The buyer, on the other hand, may come back

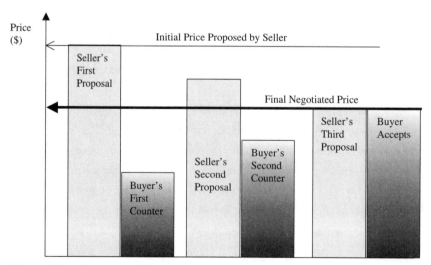

Figure 7.5　Negotiated Pricing Agreements

with a different dimensional play: "I have an alternate seller who is willing to sell 500 units at 15 percent discount, and is willing to provide on-site service for no charge."

Multidimensional negotiations are an aspect of social interaction between parties, particularly in the B2B world. Software and automation of such complex processes may be interesting, but are far more difficult to achieve than direct contact or emailing between the parties!

At a simpler level, imagine software negotiation agents that can negotiate on a two-dimensional level, such as on quantity and price. Algorithms for such two-dimensional negotiations may be easy to achieve based on a scale of price and volume on both the seller side and buyer side, but the real dynamics arise in the style of negotiation between buyer and seller, which adds zest to the negotiation.

Figure 7.6 depicts how this plays out, graphically. Nothing, however, can depict the dynamics when personalities are added, and this is closer to achievement in an interactive online environment where the give and take cannot be automated—yet.

These software based "pricebots," which can carry buyer's and seller's algorithms of price-volume and other boundaries, might enormously simplify negotiations and achieve considerable efficiency. Such software negotiations may allow each side to reveal their solution patterns selectively and offer a preliminary basis for an agreement. The buyer and

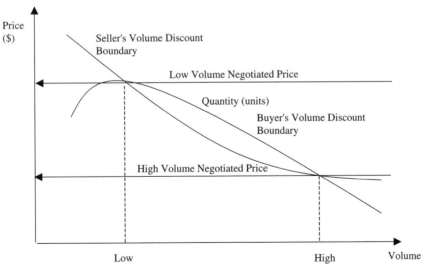

Figure 7.6   Negotiated Price at Low and High Volume Points

the seller can then ratify that agreement without potentially winning or losing face. Those pricebots are beginning to emerge, particularly in B2B e-commerce, to eliminate some considerations and qualify buyers, but wider use is still limited by the functionality.

The "Negotiated Price" model is mutually beneficial to the buyer and the seller when:

- Sellers are usually willing to discount to sell more goods
- Buyers are willing to secure advantageous pricing even though it might mean volume pricing
- Both sides achieve their mutual objectives and derive satisfaction from the deal
- Successful negotiations often lead to long-term contracts and a buyer-seller partnership
- The customer is ennobled and made a participant in a community (see Chapter 5, "The Community Stack"), which in turn spreads via viral marketing and makes the merchant more important to the community

Auctions

An auction is a dynamic price-setting mechanism, governed by the premise of limited supply or limited demand. eBay launched consumer auctions just a few years ago and it ignited an explosive growth of consumer-to-consumer, business-to-consumer, and business-to-business auctions. Forrester Research anticipates the online auction economy can grow from $1.4 billion in 1998 to almost $20 billion in 2003, with two-thirds being due to business-to-consumer auctions.

Auctions offer the following features:

- Reflections of a sparse supply or limited need
- Limited quantity transaction model
- Defined separation from alternate sales channels
- Competitive environment that encourages market activity
- Pricing model that changes with activity
- Efficiency of operations leading to a low cost model

Arguably, online auctions are one of the most interesting and compelling transaction devices on the Internet. In effect, there is an ongoing dynamic price adjustment based on real supply and demand. Online auctions widen the opportunity for participation by buyers and sellers. In such a situation, online auctions are a popular device that sets prices and provides several social benefits to consumers and sellers, unlike offline auctions or other price setting mechanisms. For the merchant, captive localized inventory can be released, and dormant unexpressed needs can be satisfied.

Dynamic growth in auctions is most noticeable in consumer-to-consumer auctions, which are displacing a lot of revenue that was generated by newspapers supporting classifieds and garage sales. Auctions are often the primary *used goods exchange vehicle* in certain markets.

How important is this to others beyond businesses or consumers with goods and services for sale? Classified ads are an important part of a newspaper's profit structure. The advent of eBay, Amazon, and others is forcing offline media that depend on classifieds to adjust their pricing and operating models to compete with online auctions! Some local newspapers are turning part of their online presences into auctions, knowing that they run the risk of cannibalizing sales offline, but keeping the revenue stream from other online auctions.

Variations on the many themes in auctions are also making headway in areas such as mortgages, insurance, new stock market issues, sales of domain names, real estate, car sales, business procurement, software development and contracted services, just to name a few.

Online auctions offer the following advantages:

- Price adjustment to adjudicate demand and supply (to a limited extent). Auctions provide price flexibility in response to demand from parties to the auction.
- Enable interactivity to a sale (particularly as distinct from fixed prices).
- Enable efficient clearing of inventory goods.
- Can be used as an alternate channel even for new goods.
- Greater participation of buyers improves auction quality.
- Online information sharing reduces fraud, which is the bane of auctions.
- Parties can participate from any global location.

The following disadvantages or current risks should be noted too:

- Auctions may be hostile to buyers or sellers. As noted earlier, auctions are inherently hostile to one party. In a seller's auction, the buyers are disadvantaged and compete with each other for the sale, rather than with the buyer. They compete with each other to provide the maximum benefit to the seller. The reverse is true for the buyer's auction, where the sellers are disadvantaged.

- The excitement of the auction may carry bidders away, and they might end up paying more than the legitimate value of the item. Impulse purchases like this are part of the online mystique and we cover them in greater detail in Chapter 9, "Application of Business Models." Competition to win the scarce item in a seller's auction or the purchase order in a buyer's auction, on the basis of price alone, produces the winner's curse of having "paid" the highest of all bidders. But this could also reflect perception of increased value, as with a painting from Sotheby's or Christy's.

- Collusions among buyers or sellers could skew the results of an auction. Elaborate auction strategies are propagated on the Web, and collusive bidding may be unfair and adversely affect some participants.

- Seller may not have the product indicated or may not ship the product. In C2C auctions, such as eBay where sellers post products for auctions, there is no guarantee the product is actually available and in good condition. Furthermore, there are cases of sellers accepting the money and not shipping the merchandise or shipping defective ones. This has already happened on commercial auction sites, leaving the sites exposed to lawsuits. Escrow services and appraisers are emerging as an important pair of online community services. Some are separate business lines maintained by eBay and others.

- Buyer may not pay after winning, leaving the seller stranded. Again, this is partly remediated by implementation of escrow services. Otherwise, the seller might believe that the auction is complete and waits in vain for the buyer to complete the transaction. Similarly, buyer's remorse or other motivations may cause the "winner" to back off from the transaction.

- Quantities available may be deliberately minimized to imply a shortage of supply, leading to a feeding frenzy. It is not uncommon to break up the available supply into multiple auction slots, thereby boosting demand for the items.

- Auction items may be stolen, in questionable taste, or otherwise illegal. Human organs, WWII weapons, and fake antiques are frequently offered on the prominent auction sites, generating more than enough negative publicity for all concerned. The more prominent the auction site and the greater the volume of goods, the more difficult it becomes to police the items offered, though Yahoo! is responding to public pressure by banning Nazi items from its auctions.

• Transaction fees to an intermediary may be hefty. This reduces net proceeds to the seller, who clearly has to evaluate the trade-offs to alternate ways of selling.

Most of these issues represent fraudulent or unethical business practices on the part of the seller, not the host of the auction site, per se. As so often happens in the online space, one party (buyer, seller, or infomediary) operates outside the pale of acceptable practices and ruins the reputation of all others involved. Unfortunately, as in the offline world, this is difficult to defend.

There are three dimensions to auctions, starting with the most specific and ending with the most general:

1. Auction Environments: Consumer-to-Consumer, Business-to-Consumer, and Business-to-Business
2. Auction Styles: English, Dutch, sealed bid, etc.
3. Auction Types: buyer or seller

Auction Environments

The most visible and dynamic auctions are in the consumer-to-consumer space with the launch and explosive acceptance of eBay. Here is a market with an ever-growing inventory of consumer purchases accumulating in the home. Disposing of these items through classified advertisements and garage sales has a very limited scope and reach, leading to low transactional volumes.

eBay introduced a categorization and auction engine, and suddenly C2C sales were international or national in reach and comprehensive in scope. Furthermore, the perception of bargains on eBay is creating an addicted online population who craves the action and excitement of putting up items for auction or bidding for goods.

Merchants and would-be garage shop businesses see this as an opportunity to move into such a consumer environment and use these auction sites to dispose of slow-to-move goods from inventory. Auction formats are being adopted by B2B, but at a much slower rate. Table 7.3 depicts the dynamics of auctions in C2C, B2C, and B2B.

Table 7.3   Characteristics of Auctions in C2C, B2C, and B2B Contexts

	Consumer-to-Consumer	Business-to-Consumer	Business-to-Business
Relevance	Sells one-of-a kind items and used goods	Alternate sales channel Clearance items Generates excitement	Commodity products Competitive bidding Efficient procurement
Information Quality	Low to high	High	High
Seller Auction	Yes	Yes	Less likely
Buyer Auction	Less likely	Yes	Yes
Quantity Available	Very low (often one or two items)	Higher than C2C	Low to medium
Automation Desired	Low to high	High	High
Interactivity Desired	Low to high	Low	Low
Sense of Community	Very high	Low	Low
Need for Intermediary	High	Low	High
Trust Basis	Other buyers and sellers	Merchant	Intermediary
Potential for Fraud	High	Low to moderate	Low

Auction Styles

There are several different auction models emerging online, however, the three dominant and most popular ones are:

- The English auction
- The Dutch auction
- The First Price Sealed Bid auction

The English Auction

This is the most traditional auction type and still the most common. In the offline world, traditional auction houses use this model to sell works of art, antiques, etc. (see

Figure 7.7). The auctioneer, on behalf of the seller, sets a minimum reserve price on the item and solicits a counter higher bid in an open outcry model. The counter bid is then followed by a subsequent higher bid and so on, until there are no further bidders. The sale is then completed to the last bidder at the highest price bid.

The online adoption of the English auction has some interesting themes. First, in the B2C and C2C space there is a conscious attempt to build buying excitement, creating a carnival-like atmosphere. In the offline world, there are previews of products, and even great quantities of publicity by the auctioneer beforehand.

Second, a virtual community is constructed with messaging, email, chat, and commentary. Third, a game-like scenario is created, with "winning" being an important aspect, as distinct from "price-value." Both environments are not without means by which the unscrupulous can manipulate outcomes.

Finally, there is continuity, an endless gambling environment with electronic addiction where the next round is always ready to begin—often with the same competitors involved.

The English auction is severely adverse to the buyer for the following reasons:

- The seller is in full control and can intervene to stimulate the auction
- Buyers compete with each other, rather than negotiate with the seller

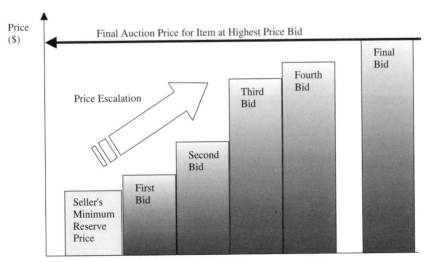

Figure 7.7 English Auction

- Competition often produces "unreasonable" price escalation
- The auction implies a shortage of availability on which basis a price escalation can be presumed. However, this demand-supply imbalance is often artificial and strictly contextual to a given auction
- Open outcry system can produce tampering such as non-serious bids and seller-spiked bids
- Final winner purchases the product at the highest price
- The seller reaps the benefit of a buyer's tussle to obtain the product

Table 7.4 shows auction issues a merchant faces in online and offline environments.

Table 7.4 Auction Issues

Function	Offline Auctions	Online Auctions
Reserve price	Benefits seller	Benefits seller
Number of items for sale in this auction.	Limited because of time available to conclude an auction in hours, at most a day. Land auctions some-times spread over several days.	Unlimited. At any one time eBay might have as many as a million items in the auction queue.
Number of similar auctions for same item.	Limited. Unique items, such as art or a parcel of land, are one-of-a-kind. Professional diligence limits fraudulence in multi-posting.	Unlimited number of compet-ing auctions. Seller might post same item in several auctions and wait out best bid. Auction sites are begin-ning to institute many mea-sures to combat against these practices.
Duration of auction (number of days or hours).	Usually a period of viewing precedes the auction, and this is a "community" event for participants.	Community arises during and after the bidding process among buyers.
Number of bids.	Limited to audience at hand, or mail-in process.	Unlimited.

(continued)

Table 7.4 Auction Issues (*continued*)

Function	Offline Auctions	Online Auctions
Bidding rate/number per hour.	Limited to ability of auctioneer to manage bidding process.	Unlimited.
Interactivity between bidders and sellers (messaging, email, collusion).	Very high, if seller is present and called upon to provide information about the offering.	Low and discouraged by auction sites. When interactivity exists, it is usually between sellers or buyers, not across the line.
Final bid price.	Function of how long auctioneer can keep interest flowing, preparation of collateral materials, pre-auction "buzz" for high-profile items.	Independent of auctioneer. Based almost exclusively on popularity of the item. There is little either party can do because of volume and amorphous nature of the audience to inflate or deflate pricing. Comes closest to pure supply and demand influences.
Margin.	Margins from sale can be quite high on large ticket items. Auctioneers have high margins for their efforts.	Because of sheer volume of low-ticket transactions and approaching garage sale proportions, margins to both parties are low. eBay and others make up for low margins by charging minimums for posting.

The Dutch Auction

As shown in Figure 7.8, the auctioneer sets the highest expected reserve price for the item and then solicits a response. If there is no bidder, the price is then lowered to see if there is a bidder. The auction continues until there is one bidder and the auction concludes with a sale to that bidder.

Online adoption of the Dutch auction is much slower than the English auction. It lacks interactivity and there is a complete lack of information on the behavior of the other potential participants.

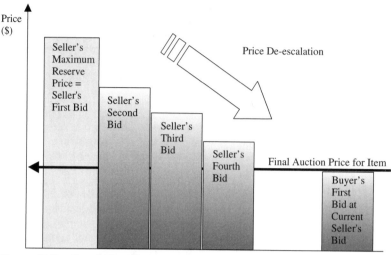

Figure 7.8   Dutch Auction

First Price Sealed Bid Auction

In this auction model (Figure 7.9), bidders submit sealed secret bids, all at one time. There is no allowance for modification of the bid once submitted. The sealed bids are opened and the winner is the highest bidder.

In this model, there is considerable risk of over-bidding because there is no information at all, either from the seller's side, as in the Dutch auction, or from the buyer's side, as in the English auction. Government contracts are awarded this way offline and, because of this, there may be some instances of Sealed Bid auctions as governments become more accustomed to the online environment for working with the business community.

There is also a Vickrey auction, which operates somewhat similar to this. In addition, some government agencies apply what is called an "average auction." The agency sets a price point based on average high to low bids and then grants the contract to the one closest to that average.

Auction Types

At the most abstract level, there are two types of auctions: seller's and buyer's auctions.

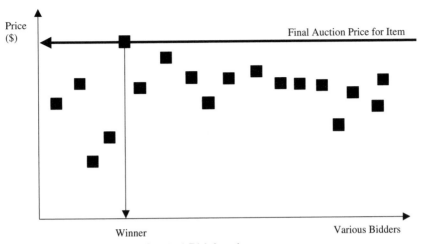

Figure 7.9   First Price Sealed Bid Auction

Seller's Auction

A seller offers to sell a product (in limited quantities). Multiple buyers then vie for the product and bid against each other. Based on the rules of the auction model, the winner is determined.

In general, this process gives the product to the buyer who values the product the most. In a Forward auction, the seller controls the rules, how long an auction runs, the volume or how much quantity is offered, and the openness (are the competitive bids open for viewing or are they closed?). Online, the third-party intermediary controls the clock and sets the bidding rules, etc.

Seller's auctions are common in the offline world for antique items, excess inventory, or items whose values are only determined through the competitive eyes of would-be beholders.

In the online world, however, auctions are increasingly being used as a basis to make a sale for items that are not necessarily scarce or unique. Seller auctions are relatively straightforward to set up. Auction software is readily available to install and many online stores have auctions, in addition to regular fixed price sale formats.

Figure 7.10 shows how a Forward auction works.

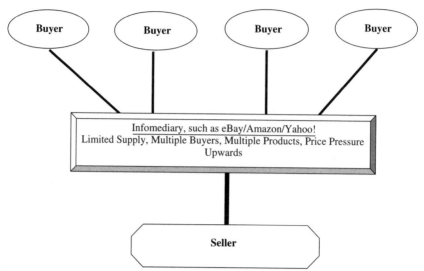

Figure 7.10 Forward Auction

Buyer's Auction

An individual buyer, a large company, or a group of buyers offers to buy a product in stated quantities (see Figure 7.11). Multiple sellers then vie to supply the product and bid against each other. The sale goes to the merchant who most aggressively wants to sell the product.

Such an auction is controlled by the buyer or by the buyer's intermediary. A reverse auction is mostly an Internet invention because it needs the following elements to come together: an aggregation of merchants willing to supply identical products, an accumulation of buyers for specific items, and a process to interface the two parties.

That process is technology, our Internet platform.

Sellers often dislike this model when they have higher margin products because it "commoditizes" their value, while at the same time it levels the playing field among suppliers. Suppliers are forced to compete for the sale on particular items that might fare better outside of the auction process.

Typically, larger merchants are adverse to playing, while the smaller ones, with smaller marketing budgets and lower influence, are eager to participate. This model is

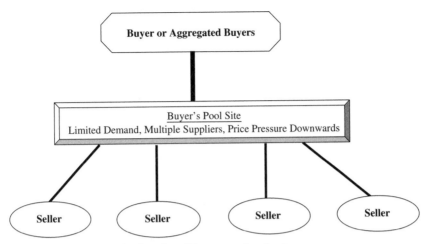

Figure 7.11 Buyer's Auction (Reverse Auction)

good for products that are easy to describe, standardized in terms of features, and do not have complex delivery or servicing requirements.

Table 7.5 contrasts the buyer's and seller's auction.

Barter

The Web is enabling a truly ancient trading mechanism, the barter, to make its comeback. Barter is perhaps the oldest method of exchanging goods and services. The carpenter trades labor for obtaining a sack of rice from the farmer, and so on.

Barter exchanges typically are local and suffer from the lack of portability of the goods or service being exchanged. For example, a farmer in one village cannot easily barter for services in another village. A standard currency resolves this issue: it is able to transmute value between multiple buyers and sellers in isolated transactions.

Barter can be a basis of trade between countries and organizations. Trade between the former Soviet bloc countries was often based on an exchange of goods: one province delivered coal, another processed steel, a third delivered automobiles, and so on. Instead of monetizing each transaction, suitable bartering arrangements were established.

Table 7.5   Characteristics of Seller's and Buyer's Auctions

	Seller's Auction (Forward Auction)	**Buyer's Auction (Reverse Auction)**
Mechanism	Floor price set by the bidder. Bidders compete against "scarce" supply	Ceiling price set by buyer. Sellers compete against "scarce" demand
Role of Intermediary	Encourages higher prices	Encourages lower prices
Commission of Intermediary	Percent of sale and incentives based on sales price; often posting fee	Percent of sale
Price Pressure	Upwards	Downwards
General Comment	Hostile to buyers "Winner's Curse" effect	Hostile to sellers
Proper Role	Scarce items Consumer-Consumer Used goods	Multiple sellers in a competitive market. Aggregated buying environments for schools, co-ops, etc.

Similarly, large corporations have established such agreements in both domestic and international environments.

Three kinds of barter systems can be recognized:

1. Direct Barter
2. Pseudo Cash Barter
3. Brokered Barter

Direct Barter

In a direct barter system, both parties are buyer and seller. They exchange a specific set of goods or services without the medium of a standard currency, such as dollars or pounds. For example, one company may provide 100 desks to another company in exchange for 150 chairs. The deal concludes with no residual transactional carryover to another deal. As is obvious, taxing authorities have problems with this method of exchange.

Table 7.6 lists some of the advantages and disadvantages of a direct barter system.

Table 7.6 Advantages and Disadvantages of Direct Barter

Advantages	Disadvantages
One-to-one negotiation	May not be competitive; exchange pricing of both sets of goods may not reflect market conditions
Transactional simplicity; easily recorded for accounting purposes	May not be fully utilizable; what if Company A wants to sell 100 desks, but Company B can only use 80?
No cash outlay, invoicing, or collection issues	Pricing and negotiation complexity

Pseudo-Cash Barter

E-commerce is spawning many new variants of "digital cash," all with one principle in mind: make it easier for consumers to conduct safe and secure transactions online. In this model, virtual or pseudo-cash, like Flooz or Beenz, is created. Many industry pundits feel that when customers become more accustomed to using relatively safe media of exchange, they spend more online. Many of these pseudo-cash mechanisms are designed to facilitate small sales as well.

This is good in theory, but often the media of exchange are cumbersome and/or carry other features that make them less desirable than traditional media: credit cards, purchase orders, etc.

To instill trust in the auction process, for example, eBay offers PayPal *(www. paypal.com)*, an email money transfer system that is now part of x.com *(www.x.com)*, an

Baseline Measurements for Barter Exchanges

1. Number of participatory merchants
2. Business categories covered by the exchange
3. Total products listed
4. Registration, support, and transactional fees
5. Average selling product margin (for selling merchant)
6. Average purchasing product margin (for buying merchant)
7. Eventual liquidity into normal currencies
8. Currencies available for exchange

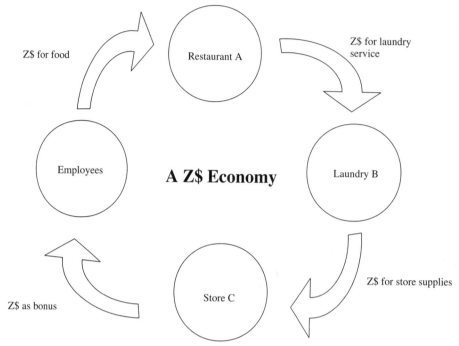

Figure 7.12   Pseudo-Cash Barter Economy

online bank. Customers set up accounts with all parties and transfer cash back and forth between the bank and their online wallet. Various payment mechanisms and accounts can be used, including both major credit cards and debit cards. PayPal, like many participating in the alternative cash environment, receive their compensation on the basis of earning interest on cash in the float.

For our purposes, we'll call ours Z$. For a community of participants (individuals, businesses) participating in this transaction model, the Z$ becomes the basis of acquiring goods and services, as illustrated in Figure 7.12.

Naturally, this is not much different than a traditional cash economy. Table 7.7 lists the pros and cons of such a structure.

It should be noted that these are fundamentally similar to airline frequent flyer points, which allow a cashless transaction (reward to customer for patronage) to be extended to the purchase of other goods and services such as airline flights, hotel stays, etc.

Table 7.7 Advantages and Disadvantages of a Pseudo-Cash Barter System

Advantages	Disadvantages
Community centric, bonding merchant, and customer alike to each other	Not usable outside community
Extends barter transaction to multiple players	Not all goods and service providers in community may participate
Builds integration between local merchants	Adds accounting complexity for taxes and reporting
Reduces or eliminates the need for credit cards and other media of exchange that can be criminally taken	Customers may have little faith in alternative currencies
Facilitates small transactions that are too expensive for merchants when credit cards are used	Too many small, "facilitated," transactions carry with them the expectation of free shipping and other perks normally associated with online purchases

Brokered Barter

Brokered barter transactions, which exist in the offline world, are now mushrooming in the online world. Thousands of U.S. companies barter. There are more than 4,000 barter exchanges in place, transacting over $10 billion worth of revenues annually to serve them.

An online barter exchange works on the principle of a large community of businesses that have enough in common on the aggregate. Such a community gains strength as more businesses join. The potential benefit to all accrues when more goods and services can be transacted within the barter exchange.

The basis of the transaction may itself be fixed price or negotiated between the parties. The barter exchange may also set up auctions or other market mechanisms to enable sales.

As shown in Figure 7.13, the barter exchange recruits members and collects subscription fees and monthly fees in cash. It loads the value of the individual member's inventory that they want to barter with into the master barter exchange database. Exchange merchants then "buy" goods or services using their account balance. The barter exchange collects real cash in the form of registration fees, support fees, and a transaction fee for each purchase.

Various online services are springing up to conduct barter exchanges. Their distant cousin is the micropayment. Each normal transaction is sliced into little pieces and every

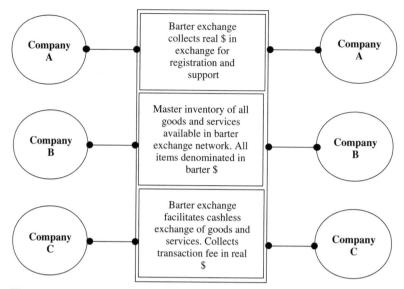

Figure 7.13   A Barter Exchange System

service that participates takes a small portion. Ostensibly, the customer never sees it and the carrying cost to the merchant is relatively small, hopefully less than the fees associated with credit cards.

One such service is iPin *(www.ipin.com),* which sets up a mechanism involving ISPs as the facilitator of an exchange. iPin accepts payments and bills them against an ISP account.

The business model for a barter exchange implies that barter trading occurs at the full market price. On the face of it, this looks attractive. What merchant would spurn a sale of goods at full market price? However, cash must ultimately be tendered. It's very hard to cover rent and other non-bartered items without cash or other fungible assets (see Table 7.8).

Any beneficial sale at "full market price" is cancelled out by the not-so-beneficial buy at "full market price." In addition, there is usually a toll due to the barter exchange itself. Consequently, a merchant who can sell products in the open market is better off selling at the best price possible and using the cash received to obtain other products and services.

However, there are some areas where barter exchanges could have value. Consider, for instance, companies with stale inventory, clearance items, equipment disposal needs,

Table 7.8 Advantages and Disadvantages of Barter Exchanges to Merchants and Customers

Advantages	Disadvantages
Forms an electronic business community	Not necessarily the "best of breed" or most cost-effective merchants; no quality control
Extends barter transaction to multiple players	Limited merchant choice in categories
Mostly cashless exercise except for transaction fees to exchange	Loss of margin due to transactional costs
Alternate market channel	May devalue offering in primary channels
Can list products at "full market price" for exchange credit	Tendency for all merchants to hike up listing prices to cover transactions
Exchange plays role of trustee in transaction	Some loss of control over one channel
Easy to enter and participate	Credit not fungible for usage external to exchange; no recourse if barter exchange itself fails
Hard-to-dispose-of goods that are time-sensitive or perishable can be moved to some one who has use for them, thus removing high inventory carrying costs	When expiration occurs, they are useless to the acquiring party who then assumes carrying cost and possible disposal issues

used machinery, dated models, etc. Such products may not have a ready market, or might be unsuitable for auctions, yet may still be needed by someone else who similarly has a product no longer needed. The two could strike a deal and exchange title to the goods on some basis—not too dissimilar to our silent auction in the 15th Century! And it could be done online.

Another important area of usage is in the case of items that are time-sensitive. Examples: produce that has limited shelf life, products approaching expiration dates, and capacities in service companies such as temporary skill agencies and software development companies. In reality, the "option value" of these goods or services approaches zero in the real external market. The barter exchange may serve to capture some value before the expiration date of the option. In these cases, then, it may be better to trade these for barter exchange credit that may be redeemed for other productive purposes on a later occasion.

Dynamic Exchanges

Fixed price, as we saw, is a norm in established retail stores. The same product can conceivably be had at a cheaper price at a neighboring store, but the merchant does not normally change the price even at the cost of a lost sale. Price adjustments do happen, usually on a quasi-dynamic basis.

A retail store holds to fixed price due to the following considerations:

- Customer is "geographically captive," and once within the retail store there may be significant physical and mental costs in going to an alternate store.
- Physical "search costs" are high, and the customer has to locate the same product at a cheaper price at a geographically proximate location.
- The basis of marketing is often product that is featured in advertisements. The products featured may often be deliberately distinct from offerings of competitors, thus allowing little basis to form a judgment on competitive prices.
- Strong private label "store brands" may confuse the values of the underlying product and the quality of the OEM manufacturer.

Similarly, in the online space, there is also competitive price pressure, due to the following:

- Customer is mobile and can move to a competitive site with a click.
- Online "search costs" are lower. Pricing search engines such as "pricebots" can retrieve competitive pricing, albeit in relatively narrow contexts to date. For example, a customer can visit *www.pricescan.com* and get a comparison of prices of books at various online bookstores and directly visit the store with the lowest price. This is the "bid price" of those merchants.
- Customers are more likely to shop for "manufacturer brands" rather than "store brands," which provides a sharper basis for differentiating on prices.

Against this backdrop, many see the emergence of online exchanges as a way to introduce dynamic pricing into e-commerce. Dynamic pricing is often seen as real-time auctions, where buyer and seller negotiate price on the spot and conclude a transaction when all deal terms are met. Price floats while terms are being resolved.

Are such exchanges easy to set up and maintain? Far from it. It has taken the stock market over a hundred years to settle into a reasonably reliable and efficient model to broker between buyers and sellers of equities. Enter technology, which is changing the way financial markets operate, opening them up to day traders, etc.

Financial markets can be bellwethers for other segments of the economy, and the forces driving adoption of technology-based business practices and business models are inevitable. The following considerations exist for a viable online exchange, many of which currently exist in financial services:

Commodity-Like Product or Service: The product or service should be specific with an absence of qualifying attributes. For instance, a customer order for 100 shares of a stock at a fixed price is a commodity purchase. But, a 4-head VCR may be fundamentally different than a 4-head VCR with an auto-stacker.

Liquidity: Enough qualified sellers can create multiple "ask" prices, which engenders a viable and dynamic market. Sellers need to warrant that sufficient quantities of goods are available at the "ask" price defined. To ensure market liquidity, however, and ensure a dynamic "bid" mechanism, there needs to be a sufficient number of qualified buyers.

Trusted Market-Maker (brand): Performing the role of a broker, or infomediary, a market-maker facilitates the transaction between the buyer and seller.

Robust Delivery Mechanism: Once a buyer and seller conclude a deal, the exchange has to ensure that the product or service promised is actually delivered. This may present issues of order management, packaging, shipping, receipt, product performance, and verification of acceptance. Delivery of a service may be even more complicated, associated with subjective metrics of satisfaction, such as when the meter for an hour of a plumber's time is turned on. Once the product or service is delivered, then the market-maker needs to collect and deliver the payment to the seller.

Escrow Services: Under certain conditions, escrow services for the transaction may be helpful. A neutral party certifies quality and authenticity, which then triggers payment and shipment of goods to the buyer.

Figure 7.14 shows how an exchange for goods and services works.

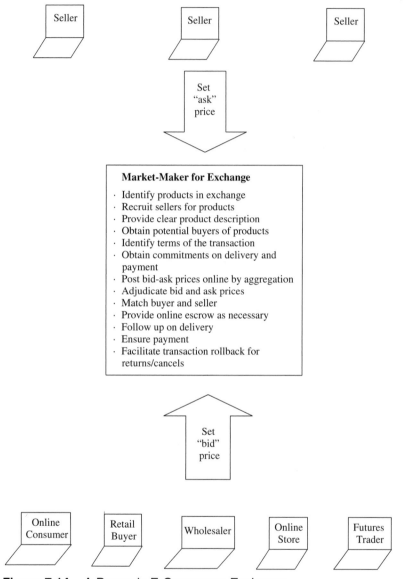

Figure 7.14 A Dynamic E-Commerce Exchange

In this pricing model, the price is set only by almost instantaneous demand and supply. Exchanges are a market mechanism, inherently geared to eliminating arbitrage and dynamically ensuring market equilibrium. The most common example is of course the stock market, where the price of a public company varies dynamically by the value placed by a holder of a security and a would-be owner of that security.

Variations of price are associated with new information in the market and buyer/seller compulsions, leading to a transaction that pushes the value of the stock upwards or downwards. This model of dynamic pricing is now making its way to sales of products or services.

What conditions are to be associated with creating an exchange? Consider the following issues:

- The product or service must be completely described without further qualification. Just as a unit of stock prescribes an "atomic," small portion ownership of a company, the product in question should be easily and completely described. Commodities are good examples for dynamic pricing. Exchanges are already in place for sale of electricity, steel, plastics, and chemicals.
- Buyers and sellers are prequalified to place offers to buy or sell. This may require membership and proof of products or funds.
- The system enables easy facility for placement of bids in real-time. Liquidity and movement are essential to the success of an exchange. Some exchanges may require market-makers to establish and sustain the market.
- The exchange has suitable facilities for credit checking, escrow services, etc.
- A typical product exchange is specialized, namely, focused on a particular commodity-like product. As the product exchange markets mature, it is likely that exchange portals that cover multiple vertical exchanges may come to the fore.
- A robust independent intermediary hosts and runs the exchange.
- Most vertical industry segments do not "tolerate" more than one or two dominant exchanges. Markets with the most liquidity and transactions eventually dry up the other thinly traded exchanges.

Table 7.9 illustrates the structure of dynamic exchanges, which brings together into one buying-selling environment buyers, sellers, and one or more market-makers. Bids may flow in from a variety of channels, both directly into the exchange or indirectly through affiliate networks and shopping bots. Intermediaries such as the market-maker, the escrow agent, and credit agencies may mediate the transaction.

It is noteworthy that most dynamic markets outside financial services are primarily B2B. These markets are characterized by many-to-many transactions and are relatively rare in B2C.

Table 7.10 outlines metrics for evaluating when and how to establish dynamic pricing at a site or on an exchange.

Are exchanges viable for all products? Certainly not. As noted earlier, exchanges are most suitable for near commodity items. However, as technology sophistication grows, it is not inconceivable that exchange pricing may occur for more complex products.

If we set up a trading exchange for washing machines and one of the offerings was a Whirlpool washing machine, delivery of such a product is sensitive to shipping charges.

Table 7.9   Structure for Dynamic Exchanges

Function	Detail
E-Commerce Role	Provides a dynamic price for a specific product or service
Participants	Buyers, sellers, market-maker
Offerings	Goods and services
Infrastructure	Market-maker site Real-time buyers and sellers connected to market-maker
Customer Acquisition	Directly to store Through affiliate networks Through embedding in search engines
Role of Intermediary	Trusted middleman Sets price based on bid-ask system Provides escrow services Maintains buyer and seller accounts
Pricing Models	Dynamic pricing
Revenue Breakup	Transacted price from buyer Transacted price to seller Fixed fee for transaction or commission fee
Examples	Gas, oil, electricity: Altranet.com Telecom: Band-X.com Bandwidth: Arbinet.com

Table 7.10 Metrics for Establishing Dynamic Pricing in an Exchange

Function	Metric
Number of products in the exchange	Number of SKUs, items per SKU and variations such as color, size, etc., or other kinds of measurement, such as for water, energy, etc.
Participants	Buyers, sellers, market-maker.
Number of buyers for each product	Market research estimates on total available market versus target audience with a proclivity to buy.
Number of sellers for each product	Competitive analysis. If more than three, find a way to differentiate to make it a three-horse race, or less!
Operating hours	24 X 7 is mandatory.
Role of intermediary	As with all exchanges, is the host buyer-centric, seller-centric, or neutral? (see Chapter 6, "The Commerce Stack.")
Pricing models	One size does not fit all. From those presented, pick the best for product/service and channel.
Minimum lot size	Factor in flooring or other carrying costs against cost of transaction and fulfillment.
Allowable bid-ask increments	Narrow spreads send a different signal than wide spreads. The narrower the spread, the less room for maneuvering for buyer. Time is the driver.
Back-office requirements for accounting, transaction management, etc.	A significant cost component to set up business rules incorporating metrics, interface with others in the supply chain, databases of products and customers, etc.
Updating mechanism by time, price, and quantity	Dynamic exchanges, by definition, must update on changes; otherwise they are not dynamic.
Payment methods	Tailor to fit size and nature of transactions.
Number of trades allowed per day	Scale the supporting systems for 80 percent of expected maximum, and then keep moving the number up and down as forecasts rise and fall.
Number of trades allowed per seller	As above, scale to market conditions.
Cost to set up seller	Keep as small as possible. Some exchanges charge setup and installation fees to keep transaction costs down.

(continued)

Table 7.10   Metrics for Establishing Dynamic Pricing in an Exchange (*continued*)

Function	*Metric*
Maintenance cost by seller	When does an inactive account drop off the list?
Exchange volume (number of open bids)	How long will open bids be entertained? Is there a notification system in place to alert bidders to status of offerings?
Number of linkages to exchange (live users, price-bots, other exchanges)	What technologies are required to implement new features, and when? Are provisions to interface with other exchanges considered?

An additional parameter may be associated with a dynamically varying price of such a product. Specifically, the price to ship to different locations may be denoted (for normal or express delivery), which would be additive to the dynamic price of the washing machine. Similarly, more dimensions could be handled through suitable algorithms, such as variations on size, options, etc.

Figure 7.15 illustrates the gyrations of pricing that occur in a dynamic pricing environment. Note that over time the bid and ask prices begin to narrow in an efficient exchange. However, when new variables are introduced, the "system" moves the items

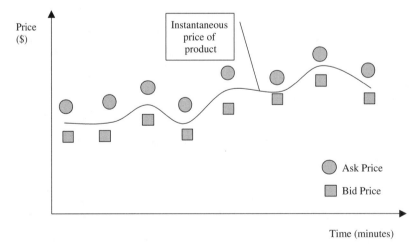

Figure 7.15   Dynamic Pricing in an Exchange

apart, perhaps only temporarily, before narrowing the spread. This also happens in financial markets for stocks, options, and commodities futures.

Looking even further into the future, there is reason to believe that futures markets may evolve for services pricing. Just as options exist for stock and semiconductors, we may soon see call and put options on the right to buy 1 Gigabit per second of bandwidth six months into the future, and the price of such an option might vary dynamically.

Enron operates a successful marketplace for dynamic leasing of bandwidth as well as energy resources.

Summary

In this chapter we took a detailed look at various pricing possibilities for the sale of goods and services online. In the quick paced evolution of the Internet, there is considerable confusion in the press about the distinction between a business model of a company and the pricing model(s) adopted by the company.

The public perception links the business model and the pricing model. Companies are stores, auction houses, infomediaries establishing exchanges, etc. In reality, any company selling goods and services can apply a variety of pricing models, depending on the context.

While differing price models can be encapsulated in a business model, the entrepreneur should understand that pricing of any type is but one dimension of presenting an offering to a customer. Quite often, different pricing models may, in fact, hide, expose, or canvas other aspects, such as service, warranty, availability, shipping, branding, etc. Be cautioned, however: Those that live by price competitiveness also die by it!

A Christmas toy may be offered to the consumer at a fixed price until November 15, in a "name your price" auction, until December 25, and on eBay after that. A company selling widgets to other businesses may have a fixed price at its regular corporate store, while concurrently offering auction lots of the item and making it available for "negotiated pricing" in a business marketplace. Management should understand the different contexts in which a sale can be made to a potential customer and make available the most appropriate pricing model for that context.

We also looked at the advantages and disadvantages of the various pricing models. Pricing is an essential consideration in the purchasing decision and can attract or deter the purchase.

Typical consumer behavior at an online store indicates a very low rate of conversion from a visitor on a site perusing a product to one that becomes a customer who places the item in a shopping cart. A significant part of this reluctance is attributable to the price and medium of exchange.

The customer may decide, rightly or wrongly, that the merchant does not alter price to attract the sale. In reality, many merchants under the right conditions would be more than happy to obtain the sale at a lowered price if this could be done without affecting other customers and/or profit margins.

Merchants might be better off with offering alternate pricing options to customers based on various channels used for marketing, promotion, and fulfillment. A merchant could place one category of products in an exchange rather than utilizing very expensive marketing approaches such as personalization, which has high capital costs for software, or targeted advertising, which has high operational costs for customer acquisition.

In B2B marketing, technology and connectivity are setting the table for new frontiers of transactional efficiency. The different auction formats can speed up removal of inventory and overstock items. The "Name Your Price" mechanism is allowing merchants to operate more efficiently with individual customers because of many factors unique to online, anonymity for one.

Business rules are critical, irrespective of which pricing model is used by the merchant. For example, setting up a process for negotiated pricing can facilitate a convergence of bid and ask prices. Putting the human-in-the-loop is reserved, if necessary at all, for the final conclusion of the deal.

Bartering business communities are evolving, leading to cashless transactions, which may or may not contribute favorably to positive cash flow for other company operations. And finally, in the narrower arena where digital exchanges become viable for near commodity items, there will be greater transparency of pricing, and a more efficient market structure, providing more value to buyers and sellers alike.

Customer Acquisition Models for E-Commerce

In spite of a growing customer base on the Internet, branding and customer acquisition remain the most complex and costly issues facing the merchant. Old time retailers and brand new e-tailers are all struggling to get their marketing strategy "right" and, in the process, are spending ridiculous amounts to acquire a customer.

The frenzy comes from a mixture of branding necessity, attracting eyeballs, and delivering traffic numbers that are presumed to make partners, advertisers, and investors happy. In a crowded field where customers are only a click away from bolting to the competition, an online presence for most can be an ephemeral experience.

Visibility, which is a prerequisite for branding and acquisition, comes at a price. Visibility, however, does not always translate to revenues. Yet 1999 through the start of 2000 became a period when e-tailers splurged their way to a spot in the Sun. If 1999 was the year of excess, 2000 was certainly the judgment year, because by mid-year visibility programs were beginning to shrink as one B2C after another either flamed out, filed for Chapter 11 . . . or worse.

How and why did e-tailers lose their grip on fiscal responsibility? What issues confront an online merchant or e-commerce entity in making itself known, driving targeted traffic to its site, ensuring visitor stickiness, then convincing customers to fill their shopping carts and take them to the checkout and return again as customers?

These are complex questions, made doubly so because of the very newness of the online experience as a means to conduct commerce. It is often forgotten that the Internet as an additional sales or distribution channel is only a few years old, and many an organization is still finding its feet, polishing its business model, and confronting a highly fluid and dynamic scenario.

It is now acknowledged that while setting up an online store or commerce activity is relatively easy, doing business and earning revenues is more complicated. The barriers to entry are low, but the cost to get a customer in and become loyal is very high.

Companies, therefore, are pressured to build awareness among their target audiences. Awareness has to be followed up with an incentive to visit, and the visit itself has to be a compelling enough experience that browsers become customers. Advertising and marketing are the two traditional disciplines charged with these responsibilities. Not surprisingly, this is where companies spend the most—unfortunately, with the least idea of whom, how, or when they are grabbing customers.

This chapter focuses on the premise of branding and how advertising and other marketing issues are applicable to the Internet space. It should also help you begin to understand their effectiveness in terms of return on investment.

Analogies involving the offline world are helpful because more and more online marketing programs entail heavy spending in the offline world. Advertisers use a variety of channels—billboards, print media, radio, TV, direct marketing, and offline marketing techniques. In most cases, objectives are "almost" identical in technique between offline and online. Online marketing can take the form of: various modes of advertising from banner ads to interstitials, affiliate partnerships, email programs, personalized content delivery, and so on.

Some of that is unique to online marketing. Some of it has a direct counterpart in the offline world.

In particular, the aim of this chapter is to discuss both branding and marketing in the context of a company's desire to increase revenues and the cost incurred to achieve it. It will seek to understand the basis for these expenses and analyze the effectiveness of various methods that reflect the costs.

Effectiveness is very much an objective criterion and needs to be discussed in an analytical framework. To this end, the chapter will utilize sample metrics to evolve a model by which to test various assumptions and their fallout.

In this chapter, we concentrate on the following issues:

- Basics of Branding
- Direct Marketing, including Permission Marketing (personalized targeted email)
- Affiliate Marketing
- Internet Advertising, including Banner Advertising, Slotted Positioning in Portals, and Dynamic Positioning in Search Engines
- Analysis of Marketing Effectiveness

The average online retailer spends from $75–$100 to acquire a customer. This compares to $12 for online selling spent by an average offline retailer (i.e., store-based but also selling online) in 1999. In a remarkable testimony to the absurdity of current online branding efforts, online revenues in 1999 for a pure e-tailer were only $70 per customer! Anyone can see that in marketing cost alone, the means are not justifying the end.

Thus, online e-tailers spend about 11 percent of revenues on marketing, approximately 62 percent of which is in offline marketing and 38 percent in online marketing. In contrast, offline retailers spent an average of 36 percent of revenues in marketing efforts devoted to selling online, which translates into 66 percent in offline marketing and 34 percent in online marketing.

Specific objectives for expenditures by online e-tailers are identified in a Boston Consulting Group (BCG) study: 58 percent in customer acquisition, 31 percent in brand awareness, and 11 percent in customer retention. To put this in terms of the 1999 expenses, this would mean $69 for customer acquisition, $37 for brand awareness, and $13 for customer retention. With acquisition costs so high, it would seem more prudent to spend a higher amount on retention than acquisition!

The most effective media for developing brand awareness are broadcast media followed closely by outdoor advertising, and then sponsorship on online sites. Other techniques for building brand awareness include email, cross-links, and, lastly, banner ads. For generating customer acquisition, we find email outweighs all other forms of communication combined. Broadcast advertising and cross-links are equal in efficiency to search engine placement—all of which are fairly low when compared to personalized and targeted email.

These statistics do not equate with effectiveness, but with spending levels. In light of the dot com failures one can make an argument that any effectiveness from these expenditures is woefully lacking as currently practiced.

The popularity of personalized/targeted email is particularly significant. It appears to be the one channel of communication that is notably effective in both brand awareness and customer acquisition. The second runner-up is, interestingly, broadcast advertising, which is a mainstay for traditional brand building. Its relatively low effectiveness in customer acquisition suggests that more study should go into what sets a condition for success in making a link between the offline and the online world. The cross-linkages between broadcast television and online might increase in significance as we approach an era of "always-on" Internet connections in households, such as from cable modems and DSL connections.

We are noting that there is still a low preference for overpriced "sponsorship deals" or slotting in portals and ISP environments. Such deals (often multiyear, multimillion dollar contracts) account for over 11 percent of the brand awareness activities.

Ranking third in effectiveness for combined brand awareness and customer acquisition is linkage from other sites. These are especially appropriate for online merchants and are often evident in affiliate marketing initiatives. Affiliate marketing arrangements are typically "pay-by-the-click" mechanisms to provide an incentive for the site to find and close the sale.

The much-touted banner advertising is increasingly seen as ineffective, recording abysmally low click-through rates that are less than .06 percent. Consumers are ignoring this type of visual noise more and more.

Basics of Branding

First off, a definition: The brand is the name and what the company and/or its offering represents to the customer; branding is the process of establishing, demonstrating, and expanding emotional and market equity in what the venture is. The brand is the result of customer perception, not the intent of branding programs.

Branding is not a single element but the collection of all the devices used to create the intricate mosaic of a company's reputation. It is more than the sum total of these efforts. It is the value that the customer perceives and the company demonstrates time and time again.

Savvy professionals in the brand arena know that the customer intuitively or cognitively registers values and connects them with values that prevail in society at that moment. The values are discounted if the brand value of yesterday is presented to today's consumer—hence, the reason for staying current with not only the prevailing opinions in society but also the underlying media that support them.

Enter the Internet and its sibling electronic commerce.

Like no other moment in the history of commerce, this one means of reaching the customer is both part of the branding process and the brand itself. We say that "The Internet (Web, etc.) delivers your brand." The Internet, especially in online commerce, exposes each and every part of the enterprise to the customer and others who are influenced by our actions.

If we excel at marketing, yet fall short in site navigation, handling the transaction, or carrying out every nuance of back-end fulfillment and logistics (including customer service), the branding process has failed. In offline commerce, there are as many failure points, but because of the longevity enjoyed by many companies and the slow pace at which brick-and-mortar operations move, a branding faux pas can be covered up and the moment made good for the customer.

Not so in the real-time world of e-commerce!

The starting point for brands and branding processes is in finding attributes that resonate well with consumers. Developing a brand takes many forms, but an ad agency or other creative service usually inspires it and is given credit for being the initiator of a branding effort. Branding, however, is a process that must begin long before the agency is called in—and it never ends. Just about everyone in the organization participates in supporting and enhancing the image that the brand represents.

A powerful brand not only distances you from the competition, it cuts you some slack if there is the inevitable mistake at any step along the online continuum, from first attempt at communication through reverse logistics (returns).

The primary goal, as always, is to establish a strong brand presence. The measurable result of the branding process is customer evangelism—when the customer not only *cannot get enough* of your offering, but becomes actively involved in promoting it as well.

Most branding attempts in the online world are, unfortunately, modeled after their offline counterparts. They follow disciplines established by either billboard advertising or television. Banner ads tend to reflect billboards, while larger presences are akin to television. Few, if any, tap the true interactive nature of the online world because of technical deficiencies—there is not enough bandwidth, yet, to support any but the crudest attempts at interactivity.

For those who are working at branding on the Internet, the attempts somewhat mirror their offline strategies: heavy advertisers are using Web advertising to complement their efforts offline; those with low profiles offline are using content as a way to convey their online brand stances.

The soft underbelly of online branding is in its ability to focus message and medium almost one-to-one. From a branding effort on the Internet, the organization can do what is not available in any other medium—demonstrate service, support, and usability and do so in the context of content that supports the message!

There are demonstrable benefits associated with a strong brand:

- Consistently larger volume/revenue year after year
- More leverage with the channels or intermediaries because customers will request the strong brand, or go to competitors for it
- Can resist price competition which equals margin protection/enhancement
- Can support assertions around high ground market positions
- Longer life with greater levels of loyalty
- Can support the launch of new offerings
- More forgiveness when quality slips or position is temporarily lost

Strong examples of firms that recognize the power of interactivity to provide more than another means of blasting their image to customers abound all over the Web. If the online marketer tries to use the Web to entice customers into hitting the site and lingering long enough to absorb a few carefully crafted messages, branding cannot occur. If, however, the marketer openly tries to deliver information value through content and community, as we have discussed, branding naturally follows.

Branding on the Internet

Here are some truths about branding in the online world:

- The process of branding a product or organization used to be a painstaking process that evolved over time, paced by the rate at which media could publish or broadcast positioning messages. Now extreme time demands can be met by using the Internet.

- In this hyperintensive, fast-moving environment, branding techniques can go into play much swifter.
- Branding the firm and branding the offering were formerly parallel paths that eventually converged; however, in the online world, they quite often start to diverge to avoid becoming identified inextricably with an identity that might require downstream change.
- The value of the brand is doubly critical in the ephemeral world of electronic commerce.
- The online world provides something no other medium can: immediacy and a direct interactive link or connection with the customer or influencer. If these are traits to be identified with, then the branding process is consistent with the market presence of the company.
- In the online world, the product can be demonstrated quickly at varying levels, which speeds adoption rates.
- Online branding provides more of an opportunity to neutralize counter-claims before they arise, and get the transaction made at the moment of sampling.
- Before, it was assumed that brands could live indefinitely—not any more! It is possible for a brand to flame out in the online world within a year, where its life expectancy in the offline world might have been much longer.
- The online, interactive world is more dynamic and subject to immediate modification to support changes that might expand recognition.
- Online media can be used to refresh the brand, but offline media can actually shape the brand.
- The uniqueness of the offering can be tuned to market needs—immediately.
- Online media embody traits evident in all elements of the marketing mix.
- If the online presence is left to banners, not enough time or screen real estate is available to establish or support branding. Banners are to branding what bumper stickers are to philosophy.
- The entire communications mix must support the online image and impression.
- As an alternative medium, the Internet can be more affordable because it appeals to a largely focused target audience; but, as more and more differentiation takes place, this is becoming less and less so.
- Weakness in brand attributes can intensify the decline of a product or organization, and, in electronic commerce, the pace of degradation can be extremely swift.

- The Internet is more likely to be better as a transactional and promotional medium because of several qualities that make its impact short term.
- Trust, or the absence of it, is the single most powerful attribute that must be cultivated and nurtured, and it does not happen easily, but is earned through practice and perhaps the most elusive quantity of all: time.
- In summary, conventional branding using offline media must bolster the electronic commerce presence.

Ultimately, loyalty to a brand is based on affinity. The online world graces and illuminates affinity. Loyalty requires collaboration between the enterprise and the customer. Online, collaboration can be facilitated with almost as much intensity and impact as when going one-on-one with the customer. With e-commerce, it happens on a larger, often global scale.

In addition to borrowing techniques from older, offline media, those building an electronic commerce presence are beginning to add new techniques and layers of new media forms. In every branding experience, no one medium can accomplish all there is to do. Those adept at pursuing a stronger brand mix their media in some fashion for optimal strategic advantage. This includes establishing a proper mix of offline and online branding programs.

Interactivity and the opportunity for collaboration with the consumer that occurs when using the Internet are important take-aways for the marketing portion of the branding process. If the customer doesn't become involved with the company or its message, the branding effort is wasted.

Some see the branding process as taking no more than six months to complete—a period in which (estimated by the Gartner Group) some companies in the B2C space spend close to $60 million to establish their brand!

Some tactics and techniques are powerful brand builders, especially those that capitalize on inherent strengths and weaknesses of the Internet. As the Internet generates more than a sea state change in branding, it has the potential for becoming a testbed for new techniques that can then be picked up by other media looking for new and exciting ways to tell a story—or brand an offering.

Branding is based on a customer experience. If the customer can't begin to relate site reality with what you say or how you say it, branding cannot occur. Simple as that.

Branding online is still an immature and inexact process. Where online helps in the branding process is in *demonstrating* various tangible qualities associated with the brand. You demonstrate trust by respecting privacy and security. You demonstrate customer responsiveness through fast downloads and dialing interactive communications into your site. And you demonstrate respect by not spamming.

These and other qualities vary by product category. However, despite the mercurial nature of online branding, these qualities along with others are necessary in building brand equity into a site or offering available through electronic commerce. Table 8.1 arranges some of the elements of a branding program by offline and online as a grid the planner can use.

Media usage in each stage varies by virtue of the inherent strengths and weaknesses of each channel of communication. It is helpful for establishing a benchmark to break down the channels of communication with the customer into pre-sale, sale, and post-sale.

During the pre-sale period, the marketer is looking for awareness and preference. When communicating with the customer in the sale process, the focus is on concluding a purchase. In the post-sale segment, the emphasis is on how the customer uses the offering, whether or not such usage and the experience with the company results in a return visit.

The sum of each outcome should generate the kind of loyalty that stimulates a customer to refer the merchant, site, and offering to friends.

Table 8.1 presents a checklist for taking a top-down view of the use of various channels and, when most appropriate, for each of the three phases of branding. Some boxes are filled in, suggesting the channel is less effective in this particular phase; that is, when someone is using an offering, he/she might be offline, hence, a banner ad is inappropriate as a channel of communication.

In the following sections we look at several techniques used to further branding, awareness, and direct contact with the customer. None are more or less valuable for B2C than they are for B2B. Each market situation stands alone and apart from others.

Direct Marketing

Direct marketing refers to targeted communication to a potential customer. In the traditional offline world, this usually means unsolicited "junk mail," while the online world

Table 8.1 Media Planning Grid for Branding

	Awareness	Preference	Purchase	Use	Repurchase	Refer
ONLINE						
BANNER	X	X	X	X	X	
SEARCH			X	X		X
CHAT					X	
EMAIL						
SITE						
HOTLINK						
OFFLINE						
ADVT.			X	X	X	
DIR. MKT.				X	X	
PROMOTION				X	X	
POINT OF SALE	X	X		X	X	
PR		X	X	X		
PERSON-2-PERSON				X		

282

refers to this concept as "spam." However, under specific conditions, personalized direct marketing is extremely effective and can selectively serve the needs of both the merchant and the consumer. Since the consumer controls the activity, the effectiveness of direct marketing depends on three factors: permission, demand, and needs.

Permission Marketing

This is a form of promotional email direct to a recipient who consents to receive such mailings. In the absence of "permission," unsolicited email is usually considered objectionable. In particular, bulk email sent to a large number of recipients who do not agree to receive such mail is spamming and may be illegal, depending on the source of the email lists.

Permission marketing programs enjoy a surprisingly high approval rate from consumers. Moreover, click-through rates can be as high as 15 percent for permission marketing versus less than 0.6 percent for banner advertisements.

Considerations for Permission Marketing

The following are some considerations for engaging in permission marketing. Because this can easily cross the line of tolerance, its success largely depends on explicit rules of engagement, tight focus, and defined run rates.

- Specific permission for email campaign—single location of permission given, no multilevel play with email addresses handed down to other parties.
- Tiers of "permission"—from a high degree of limitations to "open season" advocated by some.
- Email campaign starts immediately when the permission is given, and for a specific time period.
- A sampler campaign is well worth the effort to test the market and refine the offering.
- An offering in the email campaign has some value, especially when originally promised with permission.
- The offer is specific and limited: excessively broad offers or too numerous ones are usually less effective. For example, it is better to have one specific offer: A *20 percent discount on a SONY Home Theatre* rather than a *20 percent discount on*

the entire store or *15 percent off on Toshiba, 20 percent off on SONY, and 18 percent off on GE.*

- Email must have links that lead directly to the online offer and not to a home page requiring further additional navigation.
- Follow through on a click-through or purchase must be timely and professional, and validate the "value" provided.
- Frequency is not excessive—say no more than once a month.
- The email campaign is analyzed for effectiveness.
- Value provided is reinforced and enhanced with further personalization.
- As relationship is reinforced, the permission marketer may request referrals.
- At all times, the consumer has the ability to "opt-out" and withdraw permission for further targeted marketing.
- URL or other feature might be different to track action as a result of direct marketing.

Table 8.2 sets forth some metrics for measuring the effectiveness of a permission-marketing program. This template can also be used for other marketing and branding programs discussed in this chapter.

Email is an important component in a permission marketing program. To set a proper framework for a program that can be measured, first and foremost is an examination of a company's intentions and goals. Is the object of the exercise to attract more customers? Retain customers? Reward them for loyalty? Possibly make a (hopefully) credible case of providing value? Could it be more than one, even all, of these? What does the company sell anyway?

A mass email-based campaign, even one approved by the customer, can run the danger of becoming a scattershot affair, lacking a clear purpose. There must be a deliberate means to achieve it and the ability to conduct a post-mortem to learn from that analysis.

Email lists can be chosen with a good deal of specificity defined by the kind of demographics the company wishes to go after. Demographics encompass attributes such as occupation and targeted income bracket, geographical boundary, lifestyle issues like interests and hobbies, travel preferences, and purchasing profiles.

The constituents are chosen, the message is now ready—the time to roll out the campaign is here. Campaign issues combine logistics with a feel for when and how a

Table 8.2 Metrics for Permission Marketing

Type of Interaction	Metrics
Email list rental cost	• 8¢ per email ID for external list; zero cost for internal list
Emailing costs	• Inbound emails as percent of total order backlog • Breakdown of inbound emails @10 minutes per email • Email sorting required for major sites • Zero cost for in-house software versus est. 5¢ per email sent using an ASP service to send email
Total cost of campaign	• Mail list cost + emailing cost + other costs (time spent @ hourly burden rates, etc.)
Click-through percent	• Number of emails clicked on that link back to site or offer
Conversion rate	• From click-throughs to order
Gross return from campaign	• Total sales from campaign; average revenue per order minus total cost per order • Total sales—total cost of goods sold through this campaign • Total sales from campaign/total cost of campaign
Return on Investment	• Gross return from campaign/total cost of campaign

message may be accepted by the receiver. For example, registration at a retirement planning site could form the basis for a permission campaign to promote complementary or value-added products and services such as life insurance, estate planning, vacation time shares, and so on. These services may be in partnership with AARP and included within its periodic programs, timed to coincide with identified activities.

In another example, an online photo processing service might partner with a vacations carrier and offer a free trial of its services. A discount can be applied to a future purchase or the price of the service credited towards frequent flier miles.

Often, "test rounds" that seek to fine-tune each permission-marketing instrument precede such campaigns. Are the offerings in line with the audience demographics or is there a complete lack of congruence? Does the message evoke interest and inclination to purchase? Is there a perception of value and derived benefit among the respondents? Are

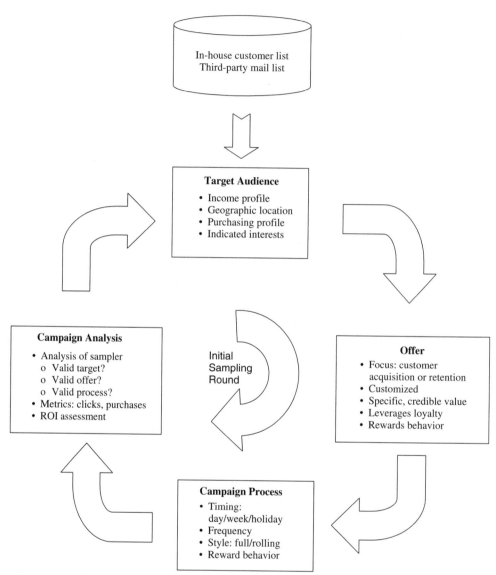

Figure 8.1   Campaign Management for Permission Marketing

there kinks in the process that need to be ironed out? Could the exercise be substantively measured—in other words, were useful metrics generated that can be subjected to a return on investment test?

Subjecting a permission-marketing campaign to the rigors of a test round may reveal assumptions that are not valid and metrics that are either useless or difficult to come by. The mail lists themselves may prove to be less than perfect for the specific purposes of a company's campaign and its product profile. Figure 8.1 depicts the interlinking relationship between the key processes.

Affiliate Marketing

With over five million Web pages being created per day and nearly three billion accounted for so far, it is no wonder that getting people to pay attention to any site is one of the most difficult problems to solve. Dot coms spend from $75 to $150 to attract a customer. It would be great if, magically, customers were brought effortlessly to your site and you only paid if they bought something from you.

Such a world, albeit in a less than perfect form, is available through affiliate marketing.

Affiliate marketing occurs when links from other Web sites generate traffic for the host merchant, thereby getting exposure, clicks, and perhaps even sales. Amazon is a pioneer in this form of online marketing and continues to pull in leads from an extensive affiliate network of hundreds of thousands of people around the world.

Amazon has two commission structures: a low one, about 5 percent, for traffic driven to the Amazon site, and a higher commission, about 15 percent, for a contextual link of a specific book for immediate purchase. This merchant also has a patent in this area, although Amazon has not yet exercised its patent privilege against potential encroachers on this marketing model.

Forrester Research reports that in a study of *new affiliate marketing models,* e-tailers with active affiliate programs for at least three months have, on average, 10,270 affiliates generating 13 percent of the online revenues. Simply put, this means that one-eighth of an e-tailer's revenues from affiliate programs could be generated with no particular involvement on their part. Imagine! Every time a person sees a link to your site on a third-party site and decides to click on it, you have a potential customer who arrived at no direct cost to you.

Of course, the top tier merchants with affiliate programs work their affiliate networks and make these programs pay off with higher results than those who view their affiliates in a more passive manner.

Now, of course, the affiliate approach is spreading from the B2C space to the B2B space, with business-centric stores recruiting qualified affiliate sites.

There are typically two types of affiliate marketing initiatives:

- In-house affiliate program: Merchant contacts selected sites from which to refer traffic. (This is straightforward and not discussed further.)
- External affiliate network: Merchant joins an affiliate network.

One of the most important aspects of affiliate marketing is to have a large robust network of affiliate sites to sell products and/or bring in the customer traffic. Such a requirement often argues against going to other Web masters one by one to evangelize the link to your site.

Affiliate Marketing Network

A cost-effective process is to utilize affiliate marketing networks that are matchmakers between affiliate sites and merchants. Affiliates can then choose the merchant that they want to link to based on relevance, perceived reliability, and anticipated payments. The merchant can choose to accept affiliates based on their customer profile and projected traffic, and can exclude undesirable affiliates. This kind of mutually beneficial collaborative commerce can potentially reduce the "friction" associated with e-commerce by enabling customers to locate goods and services in a convenient way, in the context of their Web activity.

The affiliate marketing network is both a marketplace of merchants with an array of offerings and also a grouping of sites that may or may not be merchants themselves. The latter generally have their own community of users or customers and traffic to match. The role of the affiliate network is to not only match the two, but also serve as a marketplace for both.

There are several such services operating in the affiliate marketing world, among them BeFree *(www.befree.com),* Commission Junction *(www.commissionjunction.com),* and CashPile *(www.cashpile.com).* Each provides a different set of services, ranging from matchmaking to collecting affiliate commissions.

What do merchants want? They have the offerings, the content in the form of a site with details, pictures, photographs, and the shopping and payment infrastructure. They also have traffic and revenues based on some conversion rate of visitors who become buyers.

Affiliates allow lateral expansion of their sales channel by including within their ambit other Web sites whose audiences may not visit the merchant site. By placing itself through a link or an ad in the affiliate site, the merchant is assured of visibility and the possibility of traffic emanating from the affiliate site.

Why would sites become affiliates? The major attraction is the possibility of earning revenue—it is an easy and relatively inexpensive means of adding an additional source of revenue. The merchant site rewards the affiliate with a commission, which is usually a percent of the revenues generated when a user at the affiliate site clicks on the merchant link and buys something.

The affiliate network smoothes the process by which merchants are able to secure affiliates, who then are able to identify potential opportunities. They also provide value-added services such as bringing the two parties together, categorizing merchant offerings for the affiliates, enabling an affiliate to track activities associated with a merchant providing and reporting payment tools. Such a marketplace role, with its standardized set of services and benefits to both parties, reduces the cost of a transaction between merchants and affiliates. This is detailed in Figure 8.2 and Table 8.3.

Figure 8.2 shows how this actually works. An affiliate Web site (this may be a community site, another merchant site—anything that has its own defined demographics and user traffic) has links, ad buttons, or promotions for a merchant site on its page(s). When a user dropping in clicks on the link, she is taken to the merchant site where a purchase may be made.

The affiliate network keeps track of both the click on the affiliate Web site and the resulting purchase by a customer coming from the affiliate at the merchant's site. On a monthly or some other periodic basis, the network tallies up and reports the activity to either party, and facilitates payment from merchant to affiliate.

Table 8.3 lists the roles of the various players and how they interact. The affiliate marketing network is shown in Figure 8.3.

Merchants often choose the payment method to the affiliate. Figure 8.4 shows the three common bases for payment: page views, click-throughs, and commissions on sales. One or more of these payments may be made, depending on the structure of the contract. Typically, merchants prefer to pay for actual purchases because this represents the highest

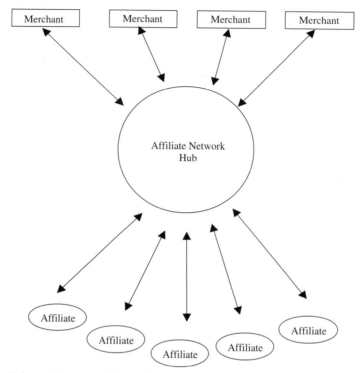

Figure 8.2 An Affiliate Marketing Network

efficiency in terms of performance. Alternatively, there may be a graded commission, with the lowest for page views and the highest for purchases made.

Merchants use the metrics in Table 8.4 to assess affiliate programs and an affiliate network. As you can see, some metrics and rules-of-thumb vary by merchant and affiliate situation.

Internet Advertising

Internet advertising is a large and growing industry, though still small when compared to offline ad expenditures.

Table 8.3 Sequence of Activities In Affiliate Networks

Merchant	Affiliate Network	Affiliate
• Join affiliate network	• Recruit affiliates into network	• Create a Web site that enjoys some traffic
• Post affiliate offering	• Recruit merchants	• Join affiliate network to obtain alternate sources of revenue
• Identify commission schedule	• Categorize merchant offering for affiliates	• Review merchant offers and select merchants who have value propositions complementary to your site
• Select from affiliates who show interest	• Enable merchants to post offer to affiliates	• Post links, promotions, graphics of merchant on your site
• Provide graphics and assistance to set up affiliates	• Enable affiliates to select merchant's offer	• Interact with merchants on strategies for increased consumer participation
• Enable tracking software	• Enable merchants to accept affiliate	• Fine-tune the number and type of merchants to showcase on your site
• Pay affiliates for sales	• Provide logging software on affiliate and merchant site	• Collect payments either directly from merchant or through affiliate network
• Maintain correspondence with affiliates through newsletters, improved graphics, promotions	• Track affiliate-to-merchant activity, including transactions	
	• Report to merchant by affiliate performance	
	• Report to affiliate by merchant performance	
	• Collect payments (by click-through, impressions, transactions)	
	• Process payment to affiliates as an optional service to merchants	
	• Provide consultant services to merchants	

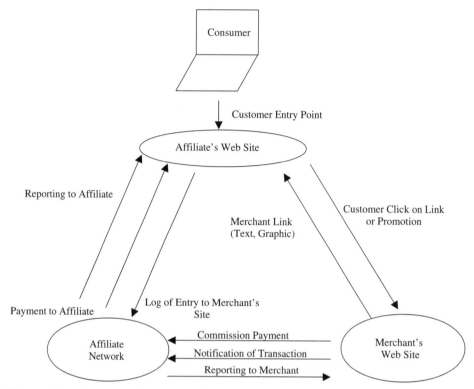

Figure 8.3 How an Affiliate Network Works with Affiliates and Merchants

Because there are many types of advertising on the Web, it helps to understand the basic characteristics and types in order to analyze their marketing and revenue implications. Advertising as a revenue model is one thing; advertising to promote a site or an offering is quite another. In this chapter, we discuss advertising's contribution to customer acquisition.

Consequently, this section discusses the following aspects of online ads and their potentials:

- Characteristics of Online Advertising
- Value Considerations
- Revenue Basis
- Types of Advertising

Characteristics of Online Advertising

The interactive nature of the Web allows for creative use of advertising. Unlike the offline world, online advertising can be highly targeted based on context and demographics, far more so than in any other medium.

There are some characteristics of online advertising that are unique to the medium. Print media offer a limited array of features for advertisers—*Bicycle* magazine, for instance, may have ads for adventure travel tours that are contextual but little more. A prospective customer would have to call the number listed and initiate a separate activity.

Contrast this with an online experience: *Bicycle* magazine's Web page may have the same ad, but it is now endowed with more uses. The reader can click on the ad *or the copy/content* and perhaps be taken to the tour package company's Web site where she can browse, get the information, and even make a booking or purchase.

That click can also trigger customer tracking, useful to both the magazine Web site and the travel company. If the Web site requires registrations, the user's profile is probably already on record, allowing the Web site to intelligently display ads targeted at either the demographics or interests specified by the user.

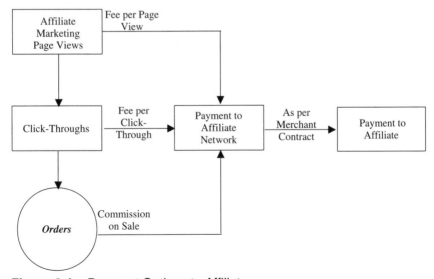

Figure 8.4   Payment Options to Affiliate

Table 8.4 Metrics for Merchant Affiliate Program

Type of Interaction	Key Metric
Size of affiliate network	Number of affiliates
Affiliate distribution by category	Type of sites, audience, traffic
Affiliate network's commission structure	Pay by impressions, click, sales leads, percent of transaction, percent of affiliate payout, etc.
Affiliate payout structure	Pay by impressions, click, sales leads, percent of transaction, percent of affiliate payout, etc.
Sign-up costs	Should be nil for merchant and affiliate
Minimum monthly payments to affiliate network	Should be nil for merchant and affiliate
Affiliate recruitment costs	Borne by affiliate network firm as cost of doing business
Net growth rate of affiliates	Attrition of affiliates
Cost of maintaining affiliate network	Data feeds, graphics, customization
Cost of special promotions to trigger sales	Effect of discount percentage on cost of goods sold
Impressions through affiliate network	Counts towards branding
Total click-throughs from affiliate network	Top-tier 20 percent of affiliates generate 80 percent of volume Conversion ratio from impressions to click-throughs Conversion ratio from click-through to purchase
Aggregate revenues through work affiliate network channel	Cost per customer acquired Average revenue per customer
Total commission payouts	Varies by merchant
Channel profitability after accounting for customer and servicing acquisition costs	Net revenue minus commission

Table 8.5 Pros and Cons of Online Advertising

Pros	Cons
• Can be highly contextual—location, click path, activity, time • Can be personalized based on login, history, profile • Can change rapidly • Can be "non-discretionary"—user to view or click to continue • Can be "actionable"—lead to offers, searches, rebates, etc. • Can be passive or active • Can contain multimedia—visual, music • Can be easily tracked for responses and effectiveness • Can be used to sell directly and therefore become a "sales channel" • Can "force" instant responses by limiting window of opportunity • Can be "interstitial," i.e., worked into an article or discussion • Real estate on Web site can be traded for real estate on other Web site for beneficial mutual gain	• Low click rates • Competes with other visual "noise" • Becomes part of background by usage • Can detract from page content • Difficult for any advertisement to distinguish itself among the numerous ones sold on every page

Clearly, there is layer-upon-layer of online ad characteristics that make ads distinct, specifically:

- Ads can be active or "live"
- Ads can be dynamic and change, based on user profile, promotions, etc.
- Ads can be tracked for usage patterns
- Ads can lead directly to a sale
- Ads can be buried in a specific and desired context within the content

Online ads have very real benefits apart from being sources of revenue. They also have limitations, usually because of technical restrictions, but those are ephemeral at best. In Table 8.5, the pros and cons are contrasted.

Value Considerations

Internet advertising is governed by six considerations:

- Location—where the advertising is located on the Internet, by Web site
- Position—where the advertising is positioned on a specific Web page
- Size—size and shape of the advertising copy
- Type—the static, dynamic or interactive nature of the advertising object
- Value—representation of perceived customer value
- Promotion value—any reward or incentive attached to the ad, such as a coupon, etc.

Each of these represents the potential attractiveness—or lack thereof—to the advertiser. Advertisers want high visibility, which translates to where the ad appears on a site and how it appears. Obviously, having an ad either on the opening page (home) or in a contextual position has more value than having it buried someplace deep in the site just because the ad rates were cheaper.

But are there *reasonable grounds* to value a choice location more than another? In other words, is there a way to analyze the "worth" of a particular ad placement? Media planners and buyers in ad agencies use a variety of metrics to make their offline ad placement decisions. Some are transferable online, but many more are not, just yet, because traffic numbers are either not there or inconclusive.

Four objectives define the placement of ads and what is expected of them: awareness contribution, consideration, purchase, and loyalty, all of which are shown in Table 8.6.

Revenue Basis

Ultimately, ads are seen as revenue sources. After all, a whole family of early Internet entrepreneurs wrote their business plans, some based on false hopes, seeking most or all of their revenue projections from advertisements! That era is now most certainly over.

Types of Advertising

How, indeed, does one assess advertisements as a revenue generator and come up with a credible accounting of revenue projections that are not mere pie-in-the-sky dreams of

Table 8.6 Online Advertising Objectives

Objective	Effectiveness	Rationale
Create awareness and build brand	Low	• Too much visual noise • Oversold space • Poor control of "advertising real estate"
Create consideration	Moderate	• Contextual ads are powerful • Streaming media still primitive • Dynamic
Create a purchase	Moderate to high	• Can be contextual • Can be personalized • Can be "timely" • Can be "actionable" • Can be interstitial
Reward customer loyalty	Moderate to high	• Can create specific incentives for loyalty • Could use "history" to amplify purchasing need

entrepreneurs and Venture Capitalists (VCs)? Here are three form factors for advertising, but there are others, many too numerous to mention or analyze given the imperfect nature of online advertising.

- Banner Advertising
- Slotted Positioning in Portals
- Dynamic Positioning in Search Engines

Banner Advertising

The purpose of banner advertising varies by site and marketing objective. For some, it is to get the all-important click to the sponsor's site or offer.

Given the size of the Web, there is a problem in bringing sellers and buyers of advertising space together. An entire industry exists to cater to this need. Once again, it is a marketplace intermediary that provides the medium for buyers and sellers of advertising to meet: sellers provide ad inventory, or pages, and buyers provide the ads. Beyond this rather simple function, such intermediaries provide additional services such as account maintenance, back-end technology for facilitating dynamic ad changes and renewals, and payment mechanisms.

For suppliers, some intermediaries also offer specialized services in campaign planning and serve as advisers in content creation. These infomediaries are similar to conventional advertising agencies; in fact, many of these offline-based agencies have "interactive" or "new media" divisions designed to handle online ad creation and placement.

Figure 8.5 presents us with an overview of where these various online "agencies" and other services interface with each other and the advertiser.

Advertising placements and subsequently revenue are typically based on the number of page views (often expressed in CPM: cost per thousand impressions), or in terms of fee per click-through. As the names imply, advertisers pay Web sites for the number of page views they command or on the basis of the number of qualifying customers who click on the ad or link to go to the target Web site.

Increasingly, advertisers are becoming more hard-nosed about what they pay for and are seeking numbers to justify the cost. In other words, there has been a movement towards click-through-based costing.

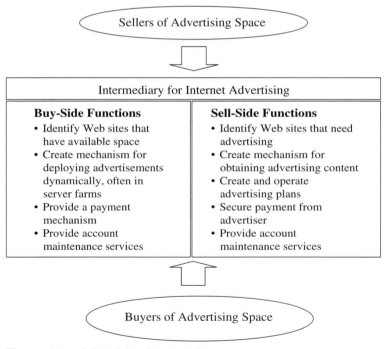

Figure 8.5　Advertising Intermediary

It is also apparent and widely recognized that banner ads are not the golden egg many Web sites assumed they were. Predictably, the market for online ads has taken a hit, with investors beginning to question any reliance on ad revenues alone. Even mighty Yahoo!, as Wall Street demonstrated in October 2000, is not immune to this change of heart.

Simple embedded links in a Web page that are bought with advertisements allow for automatic logging and reporting. Figure 8.6 illustrates this process.

Banners have their place and it behooves the advertiser to fully comprehend the benefits for the product or service and the specific location that is chosen. Directing customers to a particular site is one; coupons are another value-add for banners.

There are several important factors to consider when scheduling banner ads, either as host of the site (revenue) or as one placing a banner ad on another site (advertising/promotion). Some of those considerations are:

1. Position on the Page: The upper-left quadrant is said to be the most effective, followed by a banner at the top. The bottom is less preferable to the sides, and advertising below the normal screen display (i.e., where one has to scroll vertically) is the least useful.

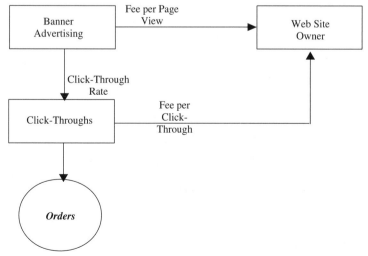

Figure 8.6   Payment Basis for Banner Advertising

2. Size: The typical banner advertisement across the top is 468×60 pixels. Because space is being sold, the cost of advertising varies, among other factors, proportionate to the size.

3. CPM: This is the industry benchmark unit for advertising sales. These costs vary considerably, often by the size. The CPM for heavily visited sites is greater because of the added drawing power implicit in the site.

4. Context: Rates increase when the context is higher. For an e-tail merchant, a shopping portal may have a legitimately higher value than a news portal because the traffic is there for a shopping purpose. An advertiser with a more sophisticated audience requirement would be willing to pay a higher CPM to be on a news site.

5. Advertising Type: With improving support from browsers and improving network performance, advertising is becoming more dynamic and interactive. If not overdone, such advertisements may produce greater click-throughs.

6. Advertising (promotional) Value: As with any other advertising, the better the value proposition, the greater the response. Advertisements that include an offer, such as "25 percent Discount," "Free," etc., do well. Where the value proposition gives something to the customer, "solution-based" ads are strong performers; for example, advertising offering search functionality for a gift, etc.

7. Click-Throughs: This attests to the final desired result, namely, the click-through to the underlying Web link. Typically, these are not guaranteed, but have the highest value.

Slotted Positioning in Portals

Portals dedicate certain areas within a Web page to have preferred positioning of merchants. This is analogous to end-of-aisle or other preferred shelf space positioning in retail stores. For such privileges, retail stores charge merchants for these "slotting" arrangements.

In the online B2C and B2B worlds of e-commerce, this practice translates to preferred positioning on Web pages. These merchandized areas may have various sizes, shapes, and locations. The value proposition that these portals have is twofold:

1. Contextual Positioning: Portals allow merchants to be visible in select locations on a continuing basis and, for enhanced branding, to be seen in a context

that supports the company stance. This constant presence is equivalent to a billboard on a commute. A business portal for office equipment may have a home page portal slot for a vendor. If Staples were to secure such a spot for an extended period, the online commuter may be explicitly or subliminally evangelized to the notion that Staples stands for all office equipment. The resulting placement could be for a banner ad or another vehicle.

2. Contextual Purchasing: This is more powerful for vertical solution merchants. In this placement, the merchant is positioned at a category or subcategory level dealing specifically with a customer need context. A customer searching for garden tools in a shopping portal may start at home and garden categories, drilling down to the garden tools subcategory. A merchant positioned here has a better chance of getting a click-through, thereby saving the customer further effort.

Figure 8.7 shows how preferential placement and slotted advertising works. For a merchant advertising on a slotting basis, the following considerations apply:

1. Location Within the Site: Usually the portal has a structured navigation tree with various branches, sub-branches and, eventually, content. Most portals

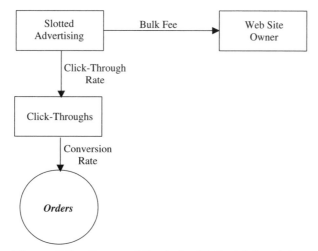

Figure 8.7 Payment Basis for Slotted Advertising

charge by proximity to the root of this navigational tree. For example, the highest charge is at the entry page, next highest at the next level, and so on.

2. Size: Just like banner advertising, advertising in slotting arrangements depends on the "real estate" provided.

3. Traffic: Guaranteed page views or impressions over the course of the contract.

4. Rotation: Movement around the site and into and out of preferred positions on some basis (for example, to the top slot, then a specific page, back to top left, etc.).

5. Audience Characterization: Representations of the demographics and psychographics are always important because the advertisement needs to be relevant to the target audience. Dog ads found on a cat-lover site are inefficient!

Preferential Positioning in Search Engines

The growth of the Internet continues to be a major driver of traffic to many sites, and both experienced surfers and newcomers rely on "search" as the method of navigation. This has placed contextual search engines—those emphasizing vertical search markets, such as for news, shopping, services, etc.—in prominent positions for those using search-based advertising. The advertising can be explicit, as in a banner advertisement, or it can be subtle by listing the preferred merchants on the top of the search result set.

Getting preferred placement is extremely important because the customer is using this third party, the search engine, to help locate your site. There are two processes to get higher listings in search engines: paying for placement and using keywords in metatags.

Similar to slotting, merchants pay search engines and search engine portals to display an offering higher in a list when the search request corresponds to their area of interest. For instance, a toy company might have an agreement with the search engine that a specific toy advertisement would appear if any user searched for a keyword of "gift for a child" in the search engine. This turns out to be quite a cost-effective method of advertising. It is based on the popularity for search-based surfing that is still the norm.

For a merchant advertising on a search engine basis, the following considerations apply:

1. Location Within Search Result Set: Once search results are returned, the location of the advertising is important, either explicitly or implicitly, by prioritizing the merchant at the top of the search results.
2. Size: If the advertising is explicit, then size matters.
3. Traffic: Consumers have preferred search engines, primarily for specialized interests (such as shopping). Metrics of the search portal (traffic, number of searches requested, repeat customers, and affiliations of the search portal) are important.
4. Number of "Preferred" Merchants: Search engines can sell the "pole position" to only a few. (Pole position refers to the allocation of the inside track placement, or seeding, to one car in auto racing. Pole position is the preferred position.) It is important for the merchant to ensure that there are no more than a specific number of preferred merchants for your category.
5. Payment Models: Most search engines charge a fixed fee for preferential positioning over a contracted period. A few charge for click-throughs, expect a commission on the eventual sale, or look for a micropayment on the transaction (see Chapter 7, "Pricing Models on the Web"). Search-based advertising is mapped in Figure 8.8.

Analysis of Marketing Effectiveness

The intent of a marketing campaign is to establish a brand, acquire customers, and obtain orders. Unfortunately, rules of thumb vary widely with every advertising and branding situation, making it important to present the following benchmarks with the understanding that their relevance in measuring the effectiveness of a campaign depends on a large number of variables:

1. Capital Cost of Campaign: This is the fixed cost associated with the advertising campaign.
2. Incremental Cost of Campaign: Depending on the type of campaign, there may be incremental costs associated with a finer-grained metric of the

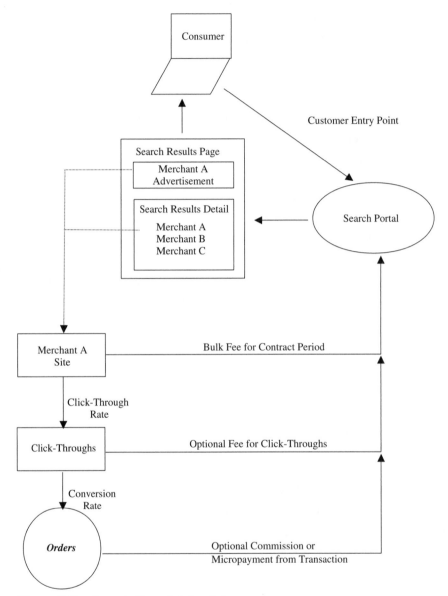

Figure 8.8 Search-Based Advertising

campaign (for example: number of emails sent in a permission marketing campaign).

3. Total Cost of Campaign: Sum of the capital and incremental costs.

4. Total Number of Impressions: This is a count of the number of times the advertisement is seen (typically, there is no discrimination between total impressions and unique impressions to a customer; in other words, the same advertisement shown five times to one customer counts as five impressions).

5. Click-Through Rate: Percentage of the advertising audience who, having seen the advertisement, click-through to the link and become "visitors."

6. Browse Time: The average number of minutes that a visitor stays at the linked site. When a site is able to encourage increased browsing time, the purchasing quantities and value of the order go up.

7. Conversion Rate: Percentage of visitors who purchase and become "customers."

8. Average Revenue per Order: The average sales attributable to a customer from this channel. This may be dependent on the type of channel: a search engine-based advertising channel may differ quite significantly from slotted advertising in a subcategory.

9. Total Revenues from Campaign: This is the total revenue over the period of the campaign, allowing for some residual time at the end for delayed impact.

10. Average Net Margin: This is the gross return to the merchant after accounting for cost of goods and cost of operations.

11. Total Marketing Value: This is total revenue value gained by the campaign and is obtained by multiplying the total number of orders by the average net margin. To allow for the "branding" component of marketing, a numerical value to branding can be associated.

12. Return on Investment: This is the traditional ROI metric expressed in percentages:

ROI of campaign = (Total Marketing Value – Total Campaign Cost) / Total Campaign Cost.

As any accountant might inform us, ROI should be a reasonable rate of return, such as 10 percent or greater, to indicate that use of funds for marketing is justified. Distressingly, it remains true that ROI analyses for marketing campaigns of Internet companies are negative, which is reflected in their negative P/E ratios. Those trying to explain away poor financial performance want you to consider the "Lifetime Value" of an acquired customer, rather than the purchase within the campaign time frame. There is some merit for the brick-and-mortar company coming online to add incremental volume to sales through incorporating online into their overall marketing strategy.

Given the proclivity of the Internet consumer to change allegiances at the click of a mouse, this is an ill-advised posture for the pure-play dot com, as we are seeing. It is prudent *not to overestimate* the lifetime value of an acquired customer in a mercurial and fickle environment!

Marketing Campaign Elements

Marketing is an uncertain science. As a consequence, there was and still is marketing money being spent without regard to objectives and with little planning. A marketing campaign should have five interlinked elements:

Campaign Planning: Clear understanding of the campaign should exist prior to commencement. This should clarify the campaign intent in detail, including:

- Objectives of the campaign (branding, customer acquisition)
- Campaign method (advertising, permission marketing, etc.)
- Target audience (demographics and, where possible, psychographics)
- Tracking methods to quantify and evaluate effectiveness
- Anticipated results

Campaign Operations: For the chosen campaign, there should be specific assignments of responsibility. Unmanaged campaigns rarely go well. The marketing manager should control:

- Time and space of campaign
- Test marketing, if possible (example: small permission marketing effort)
- Experimentation with different sizes and types
- Monitoring site logistics at the advertised site
- Working closely with the business development manager at the advertised site

Customer Acquisition: As a visitor clicks through, it is important to monitor behavior closely. Current tracking tools allow Web administrators to extract visitor behavior, such as in the following dimensions:

- Origin of entry (geography, ISP locations)
- Timing of entry (attests to when the advertising is effective)
- Responsiveness to specific media type (type of mailer, size, or location of advertisement)
- Duration of stay
- Navigation during stay
- Purchasing behavior

Campaign Statistics: As the campaign rolls forward, all data should be collated to enable cumulative analysis. Data collected should cover:

- Total impressions obtained or total emails sent
- Number of responses received
- Number of customers obtained
- Purchase detail by category and average value

Campaign Analysis: During the course of the campaign there should be a continuous loop that fine-tunes the campaign, including modifications to campaign planning and operations. When the campaign is complete, a campaign analysis should be undertaken. The following questions are useful:

- Was the campaign executed as per the original intent?
- Did each advertising site provide the environment and the impressions promised?
- Was the desired click-through rate achieved? If not, why not? What alternatives were attempted and with what result?
- Was the desired conversion achieved from visitor to customer? If not, why not? What needs to be improved for the next campaign?

Figure 8.9 interrelates the key elements in a complete marketing program. At the core is a campaign analysis. The aphorism applies: "If you don't know where you are going, you will never know when you get there!"

Sample Analysis

A sample model is constructed here for the various customer acquisition models. The model is for an online consumer store, which potentially could use any of the customer acquisition strategies discussed earlier. The intent here is to compare and contrast the various strategies and demonstrate the pros and cons of each strategy in practical terms.

The following assumptions are made:

(All customer acquisition tactics bring in 100,000 visitors, which is still relatively small for B2C but okay for B2B.)

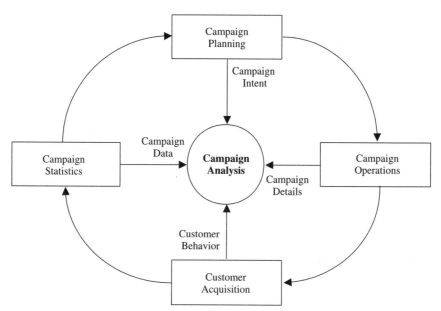

Figure 8.9   A Complete Marketing Campaign Cycle

1. The Web site campaign runs through a one-year contract term.
2. Assumptions are made for each tactic based on currently known metrics.
3. These metrics are used to obtain the cost of the specific campaigns.
4. The cost of goods sold is taken at 70 percent.
5. The cost of operations is taken as 8 percent of sales revenue. This encompasses all costs associated with salaries, rent, utilities, etc.
6. Leaving an operating margin of 22 percent, which is low (but adequate for a dot com!).

The following specific assumptions about these tactics guide the analysis:

- **Permission Marketing:** Obtaining customers from opt-in email lists is an important element in any online campaign. The cost to acquire and mail to an opt-in email name is 10 cents and the response rate is taken as 8 percent. Currently, responses for permission marketing range from 5 to 15 percent. A set up fee of $5,000 is assumed. A conversion rate of 3 percent is assumed, as this is considered an effective merchandising method for specific products and a custom message.
- **Affiliate Marketing:** This consists of using an affiliate marketing network. Commission paid to affiliates is 7 percent and the commission to the affiliate network is 3 percent, leading to a 10 percent total commission on the sale. The initial cost to set up the affiliate network is taken at $10,000. It is assumed that an average of 2,750 affiliates are signed up and they contribute 36 click-throughs per affiliate per year. A low conversion rate of 0.5 percent rate is assumed, as affiliate marketing does not offer the purchasing context to drive high conversions.
- **Banner Advertising:** The cost of advertising is assumed at $15 per CPM, with no set up costs. The click-through rate is 0.8 percent, which corresponds to the generally low impact of banner advertisements. The conversion rate is also kept low, at 1 percent.
- **Slotting:** An example of slotting inside a shopping portal is modeled here. The portal guarantees a minimum of 10 million impressions over a 12-month period at a cost of $100,000. This leads to a maximum CPM charge of $10, which is low! A conversion rate of 1 percent is assumed.

- **Search Engine Placement:** This arrangement is for preferential positioning in select categories of the merchant in a shopping search engine portal. It is assumed that the merchant is shown 100,000 times in the category context as a result of customer searches. Given the search result positioning, a high click-through rate of 5 percent is assumed, along with a conversion rate of 5 percent. For modeling, estimate that the merchant pays $10,000 per month and an initial setup fee of $5,000. This leads to a "referral fee" of $1.25 for 100,000 referrals. Additionally, a commission payment of 2 percent is made on each sale.

Model Analysis Metrics

To assess the effectiveness of a marketing campaign, the following metrics are applied:

Visitor Acquisition Cost = Total Cost of Campaign / Number of Visitors to the site

Customer Acquisition Cost = Total Cost of Campaign / Total Number of Customers Acquired

Sales Ratio = Total Sales Earned / Total Cost of Campaign

Sales Return on Investment = Sales ROI

= (Total Sales – Total Cost of Campaign) / Total Cost of Campaign

Gross Revenues on Investment = Gross Returns ROI

= (Gross Revenues – Total Cost of Campaign) / Total Cost of Campaign

Net Revenues on Investment = Net Returns ROI

= (Net Revenues – Total Cost of Campaign) / Total Cost of Campaign

The cost metric here comprises the total cost of the campaign. The "key metric" in Table 8.7 for each marketing campaign identifies that one important variable that is "controllable" by the merchant running the campaign.

Table 8.7 Comparative Analysis for the Marketing Campaigns of an Example Store

	Permission Marketing	Affiliate Marketing	Banner Advertising	Slotting	Search Engine Placement
Contract Terms	1 year term	1 year term	1 year term	1 year term	1 year term
Key Metric Value	emails sent	Number of affiliates recruited	Number of impressions	Number of guaranteed impressions	Number of times merchant shown after search
Assumed Value of Metric per Annum	1,250,000	2,750	12,500,000	10,000,000	1
Initial Cost	$5,000	$10,000			$5,000
Incremental Cost per Unit	$0.10	$0.00	$0.015	$0.010	$10,000
Cost per Month	$10,417	$0.00	$15,625	$8,333	$10,000
Click-Through Rate	8 percent	36 percent	0.80 percent	1 percent	5 percent
Number of Visitors (annual)	100,000	99,000	100,000	100,000	100,000
Total Annual Cost	$130,000	$10,000	$187,500	$100,000	$125,000
Conversion Rate	3 percent	0.5 percent	1 percent	1 percent	5 percent
Number of Customers	3,000	495	1,000	1,000	5,000
Average Sale per Order	$75	$75	$75	$75	$75
Total Annual Sales	$225,000	$37,125	$75,000	$75,000	$375,000
Cost of Goods (70 percent)	$157,500	$25,988	$52,500	$52,500	$262,500

311

Application of Business Models

In this final chapter, you will see a roll-up of the principles discussed in the earlier chapters. To highlight the impact of metrics underlying the various business models, several practical examples are presented in a series of ready-to-apply analyses.

A full business is created to relate its mission to daily operations. We then take it to the next level by relating the metrics of the business model to profitability of the company. We also analyze various marketing approaches and settle on one for implementation, measuring its effectiveness when using different promotional approaches.

In essence, a for-profit business is a machine whose ultimate design and purpose is to serve customers. As a reward for doing so, it must then make money for its shareholders and satisfy the requirements of incorporation, promote employee well being, and meet community responsibilities.

Such an economic engine always has a final report card of how its capital is utilized. The resulting machine is designed to implement the intent of the business, or goals and objectives. Management responsible for operations, resources, and technology operates this machine we call an enterprise. The report card is a return on assets or capital employed. A benchmark along the way is return on sales, or gross profits.

These returns are among the many measures of value created by a stable, ongoing concern. There are other measures, mostly by-products of management excellence. Hopefully, success in reducing the cost of customer acquisition, increasing customer retention, and raising the bar for customer service are also dialed into corporate objectives.

Figure 9.1 paints a simplified picture of the dynamic interaction that takes place as management brings in capital, blends it with internal resources, and takes advantage of external factors to create value. There are many more factors, as we will see in the pages that follow, and their relationships with each other are sometimes easy to map, but more often than not they defy simplification.

Business Structure

To facilitate a view of the business as a machine, businesses are typically constructed in the following ways. Some are explored here in some detail. Others are left for readers to explore on their own.

- **Mission:** A clearly defined and overarching goal for the company. This should be stated in a clear, simple, and precise way.

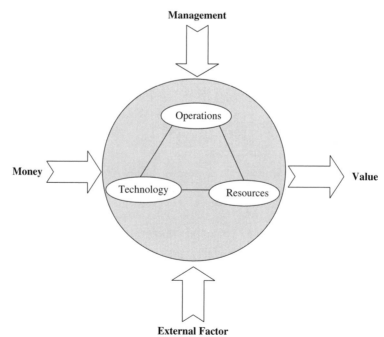

Figure 9.1　An Economic Business Engine, the Machine

- **Strategy:** Well-articulated strategic activities to achieve the mission. These should be defined for each major functional entity in the company.
- **Business Processes:** Translation of strategy to business requirements, taken down to specific functional and actionable activities. Business processes implement business requirements through specific steps. This requires detailed analysis of the various external and internal conditions that may allow or deter the achievement of business requirements.
- **Resource Assessment:** A good understanding of business processes provides the basis for identifying resources required for specific business activities. Such a granular understanding of resource requirements is invaluable for scaling up or down activities of a company.
- **Information Technology Platform:** The environment that hosts business processes. The offline infrastructure may include office facilities, warehouses, shipping and logistics facilities, and so on. For the online world, this takes the form of hardware, software, network connectivity, and site management. The entire range of auxiliary services that enables this IT platform is important in enabling the Internet platform.
- **Content:** Internally and externally developed content that enhances and extends the business to its many constituents. This takes various forms, such as product information, links to strategic partners in the supply chain, collateral materials, and inter-relationships. Online content, as we saw in Chapter 4, "The Content Stack," consists of text, graphics, video, audio, and eventually aromatic output followed by perhaps 3D or holographic images. Offline content consists of brochures, samples, catalogs, and the like.
- **Community:** To achieve business intentions, a community consisting of target markets, employees, and other stakeholders is desirable. This often results in increased "stickiness" at a site, which creates value. It also creates content which, over time, can be a valuable database of "third-party" information for use at the site or be leveraged by trading it to interested parties.
- **Commerce:** If the business intent is to achieve revenues through transactions, the ability to engage in commerce may be strongly dictated by the underlying business platform. The actual volume of commerce conducted depends on marketing campaigns undertaken. The customer base is included in the company's valuation.
- **Customer Acquisition:** As internal value is created, the company must "externalize" value to gain brand equity and expand customer interest. Online

marketing campaigns complement offline campaigns. They are not and never should be stand-alone initiatives.

- **Services:** This refers to value added by external parties for execution of business activities. Outsourcing many technology and business services is fast becoming a critical advantage to online enterprises, because outsourcing reduces the time to market and allows efficiencies of scale to be gained from "best of breed" players. This means that the diverse channels of outside resources that are available to a company should be rigorously understood and analyzed frequently.

- **Operations:** Day-to-day workings of the machine are tracked in the operational aspects of the company. This addresses daily orders, open orders, customer service, logistics, etc.

Figure 9.2 Integrates each concept and facet of a business and develops a pattern of economic activity that is mapped from the corporate mission through company operations in a dynamic way.

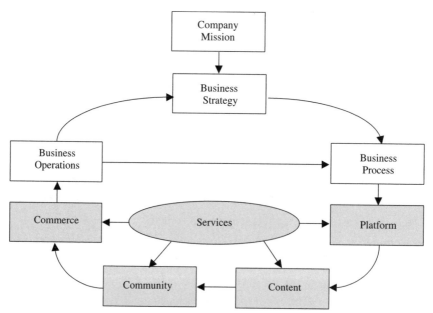

Figure 9.2 Flow of Business Activities

Evolution of Business Strategy

Strategy supports the company mission. In this section, the adoption of business strategy is treated only peripherally to provide a context for it when considering business models that work in e-commerce. The interested reader is urged to pursue references included here along with other additional materials on business strategy.

In brief, the framing of a business strategy is presented under the following four viewpoints:

- Understanding the Industry
- Understanding One's Own Company
- Setting the Basis for Change in Strategy
- Effective Implementation of Strategy

Strategy: Understanding the Industry

A good starting point for a strategic analysis, especially for a new business, is to use Porter's Five Forces Model, which takes a broad perspective on a business. (Reference: Michael Porter, *Competitive Strategy,* New York, Simon and Schuster, 1980.) In this model, the average profitability of an industry and various impacts on a specific player can be understood based on the following:

1. **Current Industry Competitors:** Who are the current players, their relative market shares, their growth rates, their competitive advantages, and the total market size?
2. **Potential Entrants:** Who are likely new entrants into this market and what are their strengths?
3. **Substitutes:** Are there substitutes to the industry that a potential customer could choose? This is particularly important to understand in the context of emerging online business models, many of which seek to supplant more established business practices.
4. **Supplier Power:** Who supplies the key ingredients to this industry (information, goods, process, infrastructure) and what is the source of their power? What lever-

age do industry players have with the suppliers? Are the suppliers fragmented? How much power do they have in setting marginal costs for the industry?

5. **Buyer Power:** Who buys the end products from players in this industry? What power do they have in setting prices? What is their ability to switch between alternative providers?

These five forces are depicted in a Michael Porter chart (Figure 9.3) that is standard fare in business classes worldwide.

Understanding One's Own Company

A good meditative exercise that management should undertake periodically (say, once a quarter) is to carry out what is popularly known as a SWOT analysis. This refers to a company's Strengths, Weaknesses, Opportunities, and Threats. This could be done at a company level or broken down to a departmental level, the objective of which is specific, actionable conclusions. A relative analysis against a target competitor or an emerging threat may also prove useful.

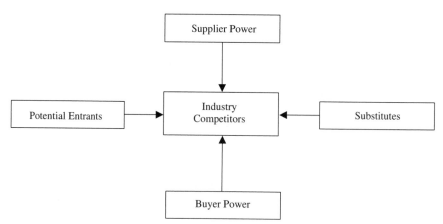

Figure 9.3   Porter's Five Forces Model for Industry Analysis

(Adapted with the permission of The Free Press, a Division of Simon & Schuster, Inc., from *COMPETITIVE STRATEGY: Techniques for Analyzing Industries and Competitors* by Michael E. Porter. Copyright © 1980, 1998 by The Free Press.)

Setting the Basis for Change in Strategy

Strategic analyses often acquire a bad rap as being intellectual debates that accomplish nothing. By its very nature, strategy is highly subjective. However, with rigor and sustained practice, strategic analysis can lead to dynamic change for the company. Specifically, it is important that the strategic intent of the company be continuously refined to adjust to changes both internal and external to the company.

In this regard, the strategic dissonance theory of Burgelman and Grove provides a framework for continuous refinement of strategy (Reference: Robert A. Burgelman and Andrew S. Grove, "Strategic Dissonance," *Califormia Management Review,* Vol. 38, No. 2, © 1996, by The Regents of the University of California. Reprinted by permission of The Regents.) This theory may be particularly relevant to the highly volatile Internet industry and is explained on the basis of five forces:

1. **Basis of Competitive Advantage in the Industry**: This is unearthed in industry analysis as in the Porter analysis shown earlier.
2. **Distinctive Competence:** An assessment of competence gained by the company, possibly as a consequence of prior strategy.
3. **Official Corporate Strategy:** The current stated strategic direction of the company (the current strategic intent).
4. **Strategic Action:** These are actual actions undertaken by the company, ostensibly to implement the intended strategy.
5. **Internal Selection Environment:** Mediates between the other four forces to allocate the company's resources for strategic action.

The authors argue that in every dynamic industry, there is "strategic dissonance" between strategic intent and strategic action. An understanding of such dissonance, in the context of the industry and the firm's internal competence, should lead to the evolution of a revised corporate strategy and modified strategic actions. This dynamic interaction is shown in Figure 9.4.

Effective Implementation of Strategy

Creating a strategy is frequently the easy part; the problems are often in the implementation. Common pitfalls include the following:

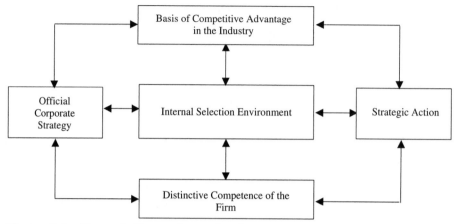

Figure 9.4 Dynamic Forces Impacting Strategy

- Inadequate management alignment on the strategic goals and objectives
- Frequent "top-down" definition of strategy without adequate feedback obtained from the ground troops
- Insufficient translation of strategy to specific departmental and manager level actions
- Inadequate definition of metrics associated with strategic actions, which is the focus of this book
- Lack of vested responsibility to execute actions
- Absence of an implementation timetable
- Absence of a periodic review of actions and results
- Too many "strategies" coming down the pike, leading to a general disregard for "strategic action"

Business Process Mapping

A scalable company can only be built on adherence to structured business processes. If processes are well mapped, then each aspect of the process is understandable in terms of the resource requirements, thus identifying the capacity of the system. Then, in conjunction with a company growth plan, the infrastructure, technology, and human resource requirements can all be adjusted accordingly.

Too many e-commerce businesses are the result of unplanned systems, which ironically break down just as the order volume surges dramatically or returns start coming in.

A company runs on the basis of structured, sequenced work. All business operations need to incorporate business processes that understand and integrate all the activities and any exceptions that may occur.

Comprehension of all possible manual and automated business activities is achieved through business process mapping. Business process mapping can be carried out to considerable levels of granularity to include all software and human steps. Table 9.1 lists the basic steps for business process mapping.

Table 9.1 Business Process Mapping Steps: A Rough Set of Corporate Metrics

Number	Activity	Examples
1	Identify each originating activity	An online customer order
2	Identify all entities that are needed to complete this activity	Web site operations Customer service staff Order management staff Logistics staff Inventory operations Fulfillment operations Delivery tracking Customer notification Back-end systems update
3	Follow the activity through each entity and track every variation of the activity	Online order is posted to the database. Order management to track order if product available in inventory. If not in inventory, customer service to contact the customer to provide back-order notification and resolution
4	Create systems and processes to support every variation	Hire enough customer service staff to process anticipated customer exceptions

Choices, Controls, and Consequences

In the operations of every company, we see that there are three C's that affect an ongoing enterprise: choices, controls, and consequences. These C's define the operational roadmap for each company and are slightly different from the more traditional 3C's of company, customer, and competition.

Choices

From a set of options for each aspect of the business, the management can choose a specific course of action. For instance, an e-commerce company may have the following, simply stated customer service options:

- Keep customer service in-house using employees
- Outsource customer service operations

Clearly, the selection of either one subsequently has fundamental impacts on the business operations. Therefore, it is important to understand and define all options available for every major business operation.

Controls

Given a set of choices, a business then has "controls" that can be used for refining operations and obtaining improved results. While this goes well with the concept of the business as a machine, in reality most companies, dot com or otherwise, operate by instinct rather than analysis. For instance, if the revenues are flat, there might be an edict to increase marketing efforts. Or, if there is to be a reduction of costs, the executive edict might well be to reduce the consulting staff by 10 percent. In many cases, inexperienced management has little understanding of the consequences of exercising such draconian control, beyond their desire to reduce costs at any cost!

For the customer service example seen here, if the business chooses to have an in-house customer service staff, then the set of controls may be:

- number of customer service staff
- pay levels

- performance metrics and requirements
- incentives for productivity

Consequences

The results of choices and controls naturally generate consequences to the enterprise. In the customer service example used for illustration of choices and controls, there are several consequences:

- Not easy to change to outsourced customer service model
- Hiring and training may take time
- Firing, even for cause, might be a problem
- Hours of operations may be limited
- Have to provide human resource benefits
- Difficult to change cost structure once hiring is done
- Can ramp up gradually to increasing need

This connectivity between choices, controls, and consequences is illustrated in Figure 9.5.

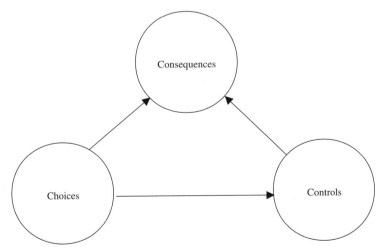

Figure 9.5 Interplay Between the 3 Cs of Operations

Consequence Analysis

An extension of this idea can be pursued to create a consequence analysis diagram for the business, which might provide the basis for strategic decisions. This is illustrated in Figure 9.6.

Modeling an E-Commerce Store

Company Name: ebiztro.com

Mission: Create a U.S.-based store that sells hard-to-find handicraft items from around the world.

Strategy:

- Target market at the outset immigrant and expatriate populations in the U.S.
- U.S. operations initially; possible global rollout after successful U.S. operations.
- Cater to ethnic and immigrant communities in the U.S.
- Use domestic suppliers from the U.S. initially; plan to stage globally later.
- Collaborate with ethnic stores in local U.S. communities where ethnic communities are prominent.
- E-commerce (multilingual) operations and sales.
- Use kiosks at affiliated ethnic stores.

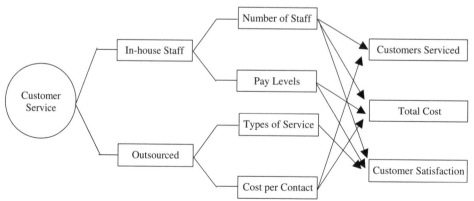

Figure 9.6   Consequence Analysis Diagram for Analysis of Options

- Fulfillment through direct shipment and pick-up at offline local affiliated store.
- Customer acquisition through advertising in ethnic radio and TV shows, local newspapers, and point-of-sale displays at affiliate stores.

Modeling Objectives: Construct a model of the e-commerce store for handicrafts and illustrate the issues of choice, controls, and consequences.

Industry Analysis

A simple Porter analysis of this industry reveals the following:

Industry Competitors
1. Predominantly ethnic stores with few selections, low inventory, and poor service.
2. A few high-end ethnic fashion stores with limited clientele and reach.
3. One departmental chain aggregating popular ethnic goods.
4. No significant online competition, currently.

Potential Entrants
1. Ethno-centric Web sites hosted abroad catering to expatriate populations (high likelihood).
2. Sites in home country fulfilling from abroad (low likelihood).
3. Expatriates with a few connections, using eBay and other auction sites.

Substitutes
1. Acceptance of "pseudo" mass manufactured ethnic items (some likelihood).
2. Acceptance of local (U.S.) handcrafted items, as in a domestic cottage industry (some likelihood).

Supplier Power
1. Distributors within U.S. are the initial suppliers. Reliability and scalability are two important qualifying attributes. Those that do qualify have high supplier power, initially.
2. Suppliers in a foreign country have lower supplier power, because there they face more competition. This supply source is more difficult to reach; and, inevitably, there are always factors of unreliability and quality.

3. Direct supply from manufacturing co-operatives in a foreign country allows for best-negotiated prices. However, these are often poorly positioned to execute speedily on demand.

Buyer Power

1. Initially, buyer power in the targeted ethnic online communities is low, given the poorly organized industry and lack of reliable sources. With proper positioning and merchandising, high profit margins could be realized.
2. With increasing entrants, buyer power increases substantially, although direct price comparisons may be difficult due to lack of standardized products. This eventually reduces profit margins.

Business Process Mapping

The following key business processes are identified:

1. Online ordering system with direct shipment method (illustrated in Figure 9.7).
2. Returns systems through affiliate store system (illustrated in Figure 9.8).

The online ordering process in Figure 9.7 shows a customer using the Web site to order an item. If the item is in stock, the credit card is processed. If approved, a notification is sent to the warehouse to ship the item and the customer is charged. If the item is out of stock, a back-order notification is issued. With customer approval, this could lead to an online order when the product arrives or substitution if acceptable. When the product is shipped from the warehouse, the customer is notified. This basic process can be extended to accommodate variations such as enhanced customer services, giftwrapping, and so on.

Figure 9.8 demonstrates the process for a customer return through a retail affiliate outlet. In this case, the customer walks in with the item, which is inspected by the store clerk. The store clerk then checks the online store database to see if the merchandise is within the warranty period. If acceptable, the customer is credited for the amount of purchase and targeted for a replacement purchase; the retail store then returns the merchandise or stocks it for an in-store sale.

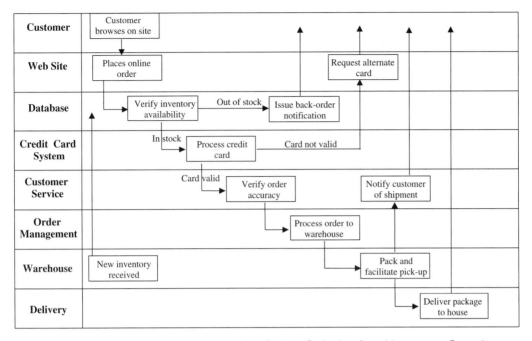

Figure 9.7   Business Process Flow for Online Ordering for ebiztro.com Sample Store

The advantage of detailed process mapping is that it allows for a discrete understanding of the load on various system resources, such as servers, network, customer service personnel, and warehousing staff.

Modeling Strategy

Throughout this chapter, the handicrafts store is modeled with respect to the four stacks, namely: platform, content, community, and commerce. The methodology is as follows:

- ❏ Identify the element of the stack
- ❏ Identify the options and make choices
- ❏ Represent diagrammatically, if appropriate
- ❏ Correlate costs and revenues to control variables

Table 9.2 provides a roadmap for the modeling that is carried out later in this chapter.

Table 9.2 International ebiztro Store Implementation Plan

Stack	Element	Considerations	Key Variables
	Business	Office space	Number of employees
	Network	Bandwidth needed for Internet connectivity	Number of site visitors
Platform	Hardware	☐ Number of desktops ☐ Number of servers	☐ Number of employees ☐ Number of site visitors
	Software	☐ Desktop software ☐ E-commerce software	☐ Number of employees ☐ Number of servers
Content	☐ Product Content ☐ Review Content ☐ Related Content	☐ Production cost ☐ Reviews by customer ☐ Content feed by outside sources	☐ Number of products ☐ Response percentage ☐ Cost per unit content
Community	☐ Creation ☐ Operations	☐ Create and maintain ☐ Provide online services	☐ Number of communities ☐ Operators per community
Commerce	☐ Operations ☐ Marketing ☐ Sales	☐ Fulfillment methodology ☐ Maximize visits ☐ Maximize conversion	☐ Time to service customer ☐ Number of site visitors ☐ Number of orders

328

For the modeling to yield results it is important to relate key variables to the smallest number of independent variables. For example, the number of customer service staff can be related to the number of orders; however, the number of products cannot be reduced to a dependence on the number of orders or number of site visitors.

Figure 9.8 takes the data from Table 9.2 and creates a process flow chart for an affiliate store supporting our international handicrafts operation.

Modeling produces two sets of results:

❑ Fixed Costs: These costs accrue irrespective of the number of site visitors or number of orders. For example, the cost of content production and maintenance of the Web site are not affected by site traffic. Fixed costs are useful in determining a base cash burn-rate per month.

❑ Variable Costs: Costs associated with goods, increased customer service, additional servers, etc., vary appreciably with number of orders and Web traffic.

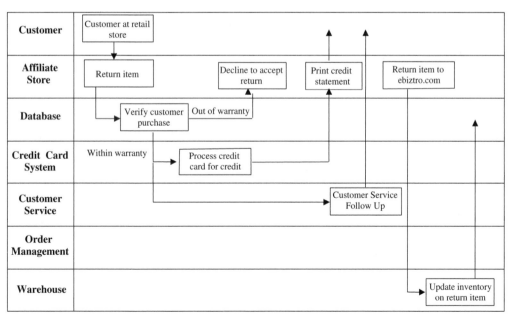

Figure 9.8   Business Process Flow for Returns Processing at Affiliate

Variable costs identify the impact of growth and enable an understanding of the consequences of increased marketing or more effective merchandising.

Platform Choices

Platform choices for business, network, hardware, and software are discussed in this section.

Business Platform

- Office space: rented office building

  Assume average of 200 sq. ft. per person and $2 per sq. ft. per month

  Monthly rental cost = $400 per person per month

- Inventory space: none required because of drop-ship operations

Network Platform

Network capacity required is predicated on servicing a peak load of concurrent users on the system. A network engineer can size the requirements given an understanding of the content on the site and the visitor behavior pattern. For our e-commerce store, a 1 Mbps network connection can handle one million visitors per month.

Hardware Platform

Desktop Hardware

Assuming that each employee gets a computer at $1,000 per desktop unit, we have:

Total cost of desktops = $1,000 × number of employees

Servers

Options: Servers with: Windows 2000/NT, Solaris, or other variations of UNIX as operating systems

Choice: Windows 2000 servers for initial lower price and quicker deployment. Known drawback is lower scalability and less operational stability. Assume that the cost per server is $5,000.

Assume 10 servers for development, testing, graphics, etc. This leads to $50,000 as the fixed cost of servers.

A system architect can compute the load carrying capacity of a server. For purposes of this modeling, it is assumed that one new server is required for every 500,000 visitors per month to the site.

Additional servers required = (visitors per month) / 500,000

Cost of additional servers = (visitors per month / 500,000) × 5,000

Example:

If site plans called for two million visitors per month, which would require a total of 14 servers, 10 for development and test, and four to support customer traffic of two million customers, or 500,000 visitors per server: The cost of additional servers is then $2 \times \$5,000 = \$10,000$.

Note: The calculations above are only for cost management, and planning purposes. Server sizing is complicated by considerations of multi-CPU configurations, memory management, and server architecture. Trained IT personnel are best positioned to address specific requirements.

Other Hardware

Other hardware required includes switches, hubs, routers, firewall, cabling, etc. Assume $50K to accommodate all of these.

Software Platform

Office Software: Assume $400 per employee

Office software costs = \$400 × number of employees

Enterprise Software

Options: In-house or ASP model

Choice: Small, low-end in-house application chosen

Initial cost = $50,000

Cost per employee = $100

Total enterprise software cost = \$50,000 + 100 × number of employees

E-Commerce Software

By choosing the Microsoft platform, the company uses the Microsoft Commerce Server as the foundation for its cataloging and commerce systems.

Commerce base package cost = $10,000

Additional cost per server = $5,000

Total e-commerce software cost = \$10,000 + \$5,000 × production servers

Content Production

Three kinds of content are required for this Web site:

1. **Product Content:** Information, pictures, description, options, etc., for each product sold on the Web site.
2. **Review Content:** This is a product review with purchase experiences gained from actual customers to the site. Such reviews for each product are powerful motivators for new customers, as well as a useful basis for feedback to manufacturers of the products.
3. **Related Content:** This content provides more generic contextual information. Examples are information about countries, regions, natural habitats, indigenous life, news stories, travel advisories, etc.

Product Content

Options in content generation are relatively limited. There is very little consolidation in the industry. Product content is obtained directly from each supplier. A few of the bigger manufacturers have good product catalogs, and some even have Web sites with pictures that can be grabbed with permission.

Content production involves the following steps:

1. Contact vendor (manufacturer, distributor, in-country host)
2. Obtain collateral (images, description, variations, pricing, inventory, delivery, etc.)
3. Data write-up (product categorization, positioning, pricing)
4. Data entry (entry into the catalog database)
5. Graphics (image enhancement, cropping)
6. Publishing to site

Content production is categorized into three buckets for planning purposes: simple, average, and difficult. Based on studies of the product production process, estimates per Shopkeeping Unit (SKU) are available for the three types of SKU complexity.

Based on content planning requirements, a SKU count of 2,000 per month is specified. Table 9.3 shows that content production requires an average of 792 person-hours per month (about four full-time workers). Most content production work is done by contract labor pegged at $10 per hour, leading to a monthly cost of $7,920 per month.

This analysis leads to the following important metric:

Cost to produce and display 1 SKU = $3.93

Review Content

When a product is purchased, the customer is sent an email approximately four weeks after the sale soliciting a review of the product. A coupon for 20 percent off the next purchase is provided as an incentive for filling out the review.

Related Content

Related content is acquired from third-party content services. Various content subscription services were evaluated and it was decided to purchase a feed of content in the areas of travel, geography, history, and news at a cost of $2,000 per month.

Community Development

The strategy of the company calls for robust development of online ethnic communities associated with handicrafts in each region. Community development is divided into two parts: community content development and community interaction.

For community content development, the world consists of five large blocks:

- Europe (France, Germany, U.K., Scandinavian countries, Spain, Portugal, Greece, etc.)
- Eurasia (including Russia, Poland, Czech Republic, Hungary, etc.)
- Indian subcontinent (India, Sri Lanka, Pakistan, Bangladesh, Nepal)

Table 9.3 Content Labor Requirements

SKU Complexity	Time Per SKU (minutes)	Number of SKUs per Month	Hours Needed per Month	Cost Per Month (at $10 per hour)
Simple	5	500	42	$420
Average	15	1,000	250	$2,500
Difficult	60	500	500	$5,000
		2,000	792	$7,920

- Asia (Japan, Korea, Singapore, Vietnam, Cambodia)
- China and Taiwan/Hong Kong

Community developers required = 5

Cost per month = \$4,000 × 5 = \$20,000 per month

For community interaction it is assumed that one in 20 visitors enter a community chat room. Two chat rooms are maintained for each community dealing with handicraft industry discussions and product discussions (namely, 10 total). One chat room moderator currently moderates both chat rooms for each community. Because the site is launched in the U.S., English is the primary language, though multilingual chat room moderators are on staff.

Chat room moderators required = 5

Cost per month = \$4,000 × 5 = \$20,000 per month

Total monthly cost for community = \$20,000 per month

Commerce Platform

The company operates a drop-ship store model as illustrated in Figure 9.9.

The e-commerce functions carried out by the company are summarized in Table 9.4.

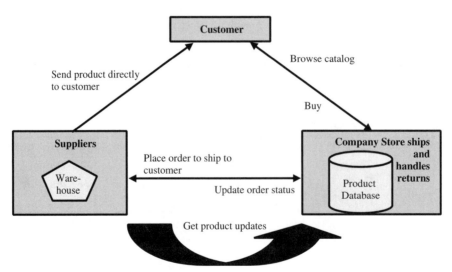

Figure 9.9   Drop-Ship E-Commerce Store Model

Table 9.4 E-Commerce Structure for Company in Store and Forward Model

Function	Detail
E-Commerce Role	• Provide a store and community for handicraft items
Participants	• Consumers, distributors, global handicraft makers
Offerings	• Handicraft items, industry news, community participation
Infrastructure	• Self-hosted • Electronic catalog of goods • Order processing • Customer service • Fulfillment from distributors
Customer Acquisition	• Permission marketing • Banner advertising • Slotting in portals
Role of Intermediary	• Intermediary used for fulfillment • Intermediary used for returns
Pricing Models	• Fixed price
Revenue Breakup	• Cost of goods/service • Marketing cost • Internal operations/administration
Competition	• Numerous

Resource Utilization

To isolate and identify resource requirements it is useful to draw simple entity relationship diagrams. For the store, the "order" is a key variable, triggering activity throughout the enterprise. The following relationship diagrams relate the order to other operational variables. This enables the order entity to be the basis of subsequent analysis.

Figures 9.10, 9.11, and 9.12 display the sequence of events and consequences that an order triggers for the online merchant.

Using an order as the reference metric, Table 9.5 is an example table that is the basis for a load estimate on the e-commerce venture's resources.

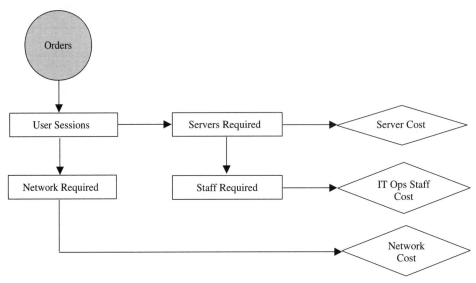

Figure 9.10   Consequence of Orders on IT Operations

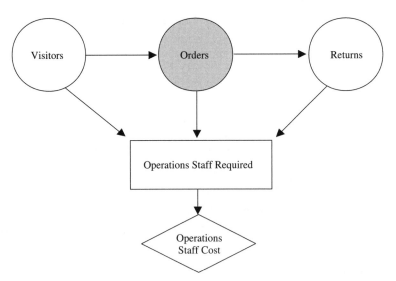

Figure 9.11   Impact of Visitors and Orders on Operations Staff Required

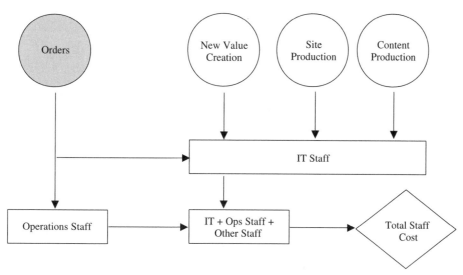

Figure 9.12 Relationship Diagram for Total Staff Required

Table 9.5 Resource Estimate for an Order

Resource Entity	*Metric Selected Based on an Order*	*Example: Value of Resource Needed*
Web Server	Time spent by a visitor on the Web site	5 minutes
Web Server	Number of visitors leading to one order (conversion ratio)	100
Web Server	Average number of hits per visitor	10
Database Server	Average number of database hits per visitor	5
Credit Card Processor	Number of credit card requests per order	1.1 (to account for wrong credit card numbers and fraud)
Customer Service and Order Management, Returns	Time required to service one order (minutes)	20 (including email, chat, phone)

Operations Staffing

The customer-facing operations staff is combined here for the following functions:

- Customer Service: Answering the phone, providing product detail, warranty information, and delivery detail.
- Order Management: Staff in this section deals with order processing, contacting vendors, ensuring process workflow, and resolving issues.
- Logistics and Fulfillment: In this group, the staff deals with ensuring the delivery of the product, installation, returns authorization, and returns processing.

Table 9.6 provides various operating details and metrics as customer-facing applications within the enterprise handle an order.

As we can see, it takes about 20 minutes in the aggregate of human time to process an order throughout all customer-facing applications. So, as an order is received and handled by the customer service department, five minutes of time is allotted. When customer service hands off the order to order management, another ten minutes of human time is required, and so on. To put an economic "burden" on each moment, with an average wage

Table 9.6   Customer-Facing Applications

Operations Department	Average Minutes per Order	Number of Orders per Person per Day (assuming 7-hour workday)	Number of Orders per Person per Month (22 days)
Customer Service	5 minutes	84	84×22
Order Management	10 minutes	42	42×22
Logistics	5 minutes (not enough)	84	84×22
Total Operations Staff	20 minutes	21	21×22

cost of $12 per hour, it cost $4 per order. Conversely, the number of operations staff can be related to the number of orders as:

Operations staff needed = Orders per day / 21

Customer Acquisition

The company reviewed various customer acquisition strategies, which are outlined in Table 9.7.

Customer Acquisition Costs

As a consequence of acquisition strategy analysis, three tactics are evaluated, namely, permission marketing, banner advertising, and slotting in portals. In the preliminary analysis, a comparison is made purely on the basis of customer acquisition cost.

Permission Marketing

Cost per mail sent = 10 cents (includes email name)

Number of emails to be sent per month = 100,000

Cost of permission marketing per month = $10,000

Anticipated click-through rate = 6 percent

Number of visitors expected per month = 6,000

Table 9.7   Customer Acquisition Strategies and Initiatives Taken

Customer Acquisition Strategy	Company Initiative
Permission Marketing	• Company can acquire vendor of mail-lists for immigrant residents • Company can contract to send directed mail merchandising its products
Online Affiliate Marketing	Investigated but abandoned as an unlikely source of useful leads
Banner Advertising	Can advertise in immigrant-centric portals
Portal Slotting	Can obtain slots in immigrant portals
Search Engine Placement	Partially useful

Visitor acquisition cost = $1.67 per visitor

Anticipated conversion rate = 3 percent

Anticipated number of customers = 180

Average customer acquisition cost = $56

Banner Advertising in Portals

Cost per CPM = $10

Contracted CPMs = 1 million per month

Cost per month = $10,000

Anticipated click-through rate = 0.6 percent

Number of visitors per month = 6,000

Visitor acquisition cost = $1.67

Anticipated conversion rate = 1 percent

Anticipated number of customers = 60 per month

Average customer acquisition cost = $167

Slotting in Portals

Cost per annum for a typical portal slot = $240,000 (paid quarterly)*

Number of guaranteed CPM for slot position = 12 million per year

Cost per month = $20,000

Guaranteed CPM per month = 1 million

Anticipated click-through rate = 1 percent

Number of visitors per month = 10,000

Visitor acquisition cost = $2.00

Anticipated conversion rate = 1 percent

Anticipated number of customers = 100 per month

Average customer acquisition cost = $200

Visitor acquisition models are summarized in Figure 9.13.

Cost per visitor for permission marketing and banner advertising is the same in this case, and is appreciably higher for slotting in portals. Assuming the site management can achieve better conversion of visitors to customers with permission marketing, the cost of customer acquisition drops to $56, compared to $166 for banner advertising and $200 for

---

*This is actually low when compared to a primary listing on AOL or Yahoo!, which can run into the millions of dollars.

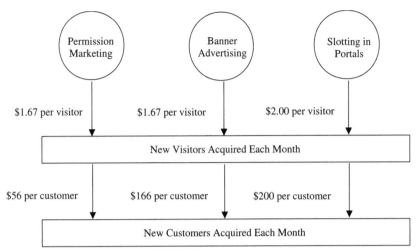

Figure 9.13 Comparison of Visitor and Customer Acquisition for Three Primary Marketing Tactics

slotting in portals. The slotting tactic is eliminated given the high costs and the requirement to commit for the full year in a shopping portal environment. Only the permission marketing method and banner advertising method are evaluated further.

Enterprise Modeling

More detailed analysis is now carried out at the full enterprise level for permission marketing and banner advertising. With modeling, the dominant cost elements of the business are tied in to produce a reasonable model of the enterprise. It is useful once again to view the business as a machine where marketing dollars are poured in to acquire new visitors and customers.

This now places demands on the resources of the system to fulfill expectations of visitors and customers. To keep matters simple, in the current model the lifetime value of a customer is not incorporated. The customer may make repeat purchases with minimal marketing expenditures on the part of the company.

Linkage between the key elements is shown in Figure 9.14. Utilizing marketing dollars, such as in a permission marketing or banner advertising, this drives traffic to the Web

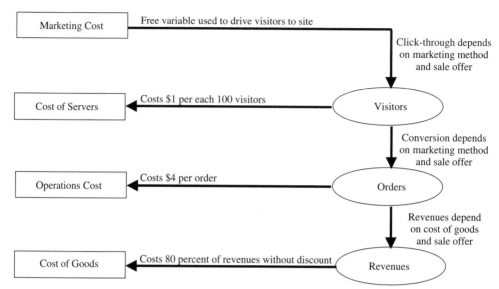

Figure 9.14   Linkages Between Marketing and Resource Utilization

site. The amount of traffic depends on the marketing method as well as the offer made to the customer, which might motivate that initial click.

The anticipated presence of visitors should drive resource requirements for the enterprise. One dominant resource may be the cost of in-house servers to accommodate demand from a new marketing initiative.

Many companies focus on elaborate marketing strategies but fail to plan for the consequence of "success," namely a higher number of visits to the site when the campaign is launched. This "success" causes server and network congestion, leading to customer dissatisfaction, and this achieves the exact opposite of the marketing intent: bring in new, happy customers!

The cost of servers was computed earlier to be about $1 for each new 100 visitors. Additional servers cause other consequences (such as additional IT staff), but these are not elaborated in this model.

Next, consider that a fraction of visitors become customers. A conversion ratio depends again on the marketing method and the offer to the customer. A permission marketing initiative targeted effectively for a well-merchandized product may have a higher conversion ratio than banner advertising for the Web site.

Once an order is placed, operations staff support is required to service the order (estimated in this model to be $4 per order). Staffing or outsourcing of this resource-need should be planned for ahead of the marketing effort.

Finally, the metric shows an obvious outcome from these orders, namely, revenues to the company. The amount of net revenues depends on gross revenues or the actual sale price to the customer minus any reductions associated with special offers such as "free shipping," discounts, two-for-one incentives, etc.

For the goods purchased, there is a consequent cost of goods to be paid to the supplier of them. In this model, this is taken as 80 percent of the original sale price of the items, or a 20 percent gross margin.

The enterprise model could be more elaborate and include other elements that are identified earlier in this chapter, such as: additional staffing apart from operations, cost of office space, cost of desktop machines and software for increased employees, and additional network costs. However, these costs are considered to be of a lower order of significance. They are, therefore, subsumed inside the model in a lump-sum as an aggregate 3 percent of sales.

Figure 9.14 connects marketing and associated costs with available resources. Metrics are derived for each cost item.

Modeling Scenarios and Assumptions

We now continue our modeling for two specific tactical scenarios:

Scenario I: Analysis for Permission Marketing

Scenario II: Analysis for Banner Advertising

In both cases, a budget of $1 million is utilized to explore the consequences of utilizing one marketing strategy versus the other.

To model the effectiveness of a business strategy that is based on a marketing tactic, some assumptions need to be made. In this case, the primary variable of interest to us is the "control" variable of discounting. Most retail and online stores utilize the "Sale" as the basis of competitive strategy in a marketing campaign. In reality, once the strategic elements of a business are in place, there are few "control levers" to utilize.

For the purposes of this exercise, it is assumed that discounting affects both the click-through rate and the conversion rate. Metrics are obtainable for the base case of 0 percent discounting.

In Figure 9.15, the assumed click-through rates are shown for permission marketing and banner advertising.

Figure 9.16 then shows assumptions for the conversion rate. For both click-throughs and conversions, it assumes that permission marketing is appreciably more effective than banner advertising. This is supported by market studies, which show that banner advertising is not very effective in making potential customers click on the banner.

Moreover, visitors who do come in by clicking on a banner ad are not necessarily as motivated to purchase. In contrast, permission marketing can be targeted with much greater specificity, leading to greater click-throughs and conversions.

Another set of assumptions is made regarding the cost of goods, the cost of servers, and the cost of customer service. It is assumed that the cost of goods is 80 percent of the nominal sale price. The cost of customer service and the increase in costs of production servers are based on computations earlier in this chapter.

Finally, different assumptions are made about the average sales price per item for permission marketing versus banner advertising. Permission marketing allows targeted offers to be made to either prior customers or targeted mail list profiles. Knowing the customer allows us to forecast the average sale price of the item at $100.

In contrast, banner advertising does not discriminate by purchasing propensity or prior history. It is therefore considered to have an average sale value of $50 per order.

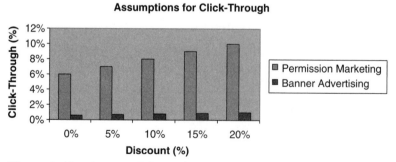

Figure 9.15   Assumed Click-Through Rate for Permission Marketing and Banner Advertising

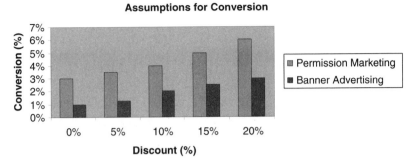

Figure 9.16 Assumed Conversion Rate for Permission Marketing and Banner Advertising

Objectives of Modeling

The current modeling effort attempts to answer the following questions:

1. With a given marketing budget, which marketing method is more effective?
2. Given a specific marketing method, what is an optimal discount value?

Results of Modeling

The promotion budget is taken as $1 million, to be utilized for either permission marketing or banner advertising.

Given that the price of the average item is $100, and the cost of goods is $80, the maximum discount that can be offered is taken at 20 percent. Naturally, at that value, the gross margin goes to zero.

Table 9.8 shows the results for the analysis of the Permission Marketing case. Assumptions specific to permission marketing are listed at the top of the table. The model is driven by the amount of money spent. That produces the number of visitors, depending on the assumed click-through rates.

Visitors then get converted into orders (i.e., customers). Depending on the discount offered, that produces the corresponding sales numbers for an average undiscounted product price of $100. Using a value of $80 per item, the cost of goods is computed, leading to the gross profit numbers.

Formulations detailed earlier let us compute the cost of servers and operating staff. The marketing cost of $1 million is restated. All other expenses associated with increased Web traffic and orders are bundled into the bucket titled "Other Expenses," which are taken as 3 percent of sales. The sum of the cost elements excluding the cost of goods is reported next as SGA (Sales, General, and Administrative) costs.

Net profits, average customer acquisition cost, and customer servicing cost are computed as:

Net profits = gross profits − SGA costs

Average customer acquisition cost = marketing cost / total number of orders

Average customer servicing cost = (SGA Costs − marketing cost) / total number of orders

Table 9.8 furthers our analysis of the efficacy of permission marketing.

In Figure 9.17, the impact of discounting is illustrated for sales and costs, where the latter is broken into cost of goods and SGA.

Corresponding customer acquisition costs per order are shown in Figure 9.18. For the same marketing budget of $1 million, sales can increase from $1.8 million to $4.8 million. The corresponding cost of goods also increases sharply from $1.44 million to $4.8 million.

SGA costs, which include the $1 million marketing expenditure, rise relatively slowly from $1.1 million to $1.4 million. Clearly, with increasing order volume, the cost of customer acquisition drops from $56 for no discount to $17 per customer at a 20 percent discount.

For these assumptions, the differences between permission marketing and banner advertising are significant for the company when incorporating various discounting options. Shown in Figure 9.19 is the number of orders for $1 million of marketing. The appreciably lower number of orders for banner advertising results from assuming lower click-through rates and conversion percentages.

The same trend manifests itself for total sales numbers as shown in Figure 9.20, but the revenues are even more skewed towards permission marketing, assuming again greater revenue per order for this marketing tactic.

The effect on profitability, though, is a different story. Both marketing methods in this model suffer deep losses. The greater loss is borne by banner advertising for discounting less than 15 percent. However, for discounting greater than 15 percent, the aggregate losses due to permission marketing are greater. Figure 9.21 summarizes costs and reveals a typical dot com profit profile—losses.

Table 9.8 Analysis for Permission Marketing

	Discount Offered				
	0 percent	*5 percent*	*10 percent*	*15 percent*	*20 percent*
Emails Sent	10,000,000	10,000,000	10,000,000	10,000,000	10,000,000
Assumed Click-Through Ratio	6 percent	7 percent	8 percent	9 percent	10 percent
Visitors	600,000	700,000	800,000	900,000	1,000,000
Assumed Conversion Ratio	3 percent	3.50 percent	4 percent	5 percent	6 percent
Orders	18,000	24,500	32,000	45,000	60,000
Sales	$1,800,000	$2,327,500	$2,880,000	$3,825,000	$4,800,000
Cost of Goods	$1,440,000	$1,960,000	$2,560,000	$3,600,000	$4,800,000
Gross Profits	$360,000	$367,500	$320,000	$225,000	$0
Server Cost	$6,000	$7,000	$8,000	$9,000	$10,000
Operations Cost	$72,000	$98,000	$128,000	$180,000	$240,000
Marketing Cost	$1,000,000	$1,000,000	$1,000,000	$1,000,000	$1,000,000
Other Expenses (3 percent of sales)	$54,000	$69,825	$86,400	$114,750	$144,000
SGA Costs	$1,132,000	$1,174,825	$1,222,400	$1,303,750	$1,394,000
Net Profits	$772,000	$807,325	$902,400	$1,078,750	$1,394,000

(*continued*)

347

Table 9.8   Analysis for Permission Marketing (*continued*)

	Discount Offered				
	0 percent	*5 percent*	*10 percent*	*15 percent*	*20 percent*
Average Customer Acquisition Cost	$56	$41	$31	$22	$17
Average Customer Servicing Cost	$7	$7	$7	$7	$7

Scenario I: Base Analysis for Permission Marketing

Assumptions

Marketing Budget	$1,000,000
Cost Per Email Sent	$0.10
Average Revenue per Order	$100
Cost of Goods	$80
Average Operations Cost per Order	$4
Cost of Production Servers	$0.01000 per visitor

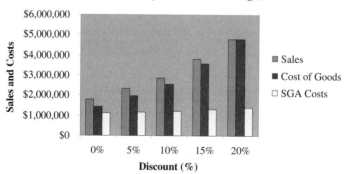

Figure 9.17   Effect of Discounting on Costs

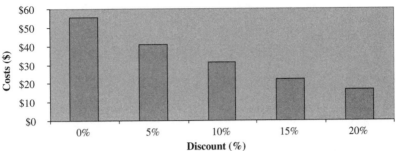

Figure 9.18 Effect of Discounting on Customer Acquisition and Service Costs

Conclusions

Based on this analysis, for ebiztro.com we can draw the following conclusions:

1. To secure a greater number of orders and revenues, permission marketing is the better method.
2. Both methods produce significant losses, with permission marketing producing lower losses at lower discount values.

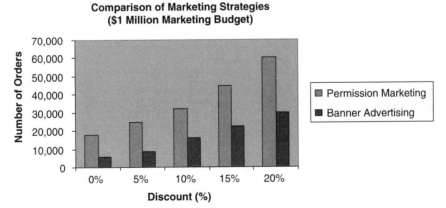

Figure 9.19 Comparison of Marketing Strategies for Orders

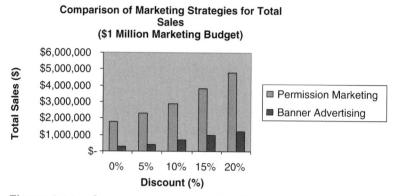

Figure 9.20   Comparison of Marketing Strategies for Total Sales

3. If the company wants to demonstrate growth of customers and revenues, a "solution" would be to combine permission marketing with discounting under 10 percent.

4. If the company wants to be profitable, then more fundamental changes are required in the business: improved profit margins through cost containment throughout operations or even major challenges to assumptions underlying strategy for the operation; better targeting to improve click-throughs and better merchandising to improve conversions; and improved operational controls.

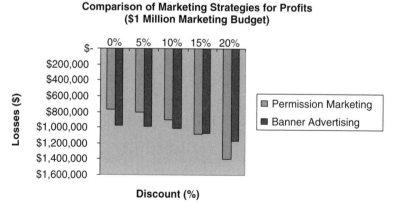

Figure 9.21   Comparison of Marketing Strategies for Profits

Summary

In this chapter, we looked at ways to model an e-commerce store, using a retailer of international handicrafts as our example. The choices confronting the four stacks of platform, content, community, and commerce were identified and specific choices were made.

This led to cost scenarios, both for launch of the enterprise as well as for continuing operations. Marketing issues were then modeled in greater detail to extract a methodology that applies the limited set of controls available to an e-commerce store operator to determine order rates, revenues, and profits.

Inevitably, modeling calls for making suitable assumptions to portray consequences of changing some key control value. Such assumptions can rarely be made with certainty. The e-commerce operator should use a combination of in-house measurement, limited testing, third-party research, and judgment to arrive at data models that identify the key controls and consequences inherent in his or her e-commerce implementation.

Our business is fictitious, but the numbers that contribute to the metrics are real. Each outline of baselines for measurement and table of metrics should be used as a starting point and guide to help understand what is required for building and launching a dot com business.

Running a business is a complicated process. Often, as any CEO can tell you, there are many more factors to success than those that are measurable. It is our premise, however, that if the variables governing success or failure can be reduced to a smaller number, then success is a higher likelihood. By measuring as much as possible to establish benchmarks and warning signals, the CEO or other operating management is free to look for areas where there is the possibility of greater ambiguity.

Finally, not every metric is appropriate in every situation. This is where management experience and expertise must come in. As we noted at ebiztro.com, some operating decisions are appropriate for the target audience and market dynamics, and some are not. It is management's role to determine and apply the metrics that are truly meaningful and discard those that are not. Metrics for their own sake are a waste of the resources used to generate them and management attention.

Every day another dot com becomes a dot bomb by showing worse than anticipated losses. Interspersed among these news accounts are often similar but far less dramatic operating problems with brick-and-mortar and click-and-mortar businesses. Running an online business is tough. Industry-specific scar tissue is in short supply.

There are not enough seasoned executives with a track record of successful online operations to go around. This means many of the others have to find their way around problems and take advantage of unanticipated opportunities in whatever way they can find.

It is our hope that this book can help make strategic decisions and analyze the consequences of those decisions against sound fundamental business principles. If a small fraction of you do "make the cut" in the generation of online businesses, then we will have succeeded in helping make the dot com world a little more reliable of an environment for launching and sustaining a business.

Categorization of Selected Internet Companies

Categorization of Businesses

Company	Company Description	Major Category	Sub-Category	Revenue Model	Web Site
1 800 Flowers	B2C store	Commerce	Services - Commerce	Store rev., ads	www.800flowers.com
11thHour Vacations.com	Last minute travel package inventory	Content / Commerce	Services - / Services - Commerce	ASP lease, ads, rev. share / ASP lease, ads, rev. share	www.11thhour.com / www.11thhour.com
About	Information content	Content	Services - Media	Advertisement Co-branding Franchises Alliances	www.about.com
Accelerated Networks	Delivery of voice and data services on diverse broadband networks	Platform	Software	Sales	
Aceva Technologies	Consolidated online transaction processing, customer service	Commerce	Services - CRM	Sales, services	www.aceva.com
AdExchange	Online media market-place for buyers and sellers of advertising	Content / Commerce	Services - Media / Services - Media	ASP, rev. share / ASP, rev. share	www.adexchange.com / www.adexchange.com
AdFlight	Self-service online marketing engine to buy and sell online advertising	Content / Commerce	Services - Media / Services - Media	Transaction fees / Transaction fees	www.adflight.com / www.adflight.com

354

AdForce	Inventory management and aggregation for Web site publishers and ad rep firms	Content	Services - Media	ASP, rev. share	www.adforce.com
		Commerce	Services - Media	ASP, rev. share	www.adforce.com
AdFusion	Enterprise-level collaboration hub to streamline media buying and selling	Content	Services - Media	Fees, commissions	www.adfusion.com
		Commerce	Services - Media	Fees, commissions	www.adfusion.com
AdOutlet	Media inventory and corporate media aggregation services	Content	Services - Media	Fees, exchange	www.adoutlet.com
		Commerce	Services - Media	Fees	www.adoutlet.com
Air2Web	Wireless Web-based infrastructure services	Platform	HW, SW, Services	Sale and lease terms	www.air2web.com
Akamai	Web delivery optimization	Platform	HW, SW, Services	Sales, services	www.akamai.com
Allaire	Provider of software to build business on the Web, including application servers, visual development tools, application framework platform for building and deploying JSP and servlet applications, editors, server-side tools, and services	Platform	Software	Fees	www.allaire.com

(continued)

355

Categorization of Businesses

Company	Company Description	Major Category	Sub-Category	Revenue Model	Web Site
Altranet	B2B provider of enterprise-wide, end-to-end solution to trade, schedule, transport and account for energy transactions including natural gas, NG liquids, power, and crude oil	Content	Services - Commerce	Transaction fees, subscription fees, software fees	www.altranet.com
		Commerce	Services - Commerce	Transaction fees, subscription fees, software fees	www.altranet.com
Amazon.com	Online B2C store	Content	Services - Content	Advertisement Co-branding Franchises Alliances	www.amazon.com
		Community	Services - Community		www.amazon.com
		Commerce	Services - Commerce		www.amazon.com
Amber Networks	Telecom equip. for edge-of-service providers of IP/ optical network	Platform	HW	Sales and lease terms	www.ambernetworks.com
America Online	Media conglomerate, ISP, community, portal store	Content	Services - Content	Multiple	www.aol.com
		Community	Services - Community	Multiple	www.aol.com
		Commerce	Services - Commerce		www.aol.com
		Platform	HW, SW, Services		www.aol.com

356

Ameritrade	Online brokerage	Content	Services - Commerce	Commission, ads	www.ameritrade.com
		Commerce	Services - Commerce	Commission, ads	www.ameritrade.com
Arbinet	B2B, neutral, central-ized online exchange to buy, sell, and physically deliver voice, fax, IP minutes across PSTN, data, VOIP, and wireless networks	Commerce	Services - Commerce	Membership fee, fee for blocks of min-utes traded depend-ing on type & quality; no commissions	www.thexchange.com
		Platform	HW, SW, Services	Membership fee, fee for blocks of min-utes traded depend-ing on type & quality; no commissions	www.thexchange.com
Ariba	Online B2B marketplace enabler	Commerce	Services - Commerce	Sales, subscriptions, contractual, commis-sions, ads, listing fees	www.ariba.com
		Platform	HW, SW, Services		www.ariba.com
Art Technology Group	CRM and e-commerce products	Commerce	Services - CRM	Revenues from brick-and-mortar companies	www.atg.com
Asera	B2B demand-chain man-agement solutions on XML-based platform	Commerce	Services	Sales and services	www.asera.com
AsianSources	B2B marketplace for global sourcing	Commerce	Services - Commerce	Commissions, ads, listing fees	www.asiansources.com
		Content	Services - Content	Commissions, ads, listing fees	www.asiansources.com

(continued)

357

Categorization of Businesses

Company	Company Description	Major Category	Sub-Category	Revenue Model	Web Site
Ask Jeeves	Search tool	Content	Services	Preferred placement fees, ads	www.askjeeves.com
Asyst Technologies	Factory automation solutions and other systems for semiconductor manufacturing	Platform	HW, SW, Services		www.asyst.com
Atrieva	Storage systems	Platform	HW, SW, Services	100 MB free, priced for additional ad rev.: $8 - $50 per 1,000 viewers	www.atrieva.com
AudioBookClub	Digitized media content	Content	Services - Content	Sales, commissions, ads	www.audiobookclub.com
		Commerce	Services - Commerce	Sales, commissions, ads	www.audiobookclub.com
Audiohighway.com	Digitized media content	Content	Services - Content	Sales, commissions, ads	www.audiohighway.com
		Content	Services - Media		www.audiohighway.com
		Commerce	Services - Media		www.audiohighway.com

358

Autobytel.com	Online auto purchase information, selection, ordering	Content Commerce	Services - Content Services - Commerce	Commissions from lead generation, ads, transaction fees, classifieds	www.autobytel.com www.autobytel.com
BEA Systems	E-business infrastructure middleware software company providing e-business platform including application server, commerce server, personalization server, collaboration, process integrator, m-commerce solution and services	Platform Commerce	Software Software	Fees Fees	www.bea.com www.bea.com
BeVocal	Interactive voice activated content provider	Content	Services - Media	Commissions, ads	www.bevocal.com
BidCom	Online B2C auction site	Content Commerce	Services - Commerce Services - Commerce	Commissions, ads Commissions, ads	www.bidcom.com www.bidcom.com
BizBuyer Out of business, Dec. 2000	B2B procurement enabler and market-place for small business	Content Commerce	Services - Commerce Services - Commerce	Commissions from suppliers, member-ship fees	www.bizbuyer.com www.bizbuyer.com

(continued)

359

Categorization of Businesses

Company	Company Description	Major Category	Sub-Category	Revenue Model	Web Site
Brience	Personalized wireless Web services	Content	Services - Media		www.brience.com
Broadcom	Semiconductor manufacturer for broadband networking	Platform	HW	Sales	www.broadcom.com
BroadVision	Online B2C media company	Content	Services - Media		www.broadvision.com
CDNow	Online B2C media store	Content / Commerce	Services - Media / Services - Commerce	Sales, commissions, ads	www.cdnow.com / www.cdnow.com
Cellpoint, Inc.	Mobile locations services provider	Content	Services - Commerce	Fees, ads	www.cellpoint.com
Charles Schwab	Click and mortar brokerage	Content / Commerce	Services - Commerce / Services - Commerce	Commissions / Commissions	www.schwab.com / www.schwab.com
Cisco Systems	Platform company	Platform	HW, SW, Services	Sales, consulting, services	www.cisco.com
CMGI	New media incubator, VC, holding company	Commerce	Services	Ownership stake	www.cmgi.com

360

CNET	Digitized media content	Content	Services - Media	Ads, fee for some content	www.cnet.com
CommerceOne	Online B2B marketplace enabler	Commerce	Services - Commerce	Listing fees, contractual, commissions, ads	www.commerceone.com
		Platform	HW, SW, Services	Listing fees, contractual, commissions, ads	www.commerceone.com
CommerceQuest	End-to-end business integration solutions provider	Services	HW, SW, Services	Sales	www.commercequest.com
CVS.com	Click and mortar pharmacy	Content	Services - Commerce	Sales, ads	www.cvs.com
		Commerce	Services - Commerce		www.cvs.com
Cyberian Outpost	Online B2C store	Content	Services - Commerce	Sales, ads	www.outpost.com
		Commerce	Services - Commerce	Sales, ads	www.outpost.com
Dice.com	Online employment listings	Content Community	Services Services	Listing fees, ads Listing fees, ads	www.dice.com www.dice.com
DoubleClick	Online media marketplace	Content	Services - Media	Volume commissions on placed ads	www.doubleclick.com
		Commerce	Services - Media		www.doubleclick.com

(continued)

361

Categorization of Businesses

Company	Company Description	Major Category	Sub-Category	Revenue Model	Web Site
Drugstore.com	Online pharmacy	Content	Services - Commerce	Sales	www.drugstore.com
		Commerce	Services - Commerce	Sales	www.drugstore.com
E*Trade	Online brokerage	Content	Services - Commerce	Commissions	www.etrade.com
		Commerce	Services - Commerce	Commissions	www.etrade.com
EarthWeb	Web hosting, ISP	Platform	HW, SW, Services	Hosting fees, ISP subscriptions, ads	www.earthweb.com
eBay	Online B2C auction site	Content	Services - Content	Commissions, ads	www.ebay.com
		Community	Services - Community	Commissions, ads	www.ebay.com
		Commerce	Services - Commerce	Commissions, ads	www.ebay.com
e-centives	Online incentive marketing	Commerce	Services - Media		www.e-centives.com
eCredit.com	Real-time credit and finishing services for e-biz	Commerce	Services - Commerce		www.ecredit.com
eForce	System integrator for e-commerce companies	Platform	HW, SW, Services		www.eforce.com

362

eGain	Online CRM software	Commerce	Services - CRM Software	Sales	www.egain.com
		Commerce			www.egain.com
Egghead.com	Online media store	Content	Services - Commerce	Sales, ads	www.egghead.com
		Commerce	Services - Commerce	Sales, ads	www.egghead.com
E-Loan	Online loan approval	Commerce	Services - Commerce		www.eloan.com
EMC	Storage systems	Platform	HW	Sales, services	www.emc.com
Entrust	Certificate management	Commerce	Services - Commerce	Fees	www.entrust.com
Epinions	Customer reviews of products and services	Content	Services - Content	Advertisements	www.epinions.com
E-Steel	B2B provider of open e-commerce solutions that connect the global metals supply chain	Content	Services - Commerce	Ads, transaction fees from members; no charge to buyers	www.esteel.com
		Commerce	Services - Commerce	Ads, transaction fees from members; no charge to buyers	www.esteel.com
Everypath.com	Wireless ASP	Platform	HW, SW, Services	ASP lease, rev. share	www.everypath.com
Excite@Home	ISP, Web hosting, B2C portal	Platform	HW, SW, Services	Fees	www.home.com
		Content	Services	Advertisements	www.home.com
		Community	Services	Advertisements	www.home.com
		Commerce	Services	Advertisements	www.home.com

(continued)

363

*Categorization
of Businesses*

Company	Company Description	Major Category	Sub-Category	Revenue Model	Web Site
Exodus	Internet data center and services	Platform	HW, SW, Services	Data center lease, hosting fees, services	www.exodus.com
Expedia	Online travel site	Content	Services - Commerce	Commissions, ads	www.expedia.com
		Commerce	Services - Commerce	Commissions, ads	www.expedia.com
FastParts	B2B neutral marketplace for electronics manufacturing industry to trade electronic inventory	Content	Services - Commerce	No membership fees; fees to seller upon completing transaction	www.fastparts.com
		Commerce	Services - Commerce	No membership fees; fees to seller upon completing transaction	www.fastparts.com
FreeAgent	Online employment marketplace	Content	Services	Listing fees, ads	www.freeagent.com
		Commerce	Services	Listing fees, ads	www.freeagent.com
FreeMarkets	Online marketplace for electronic components	Content	Services - Commerce	Listing fees, contractual, commissions, ads	www.freemarkets.com
		Commerce	Services - Commerce	Listing fees, contractual, commissions, ads	www.freemarkets.com

364

FutureStep	Online employment marketplace	Content Commerce	Services Services	Listing fees, ads Listing fees, ads	*www.futurestep.com* *www.futurestep.com*
Garden.com	Community for garden enthusiasts; now part of Burpee, Inc.	Community	Services - Community	Ads	*www.garden.com*
Gofish	B2B marketplace for seafood industry providing buyers and sellers with real-time pricing, credit reporting, news, weekly market reports, legislative reporting, and neutral trading floor	Content

Commerce | Services - Commerce

Services - Commerce | Ads, membership fees for sellers, and seller-side trans-action fee of 1.7 percent, value-added services
Ads, membership fees for sellers, and seller-side trans-action fee of 1.7 percent, value-added services | *www.gofish.com*

www.gofish.com |
| Grainger | Click and mortar B2B MRO | Content

Commerce | Services - Content
Services - Commerce | Sales, commissions, ads | *www.orderzone.com* *www.grainger.com* *www.orderzone.com* *www.grainger.com* |
| Guru | Online employment marketplace | Content Commerce | Services Services | Listing fees, ads Listing fees, ads | *www.guru.com* *www.guru.com* |
| HealthCite | Online service and communications net-work for physicians and patients | Community | Services - Community | | *www.healthcite.com* |

(continued)

365

Categorization of Businesses

Company	Company Description	Major Category	Sub-Category	Revenue Model	Web Site
HeyAnita.com	Interactive voice-activated content provider	Content / Platform	Services - Content / HW, SW, Services	Fees, ads / Fees, ads	www.heyanita.com / www.heyanita.com
HomePage	B2C community site and Web space	Community / Platform	Services - Media / Software	Ads / Ads	www.homepage.com / www.homepage.com
i2 Technologies	B2B provider of supply chain management software, collaboration, and marketplace	Platform / Commerce	Software / Services - Commerce	Sales, lease, consulting, services	www.i2.com / www.i2.com
IBM	Hardware and software company offering suite of products for enterprises	Platform / Commerce	HW, SW, Services / Services - Commerce	Sales, ads, fees, etc. / Sales, ads, fees, etc.	www.ibm.com / www.ibm.com
Infoseek	Search tool	Content	Services - Media	Ads	www.infoseek.com
InfoSpace	Commerce, information and communication infrastructure services for wireless and Web sites	Platform	HW, SW, Services	Ads, fees	www.infospace.com

Inktomi	Provider of software to develop scalable infrastructure, including network products (traffic server, content delivery), media products, search tools, commerce engines			www.inktomi.com
InsWeb	Online insurance content and quotes	Content Commerce	Services - Commerce Services - Commerce		www.insweb.com www.insweb.com
Internet Capital Group	New media incubator, VC, holding company	Platform Commerce	HW, SW, Services Services	Ownership stake Ownership stake	www.icg.com www.icg.com
internet.com	Internet news and technology portal	Platform Content	HW, SW, Services Services - Commerce	Ownership stake Ads, listing fees	www.internet.com www.internet.com
Interwoven	Software to manage content and services for enterprise Web	Platform	Software	Fees	www.interwoven.com
Intuit	Financial SW for online and PC-based individuals	Platform Content Community Commerce	Software Services Services Services - Commerce	Sales, ads Sales, ads Sales, ads Sales, ads	www.intuit.com www.intuit.com www.intuit.com www.intuit.com

(continued)

367

Categorization of Businesses

Company	Company Description	Major Category	Sub-Category	Revenue Model	Web Site
iVillage	Community for women	Content Community	Services Services	Ads Ads	www.ivillage.com www.ivillage.com
Jamcracker	Aggregator of Web-based SW from ASPs	Platform	Software	Lease contracts	www.jamcracker.com
Jetstream Communications	Broadband access for next-generation local telecom networks	Platform	HW, SW, Services		
Juniper Networks	High-performance routers for networks	Platform	HW, SW, Services	Sales	www.juniper.net
Juno	Web hosting, ISP	Platform	HW, SW, Services	Hosting fees, ISP subscriptions, ads	www.juno.com
Jupiter Communications	New media market research company	Content	Services - Media	Fee for research	www.jupiter.com
levelseas.com	Web-based chartering of bulk ocean freight	Content Commerce	Services - Commerce Services - Commerce	Subscriptions, commissions	www.levelseas.com www.levelseas.com
LivePerson	IP-based call center management	Commerce	Services	Fees	www.liveperson.com
Lycos	B2C portal, content, search tool	Content Community Commerce	Services Services Services	Ads Ads Ads	www.lycos.com www.lycos.com www.lycos.com

368

Macromedia	Web development tools	Platform	Software	Sales	www.macromedia.com
MapQuest	Online GIS content delivery	Content	Services - Media	Ads, corporate sales	www.mapquest.com
Media Metrix	New media market research company	Content	Services - Media	Consulting, analysis	www.mediametrix.com
Mercury Interactive	Provider of Web performance management solutions (functional, load, process testing products; performance monitoring, hosted Web performance, hosted load testing products and services) that help e-businesses ensure a positive user experience	Platform	Software	Fees	www.mercuryinteractive.com
Microsoft	Software company offering suite of products for individuals and enterprises	Platform Content Community Commerce	HW, SW, Services Services - Content Services - Community Services - Commerce	Sales, ads, fees, etc. Sales, ads, fees, etc. Sales, ads, fees, etc. Sales, ads, fees, etc.	www.microsoft.com www.msn.com www.msn.com www.msn.com
mobilePosition	Mobile locations services provider	Content	Services - Commerce	Listing fees	www.mobileposition.com

(continued)

369

Categorization of Businesses

Company	Company Description	Major Category	Sub-Category	Revenue Model	Web Site
Monster.com	Online employment listings	Content Commerce	Services Services	Listing fees, ads Listing fees, ads	www.monster.com www.monster.com
Mortgage.com	Online mortgage information and quotes	Content	Services - Content	Commissions, ads	www.mortgage.com
Motley Fool	B2C financial portal site	Content Community Commerce	Services - Content Services - Community Services - Commerce	Ads, sales Ads, sales Ads, sales	www.fool.com www.fool.com www.fool.com
MP3.com	B2C entertainment media provider	Content Commerce	Services - Media Services - Media	Ads, commissions Ads, commissions	www.mp3.com www.mp3.com
MyPlay.com	Online music playlist and storage	Content	Services - Media	Ads	www.myplay.com
NBCi	Online information and entertainment media portal	Content	Services - Media	Ads, corporate sales	www.nbci.com
Netcentives	B2C incentives marketing	Content	Services		www.netcentives.com

370

Netfish Technologies	XML-based B2B e-commerce solutions			www.netfish.com
NetPerceptions	Data mining, retail knowledge expertise and software solutions	Commerce Platform	Services - CRM Software	www.netperceptions.com www.netperceptions.com
Network Solutions	DNS registry and domain name registrations	Platform Commerce	Services Services	www.netsol.com www.netsol.com
NetZero	ISP, Web hosting	Platform	HW, SW, Services	www.netzero.com
			Ads, hosting fees	
ON24	Broadcast news and opinions for online investors	Content	Services - Media	www.on24.com
			Ads	
ONI Systems	Optical networking	Platform	HW, SW, Services	www.oni.com
			Sales	
OnSale	B2C store	Content Commerce	Services - Commerce Services - Commerce	www.onsale.com www.onsale.com
			Sales Sales	
OnSign	SW for users to create encrypted digital signature for email	Platform	Software	www.onsign.com
			Sales	

(continued)

371

Categorization of Businesses

Company	Company Description	Major Category	Sub-Category	Revenue Model	Web Site
PaperExchange	B2B marketplace for pulp and paper industry	Content	Services - Commerce	Sales, commissions	www.paperexchange.com
		Commerce	Services - Commerce	Listing fees, contractual, commissions, ads	www.paperexchange.com
Persistence	Provider of transaction application servers and platform for high volume transaction processing and integration with back-end systems	Commerce	Software	Fees	www.persistence.com
PlanetRx	Online pharmacy	Content	Services - Commerce	Sales, ads	www.planetrx.com
		Commerce	Services - Commerce	Sales, ads	www.planetrx.com
Priceline.com	B2C marketplace for travel, hospitality, and goods	Content	Services - Commerce	Commissions, auction differentials	www.priceline.com
		Commerce	Services - Commerce	Commissions, auction differentials	www.priceline.com
PurpleYogi	Broadcast news and opinion for online investors	Content	Software - Services	Sales	www.purpleyogi.com

372

Razorfish	New media consulting, Web design and development			www.razorfish.com
RealNetworks	Online entertainment content delivery	Content	Services - Media	Ads, corporate sales	www.real.com
Register.com	Domain name registrations	Platform	Services	Commissions on registrations, ads, services	www.register.com
Responsys.com	Online permission marketing system for customer retention	Commerce	Services - Media	Fees	www.responsys.com
SciQuest	Procurement and MRO marketplace for pharmaceutical industry	Platform	Services - Commerce	Listing fees, contractual, commissions, ads	www.sciquest.com
		Content	Services - Commerce	Listing fees, contractual, commissions, ads	www.sciquest.com
		Commerce	Services - Commerce	Listing fees, contractual, commissions, ads	www.sciquest.com
Selectica	System SW and services	Platform	Software	Sales, lease, consulting, services	www.selectica.com
Snapfish	Free photo service including film development, printing, and online storing	Content	Services - Media	Sales (above free min.), ads	www.snapfish.com
		Commerce	Services - Media	Sales (above free min.), ads	www.snapfish.com
Stamps.com	Online mail stamps delivery	Commerce	Services - Commerce	Commissions, ads	www.stamps.com

(continued)

373

Categorization of Businesses

Company	Company Description	Major Category	Sub-Category	Revenue Model	Web Site
Sun Microsystems	Hardware and software company offering suite of products for enterprises	Platform	HW, SW, Services	Sales, fees	www.sun.com
Sycamore Networks	Networking products for flexible intelligent optical networks	Platform	HW, SW, Services	Sales	www.sycamore.com
TheStreet.com	Financial news content and stock market quotes	Content	Services - Media	Ads, commissions, fee for detailed content	www.thestreet.com
		Commerce	Services - Media	Ads, commissions, fee for detailed content	www.thestreet.com
Tibco Software	Realtime e-biz infrastructure SW especially for financial industry	Platform	Software	Sales, services	www.tibco.com
Ticketmaster	Click and mortar B2C entertainment tickets	Content	Services - Commerce	Commissions, ads	www.ticketmaster.com
		Commerce	Services - Commerce	Commissions, ads	www.ticketmaster.com
Travelocity	Online travel site	Content	Services - Content	Ads, commissions	www.travelocity.com
		Commerce	Services - Commerce	Ads, commissions	www.travelocity.com

374

U-Wire	College news aggregator and content provider	Content	Services - Media	Contractual fees, ads	www.uwire.com
		Commerce	Services - Media	Contractual fees, ads	www.uwire.com
Ventro	Procurement and MRO marketplace for pharmaceutical industry	Platform	HW, SW, Services	Listing fees, contractual, commissions, ads	www.ventro.com
		Content	Services - Commerce	Listing fees, contractual, commissions, ads	www.ventro.com
		Commerce	Services - Commerce	Listing fees, contractual, commissions, ads	www.ventro.com
VeriSign	Certificate registration, management, verification, revocation	Platform	Services		www.verisign.com
VerticalNet	B2B community, content, marketplace for verticals focusing on direct material/OEM and solutions providing market design tools and market mechanisms	Platform	HW, SW, Services	Contractual, commissions, ads	www.verticalnet.net
		Content	Services Content	Contractual, commissions, ads	www.verticalnet.net
		Community	Services - Community	Contractual, commissions, ads	www.verticalnet.net
		Commerce	Services - Commerce	Contractual, commissions, ads	www.verticalnet.net

(continued)

375

Categorization of Businesses

Company	Company Description	Major Category	Sub-Category	Revenue Model	Web Site
Vignette	Supplier of e-business applications for building online businesses, extend relationships with prospects and customers, enable high volume transaction exchanges with suppliers and partners	Commerce	Software	Fees	www.vignette.com
Walgreens.com	Click and mortar pharmacy	Content Commerce	Services Services - Commerce	Sales	www.walgreens.com www.walgreens.com
WebMD	Online service and communications network for physicians and patients	Content Commerce	Services - Content Services - Commerce		www.webmd.com www.webmd.com
Webvan	B2C online grocery	Content Commerce	Services - Commerce Services - Commerce	Ads, commissions Ads, commissions	www.webvan.com www.webvan.com
Wine.com	B2C community for wine afficionados	Content Community Commerce	Services - Content Services - Community Services - Commerce	Ads Ads Ads	www.wine.com www.wine.com www.wine.com

376

Wingspan Bank	Online bank	Content Commerce	Services - Commerce Services - Commerce	Fees from services, ads Fees from services, ads	www.wingspan.com www.wingspan.com
Women.com	Community site for women	Content Community	Services - Content Services - Community	Ads Ads	www.women.com www.women.com
Xdrive	Online storage	Platform	HW, SW, Services	Fee for storage	www.xdrive.com
Yack	Internet version of TV Guide with multimedia and interactive features	Content Community	Services - Media Services - Media		www.yack.com www.yack.om
Yahoo!	B2C portal, content, search tool, shopping	Platform Content Community Commerce	HW, SW, Services Services - Content Services - Community Services - Commerce	Multiple Multiple Multiple Multiple	www.yahoo.com www.yahoo.com www.yahoo.com www.yahoo.com
Yantra Corp	E-Commerce solutions SW	Platform	Software	Sales	www.yantra.com

(continued)

377

Categorization of Businesses

Company	Company Description	Major Category	Sub-Category	Revenue Model	Web Site
Yodlee	Aggregator of personal online accounts including email, banking, brokerage	Content	Services	Ads	www.yodlee.com
ZDNet	Digitized media content	Content	Services - Media	Ads	www.zdnet.com

Disclaimer: This selection of Internet companies is for illustrative purposes and is not intended to be comprehensive. The authors do not warrant or attest to the value or utility of the products and services provided by these companies. Furthermore, companies change their business models over time reflecting market opportunities and compulsions.

378

Index

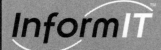

E-Commerce

ADD VALUE TO
EVERY E-BUSINESS
DECISION YOU MAKE

INTERNET COMMERCE METRICS AND MODELS
in the New Era of Accountability

SRIDHAR JAGANNATHAN | **JAY SRINIVASAN** | **JERRY L. KALMA**

About the Authors

SRIDHAR JAGANNATHAN is currently the Vice President of Technology for Softbank Emerging Markets with responsibilities for technical due diligence. Prior to working at Softbank, Sridhar was the co-founder and CTO of an e-commerce company and served as Technical Director, Internet and E-Commerce Solutions Group at Oracle Corporation. Sridhar has a doctorate from the University of California, Berkeley and a Master's degree from the Stanford Graduate School of Business.

JAY SRINIVASAN is an e-business consultant specializing in industry and market research and has consulted with companies in the B2B market. He was formerly a senior consultant with a Big Five consulting firm and worked for many years in the healthcare industry.

JERRY L. KALMAN is an entrepreneur and writer/lecturer in electronic commerce. In addition to starting three firms and serving on the board of directors of several software and Internet companies, he also teaches electronic commerce at the Singapore Institute of Management and the University of California, Irvine extension program.

U.S. $39.99 | Canada $60.00
PRENTICE HALL
Upper Saddle River, NJ 07458

www.phptr.com

Internet Commerce Metrics and Models in the New Era of Accountability delivers today's best practices for e-business investment and management decision-making, based on real-world case studies and advanced analysis techniques. It gives e-commerce entrepreneurs and decision-makers a comprehensive, up-to-date framework for understanding Internet business models—and desperately needed metrics for evaluating them.

The authors introduce an exclusive five-stack e-business model, encompassing platform, content, community, commerce, and the "services" that add value to them. Using this framework, they construct a complete e-commerce business model, analyzing the economic impact of key choices, and introducing new ways to project the consequences of your decisions. Coverage includes:

- **Content development models**
- **Community/market models**
- **Pricing models**
- **Customer acquisition models**
- **Infrastructure models: providing high-value services that support every e-business function**

Whether you're an entrepreneur, manager, investor, or consultant, this book's breakthrough framework and analytical techniques will add value to every e-business decision you make.

ISBN 0-13-028186-7